Religious Liberty in Transitional Societies

It is commonly assumed that the issue of religion declines in political significance as societies modernise. However, the upheaval associated with the shift from authoritarian to more open regimes can be accompanied by a revitalisation of religion. Individuals within these societies are struggling to find meaning in the seeming chaos of political change; religious elites are seeking to define their own role within the new order; and political elites are looking for new ways of ensuring legitimacy and building national unity. In this book John Anderson constructs a theoretical framework where he compares and contrasts the politics of religious liberty in two Southern European countries, two Central-Eastern European countries, and the evolution of the former USSR, particularly Russia. Exploring these issues of religious 'recognition' and religious diversity, Anderson attempts to expose the wider problem of creating a democratic mentality in such transitional societies, through extensive original research and interviews.

John Anderson is Senior Lecturer in International Relations at the University of St Andrews, Scotland. He is author of *Religion, State and Politics in the Soviet Union and Sucessor States* (CUP, 1994), *The International Politics of Central Asia* (1997) and *Kyrgyzstan: Central Asia's Island of Democracy* (1999).

Religious Liberty in Transitional Societies

The Politics of Religion

John Anderson

CAMBRIDGE
UNIVERSITY PRESS

PUBLISHED BY THE PRESS SYNDICATE OF THE UNIVERSITY OF CAMBRIDGE
The Pitt Building, Trumpington Street, Cambridge CB2 1RP, United Kingdom

CAMBRIDGE UNIVERSITY PRESS
The Edinburgh Building, Cambridge, CB2 2RU, UK
40 West 20th Street, New York, NY 10011–4211, USA
477 Williamstown Road, Port Melbourne, VIC 3207, Australia
Ruiz de Alarcón 13, 28014 Madrid, Spain
Dock House, The Waterfront, Cape Town 8001, South Africa

http://www.cambridge.org

First published 2003

Printed in the United Kingdom at the University Press, Cambridge

Typeface Plantin 10/12 pt.   *System* LATEX 2$_\varepsilon$ [TB]

A catalogue record for this book is available from the British Library

Library of Congress Cataloging in Publication data
Anderson, John, Dr
Religious liberty in transitional societies : the politics of religion / John Anderson.
         p.   cm.
Includes bibliographical references and index.
ISBN 0 521 82396 X
1. Europe – Religion – 20th century.   2. Freedom of religion – Europe –
History – 20th century.   3. Democracy – Religious aspects – History –
20th century.   4. Religion and politics – Europe – History – 20th century.
I. Title.
BL695.A53   2003
322.44′2′094 – dc21   2002041699

ISBN 0 521 82396 X hardback

For Jill, Joe and Caitlin

Contents

Preface

Most of the work on producing this book took place in 1999–2000, but its origins go back further. My research life started in the field of 'Soviet studies' and more specifically in the study of religion–state relations in the former Soviet Union. During the 1990s my focus shifted to political change in Central Asia, but at this time I was also teaching courses on democracy and democratisation. Gradually this led to a fusion of several interests and the emergence of a long-term research project on religion and democratisation. One aspect of this study concerned the issue of how religious institutions handled the development of political, social, cultural and spiritual pluralism that tends to accompany processes of political transition, so I was particularly grateful when the Becket Institute at St Hugh's College Oxford offered me the chance to spend nine months away from my own department to explore the politics of religious liberty. The consequence of this has been the production of a book exploring the way in which transitional societies have handled the issues of religious 'recognition' and religious diversity.

The objectives of this work are set out in the first chapter, but inevitably in venturing out of one's own area of geographical and linguistic expertise there is a danger that the historical background of some of my cases will be poorly understood, that the nuances of political life will be missed, and comparisons tend to the superficial. For that reason I have tried to keep the focus narrow, though to the extent that this still engenders over-simplification the author must take the blame. If I have managed accurately to portray the experience and politics of the eleven countries whose experience I touch on here, the credit belongs to many others. Over the last twelve years I have visited seven of the eleven countries surveyed and discussed religious questions with a variety of religious activists, administrators, journalists, academics, clergy, lay people and casual acquaintances. Equally important have been the writings of numerous academics, human rights activists and religious leaders whose works are, I hope, adequately cited in the endnotes and bibliography. In addition, a large number of people have provided support and advice, whether in the form of interviews, electronic exchanges, answering queries on specific points, providing translations, or reading parts of the manuscript. Special thanks should go to Edwin Bacon who read and offered a critical commentary on the whole manuscript. Some of his comments I have taken on board and others, at my peril, I have ignored, but all were valuable in pointing to weaknesses in this book. Others deserving of special mention include Altyrkul Alisheva, Wendy Anderson, Audrey Brassloff, Emil Cohen, Vassili Feidas, Krassimir Kanev, Bishop Carlos Lopez Lozano, Nick Nedelchev, Lyatcheslav Popov, Fotis Romeo, Soutiris Roussos, Constantine Scoutaris, Medet Sultanbaev, Anara Tabyshalieva and CUP's three referees. Special stimulus was also provided by fellow participants in the European Consortium on Political Research workshop on 'Church and State in Europe' workshop held in Copenhagen during April 2000. On Russia special debts of gratitude are owed by all scholars working in this field to Paul Steeves whose speedy transfer of Russian press articles to his website is invaluable, and to the revived reporting of the Keston News Service team which over the last four to five years has provided unrivalled coverage of the religious scene, especially in the hitherto largely uncovered regions of Russia. In Oxford the librarians at the Bodleian Library were ever helpful in opening up the riches of that particular library and, not for the first time, Malcom Walker provided the same service at the Keston Institute library. Special thanks must also go to the Carnegie Trust for the Universities of Scotland for providing the funds for research visits to Greece and Bulgaria.

Above all I owe a huge debt to the Becket Institute and its director Jonathan Rowland who gave me the chance to explore this topic. Thanks also to Jade Martin who facilitated the practical side of my stay in Oxford, to David Robertson at St Hugh's, and the participants in the Institute's Church–State seminar who provided me with many insights into a wide variety of countries. As always, thanks to my colleagues at St Andrews who gave me time off at very short notice. Thanks must also go to all the kids in the St Andrews Scorpions roller hockey club who put up with my feeble efforts at coaching and, more importantly, kept my feet firmly on the ground! Finally, as usual but without taking them for granted, thanks to Jill, Joe and Caitlin who accepted a commuting lifestyle for six months before joining me in Oxford to face the joys of English traffic, home schooling, and falling out of punts.

1   Introduction

In the summer of 1997 the State Duma of the Russian Federation adopted a law 'on freedom of conscience and religious organisation' that, after a brief delay, was signed into law by Boris Yeltsin on 26 September. Whereas the law on religion approved in 1991 had effectively created a religious free market in Russia, the new law differentiated amongst religious communities with regard to both their symbolic status and legal rights.

As the Russian text was awaiting the final presidential signature, the author of these lines was in Kyrgyzstan researching the growth of civil society in this newly independent Central Asian republic. Following an interview with the state commissioner for religious affairs he held a conversation with some relatively liberal-minded intellectuals who argued very strongly that the religious sphere could not be one of absolute freedom and that some degree of legal regulation and even restriction was essential.

In both of these countries the discussion of new regulatory frameworks for religious institutions revolved around issues of stability, vulnerability, unfair competition, a desire for order, and questions of national identity. In Kyrgyzstan the argument suggested that here was a fragile society that had only recently achieved independence, and which had since experienced a veritable onslaught by religious and missionary organisations of all sorts. On the one hand there were Muslim purists who wanted to impose their version of the true faith on a society that, whilst retaining a strong cultural attachment to religion, had also been deeply affected by decades of Soviet secularisation – and my colleagues cited above were all urban, educated women, suspicious of Islamicist motives. Against such groups were ranged a wide variety of Protestant, neo-Protestant and new religious movements, some with roots in Kyrgyz society and some attracted by the relatively free religious market created in the early 1990s. Most of these directed their evangelistic work across ethnic and religious boundaries, and it was this latter factor that led my interlocutors to argue for at least a minimal legal regulation of religious activities in order to preserve some degree of internal stability.

Similarly, in Russia – and indeed in other former Soviet bloc countries – the debates that emerged in the mid-1990s centred on the vulnerability of a population disoriented by the collapse of the USSR and subsequent economic decline. Here the argument emphasised that the traditional religious institutions had been weakened institutionally, financially and psychologically by decades of atheist repression and this had left them unable to compete with the wealthy religious missions that were flooding into Russia. At the same time those appealing for legal protection of the 'traditional churches' could draw on a widespread longing for order in a society facing the seemingly anarchic reality of 'democracy' and, so they hoped, on a popular rejection of alien forms of religion or externally determined models of religion–state relations. For that reason much of the argument in Russia had a nationalistic, sometimes chauvinistic, flavour that just occasionally led church leaders into some rather unholy political alliances.

Both Russia and Kyrgyzstan were apparently in a process of transition, from communist authoritarianism or 'post-totalitarianism'[1] to some new form of political rule. Each of them proclaimed their commitment to 'democratisation', and each maintained some of the forms of liberal democracy. In neither case had presidential and parliamentary elections been fully 'free and fair', though in Russia they had provided for some parliamentary 'circulation of elites'. In political science terms both had undergone a process of 'liberalisation' – though Kyrgyzstan's 'liberality' had declined considerably by the end of 2002 and the country could not be described as 'democratic' in any meaningful sense – but neither were 'consolidated democracies'.[2] Equally important for the future of democracy, in these and many post-Soviet societies the development of an appropriate 'democratic mentality' has proved hard to achieve. Survey data suggested that for many people strong leadership and the restoration of 'order' were more important than democratic niceties, and that society and elites had yet to imbibe the values of tolerance and acceptance of diversity that tend to underpin mature democratic states. For example, in Russia surveys carried out in 1997 showed that some 82 per cent of those polled were dissatisfied with democracy, though the majority felt that at least now they could say what they thought.[3] Other survey data pointed to low levels of acceptance when it came to social diversity, with surveys in the late 1980s and early 1990s showing that up to one-third of Russians would have liked to 'eliminate' homosexuals – as against *only* 5 per cent who wanted to do the same to members of 'sects' – and that many remained wary of some of the excesses of democracy.[4] Similar studies carried out in Bulgaria in the late 1990s demonstrated that over half of the population had hostile attitudes towards religious and ethnic minorities.[5]

For these reasons debates over religious pluralism and diversity are worth studying because of what they tell us about the wider problem of creating a democratic mentality in transitional societies. At the same time they allow us to engage with debates over the respective role of elites and masses in the process of political change. Does democratisation simply require that the elites accept democratic values and act in some rough accord with these – for example, in debate with opponents is a level of civility maintained, are electoral defeats accepted, and do politicians promote the acceptance of social and political diversity? Or is more needed, and do the mass of the population need to accept, and act in accordance with, democratic values before it is possible to speak of a secure and consolidated democratic order? In general, most sources appear to view it as desirable that both questions be answered affirmatively, but suggest that in the short term democratisation is unlikely to be successful or stable without an elite commitment to 'the rules of the game'.[6] If such is the case then do religious elites have a contribution to make, whether in encouraging other elites to 'play fair' or in pursuing their own agendas according to democratic rules? And what messages might it send to the wider public if respected national religious institutions seek to acquire institutional privilege or limit the rights of competitors? How then can they be taken seriously when they call on the military, political parties or important individuals to respect democratic norms? Yet equally, it might be suggested that successful democratisation requires a sense of social solidarity, national unity and collective values and that therefore the promotion of an over-arching 'spiritual' institution or the constraining of excessive and destabilising diversity might also be beneficial.

Bearing some of these issues in mind this study seeks to put the Russian experience into a wider context by comparing the ways in which various 'transitional' polities have handled the questions of religion–state relations and religious diversity. To this end I have undertaken five case studies, though in the chapter on the former USSR there are included a series of briefer sketches from the experience of the non-Russian republics. The five major 'European'[7] cases were chosen primarily because all have a dominant religious tradition that, at least historically, has enjoyed a privileged position within the political order. Though it might have been possible to enhance comparison by examining countries with mixed religious traditions, this would have complicated further the assessment of the factors making states respond to the religious question in different ways. The cases were also deliberately chosen from both sides of the old iron curtain in order to explore the impact of regime types on religious politics.

The first two cases are Southern European countries that during the mid-1970s made the transition from a more traditional form of authoritarianism. Here democratic political orders were clearly consolidated by the mid-1980s, with the peaceful advent of socialist governments demonstrating that traditionalist forces accepted the electoral principle. Clearly the experience of these two countries was very different, for though both had the experience of a bloody civil war, Spain had been under a dictatorial regime for nearly four decades, whilst the Greek colonels had been in power for only seven. Moreover, each had different religious traditions and patterns of church–state relations, though in both there was a single traditionally dominant religious institution. In practice, however, the Spanish state, with the longer experience of dictatorship, proved able very quickly to adapt to the norms of 'liberal democracy' in dealing with religious diversity. By way of contrast the reconstructed Greek constitutional order maintained many of the religious privileges and restrictions left over from the pre-war Metaxas dictatorship and, during the 1990s, was still facing challenges in the European Court over its handling of religious minority issues.

The second two cases are taken from East-Central Europe, from countries that shared over forty years of communist dominance but in which the shape of this rule had varied considerably. In Poland, after a brief attempt to bring the country under closer political control, the communist regime had permitted, or been forced to accept, a looser system whereby central authority was not to be challenged but in which a limited pluralism could function. Thus, the realities of Polish life, as well as the hesitancy of the local communist elite, ensured the preservation of two institutional sectors that were probably incapable of being reconciled with communist rule: a strong private agricultural sector and the Roman Catholic Church. By way of contrast, the rulers of Bulgaria promoted an obsequiousness towards Moscow in both rhetorical and practical terms, undertaking collectivisation, purging any leader who inclined to nationalistic enthusiasms, and first terrorising, then controlling an Orthodox Church with a long tradition of submissiveness to secular power, despite its occasional role in promoting resistance to Ottoman rule during the nineteenth century.

Finally, we turn to the former USSR and in particular to the largest of its successor states, Russia. Here there was no substantial tradition of democratic rule or widespread acceptance of diversity; here the Orthodox Church had been legally dominant until 1917 and then, alongside all religious groups, faced severe if changing pressures during the seventy-four years of communist rule. Political change came as a result of communist, some would say imperial, collapse and the break-up of the unique political order that had dominated Eastern and Central Europe during the post-war years. In Russia and most of the other successor states the period from 1988–1995 saw the emergence of a religious free market in which all sorts of groups flourished, but by the end of that period there were growing pressures for the introduction of legal controls on the activities of such groups. Whilst our focus is on Russia, this study will also include a series of briefer sketches of developments in six of the former Soviet republics – Latvia, Lithuania, Georgia, Armenia, Kyrgyzstan and Turkmenistan. Though larger conclusions will not be drawn from these short studies, they are all, with the exception of Latvia, countries with a traditionally dominant religion. Moreover, two are Islamic and distinctly non-European and as such can perhaps provide some useful if limited and not fully explored control element.

Chapters 2–4 of this book are essentially case studies, describing the experience of the three regions: Southern Europe, East-Central Europe and the former USSR. These chapters will present the legal and constitutional state of play during the 1990s and into 2002, exploring how this impacts upon the daily life of religious communities in general and minorities in particular. They will not deal with every aspect of religious life but will focus on two questions:

1. To what extent has the traditionally dominant religious community (or communities) sought or been granted some form of formal legal or constitutional 'privilege' or 'recognition'?
2. To what extent has this entailed, or been accompanied by, the placing of legal or administrative restrictions on the rights of other religious communities?

The fifth chapter will raise a further question:

3. Which actors or individuals have been arguing for privilege or 'recognition and/or discrimination, and what arguments have they used to justify their claims?

Underlying the whole text, and raised later in this chapter as well as in the conclusion, will be the question of:

4. What factors or explanatory models might help to explain the differential experiences under review?

In the concluding chapter we shall also ask what, if anything, does the handling of religious diversity tell us about the problem of creating a democratic order in transitional societies? However, before moving on to the cases it is worth making a few more general comments on each of these questions.

I. TO WHAT EXTENT HAVE THE TRADITIONALLY DOMINANT
RELIGIOUS COMMUNITY (OR COMMUNITIES) SOUGHT OR
BEEN GRANTED SOME FORM OF 'PRIVILEGE' OR FORMAL
'RECOGNITION'?

Historically all of the traditionally dominant religious groups in the countries we are dealing with have enjoyed a position of de facto and de jure privilege, whether spelt out in formal constitutional and legal texts, guaranteed by Concordats with the Vatican, or developed over many years of dealing with the nation-state. In some cases this was maintained throughout the period of authoritarian rule and even in the communist period dominant churches, after a period of extreme persecution, were often granted a tightly controlled status of first amongst equals. Less clear, however, was the appropriateness of 'privileging' particular religious organisations in a liberal democratic setting where constitutional orders normally promise equality regardless of religious faith and where in most cases only a minority of the population are practising members of a single religious community.

There are also problems here in seeking to define what constitutes privilege or, perhaps more accurately, what constitutes illegitimate advantage, because in principle it might be possible to have an established religion that is not thereby a privileged one. Nonetheless, insofar as the very act of separating out one religious community from others makes distinctions it could be construed as disadvantageous for those not so selected. And where, as in the English case, this gives certain ecclesiastical leaders the right to sit in the upper house of the legislature and offers special protection in the form of a blasphemy law, it could be argued that establishment clearly does entail privilege. The issue becomes still more problematic in relation to issues such as religious-based schools, the granting to the dominant religion of special prerogatives in the area of family law and sexual morality, the provision of military or prison chaplains, and the granting of state subsidies to particular religious communities. Here it might be argued that privilege is entailed, though it may be possible to undermine this by granting all religious groups the same rights. Yet even this Solomonic solution runs into difficulties stemming from the well-known legal problem of deciding what constitutes a religion entitled to rights as such in law.

In most of the situations covered in this book the dominant religious communities deny that it is privilege they seek, and prefer to speak of the need for 'recognition' of a historical and social reality. They are the body that has helped to shape and defend national interests over many centuries; they are the community with which a large part of the nation has some sense of identification; they are a social reality that cannot and should not be ignored. In such circumstance, to impose an American style 'wall of separation' and effectively remove religion from the public square might actually serve to privilege a secularist world-view rather than institute religious neutrality. There is also some resentment at the notion that when they campaign on specific issues the churches are in some sense acting improperly, for why should churches not have the same rights to lobby and persuade as other public institutions? Indeed, but problems do arise when religious institutions try to ring-fence certain policy areas. As Fleet and Smith observe in their study of Latin America, if religious institutions claim 'reserved domains' in certain areas, why should other communities such as business or the military not do likewise, and if this is the case what happens to democratic accountability.[8]

A further problem arises in the use of the term 'establishment' for in none of our five major cases is the dominant religion formally referred to as a state church, though the Greek constitution's reference to the 'prevailing' religion and the de facto operation of its constitutional and legal status effectively amounts to establishment. One might also need to make further distinctions between the act of establishment, which tells us little in itself about the impact of 'recognition' on other religious communities or on the wider society, and the wider regulatory regime affecting religious communities. Some scholars have preferred to speak in terms of the market, eschewing the word establishment and focusing on the degree to which religious institutions enjoy a state-protected monopoly position. Chaves and Cann, for example, have developed a six-point scale to indicate the degree of religious monopoly, a scale that included amongst other things asking whether there was an officially designated state church, recognition of some denominations but not others, state subsidies and so forth.[9] The problem with such formal indices – which also assume that the higher the level of religious monopoly the lower the level of religious liberty – is that they struggle to cope with cultural context. For example, the formal establishment of the Lutheran Church in Denmark has a far less restrictive impact upon religious minorities than does the de facto establishment of the Orthodox Church in Greece, accompanied as it is by a series of what have been described as 'para-constitutional' regulations constraining religious rights and freedoms.[10] Equally, in assessing the legitimacy or otherwise of religious 'advantage' it is perhaps worth distinguishing between the regulatory regime and policy involvement by dominant religious institutions. The first is more narrow in impacting upon the religious communities themselves whereas the latter has the potential to impact upon a wider, non-participant population – as in the questions of divorce and abortion.

For all this, my concern here is with elaborating on the ways in which the five traditional dominant churches – and all the main cases refer to either Catholic or Orthodox hegemony, though there are Protestant and Islamic references in the post-Soviet sketches – have either *sought* or *been granted* some form of formal status. For that reason I make brief references to issues such as education, finance and family policy, but the primary focus is on the search for a public statement about the church's position in the new polity. And in deference to the churches' own denial that privilege is what is sought, I have opted for using the word *recognition* in describing the status they seek. For that reason the primary focus of the first substantive part of each case study focuses on statements that set apart the 'national churches', whether these be found in constitutions – which may or may not bear much relationship to reality – or in specific laws relating to religious organisations.

2. TO WHAT EXTENT HAS THIS ENTAILED, OR BEEN ACCOMPANIED BY, THE PLACING OF LEGAL OR ADMINISTRATIVE RESTRICTIONS ON THE RIGHTS OF OTHER RELIGIOUS COMMUNITIES?

Clearly the privileging or establishment of one religious group does not in and of itself necessitate discrimination against others. Whilst minorities often campaign against special privileges there have been occasions where they have defended public recognition of the position of the dominant tradition. For example, in England during the Rushdie affair some Muslim and Jewish spokesmen argued against disestablishment of the Church of England on the grounds that it would effectively remove a religious voice from the public arena. Nonetheless, it could be argued that in all of the countries we focus on here some distinctions are made between religious groups, and that in at least three of the countries the public 'recognition' given to the 'traditional' confessions has been accompanied by discriminatory legislation or practice directed against minority confessions.

Exploring this question in the context of the case studies we start from the assumption that there are certain international legal norms that define the type of rights that should be available to religious communities, regardless of their relationship to the history and culture of the nation. These norms are set out in the International Covenant on Civil and Political Rights, the UN Declaration on the Elimination of All Forms of Intolerance and of Discrimination based on Religion or Belief, and in the European Convention for the Protection of Human Rights and International Freedoms. Of course the production of these documents was a political process and many of the basic understandings enshrined in their texts resulted from compromises over meaning. In particular, problems have emerged over issues such as the right to change one's religion, proselytism, religious education, conscientious objection, and the right of states to advantage or promote particular religious visions. Underlying these discussions are more fundamental debates over whether it is possible to find universal regulatory norms applicable to every cultural context. Some of these arguments surface in a number of the countries with which we are concerned, especially in those whose religious roots are Orthodox. Given that all of these countries share to some degree a common European heritage, and all, with the partial exception of Greece, have signed up to these international agreements it is deemed appropriate here to explore the question of religious rights in terms of these commonly accepted commitments, and for reasons of space to eschew a wider discussion of what is meant by the concept of religious freedom. For our purposes the case studies will focus on the extent to which states produce legislation that restricts the rights of religious minorities to practise their belief, open places of worship, carry out their rituals and worship without hindrance or harassment, educate their children according to their beliefs, not to be excluded from employment on the grounds of their faith commitments, and to be able to find alternative forms of service in countries where military conscription is the norm.

Whilst these international norms are used to define what is unacceptable in a state's regulatory regime vis-à-vis religious communities, it is worth asking whether religious liberty should always be seen as an absolute value and whether it can in some sense be 'trumped' by other needs of the political community. In particular, during times of transition when populations are disoriented, vulnerable and traumatised, might there not be a need to create a sense of solidarity, belonging and shared values? In such circumstances a religious institution that has played a key role in shaping the national past might be particularly suited to providing meaning for a society that has seen all of its old certainties collapse. Equally, can the restriction of religious liberty and diversity be justified in terms of the need to preserve social and political stability in fragile societies undergoing processes of rapid political change?[11] Or might it be possible, following the European Court judgement in the Kokkinakis case (see chapter 2), for distinctions to be made between an appropriate and inappropriate use of religious liberty rights? If so, who decides what is acceptable – the European Court unhelpfully failed to do so in speaking of proper and improper forms of proselytism – and to what extent should state authorities have the right to intervene in the religious sphere? And even if a case could be made for the curbing of some types of religious activity, does this require special laws on religion, along the lines of those emerging in the former Soviet bloc, or can excesses be adequately dealt with by civil and criminal law?

3. WHICH ACTORS OR INDIVIDUALS HAVE BEEN ARGUING FOR 'RECOGNITION' AND/OR DISCRIMINATION, AND WHAT ARGUMENTS HAVE THEY USED TO JUSTIFY THEIR CLAIMS?

The common assumption is that the claims for 'recognition' or restriction of minority rights come primarily from the traditionally dominant religious community, and it is often the case that such churches do actively seek to protect their own institutional interests, especially in times of political and social change when their position and public role may be under question. At the same time a broad array of other institutional actors or individuals within the social, political and cultural elite are often to be found making the case for 'protection'. On the part of the state this may involve government ministers using the issue for electoral or other political ends, state security agencies seeking to find new 'threats' in a post-authoritarian context, or other bureaucratic agencies – in some post-communist countries, former religious affairs administrations – finding it hard to throw off the old disposition to control any manifestation of independent social activity. Nationalist politicians are often at the forefront of campaigns for privilege or restriction, arguing in terms of the need for national and religious unity in the face of internal and external threats, or arguing against externally imposed models of religion–state relations that are inappropriate to their country's particular cultural context or traditions. Liberal intellectuals may also express the fear, sometimes in paternalistic fashion, that the current fragility of the transition period leaves the masses vulnerable to religious movements of dubious provenance and doubtful taste. Local officials, pressure groups and the media may play a key role in waging campaigns against particular groups, with the press producing sensationalist accounts that generalise about all religious minorities on the basis of the actions of the most radical. This may in turn play on, as well as create, a public anxiety about the 'invasion of the sects' that is rooted in the wider uncertainties created by the new social and political context. Finally, international factors may be at work, as in the former USSR where many of the newly independent states followed the Russian Federation in modelling new laws or proposals on religious issues, or as in Greece where the primary stimulus for a change in the church–state relationship comes from external rather than internal pressures.

The arguments that are made here tend to fall into four broad 'families':

- The first focuses on the need to recognise the 'sociological reality' in countries where the majority church is part of the very fabric of society and therefore deserving of formal recognition. This is the religious institution that has steered the nation through centuries of history and to which the majority of the population has some form of nominal allegiance. In such circumstances constitutional or legal status does not represent any privileging of the institution but a simple acceptance of a 'social fact'. Such arguments are not unproblematic, with religious institutions tending to utilise majoritarianism in a selective fashion and the national church argument raising questions about the position of those citizens who do not adhere to its institutional or doctrinal forms.

- Secondly, there is what might be called the moral guardianship approach that emphasises the role of the dominant church in protecting moral values and defends the need to strengthen this body in order to prevent a disoriented population from falling into the hands of 'destructive sects'. Closely allied to this is the notion of unfair competition, with the suggestion that in the new situation there is not a level playing field and that privileging the weakened majority community will simply provide them with proper support in their struggle against well-funded foreign missionaries.

- Thirdly, there are appeals rooted in a concern for order and stability, partly stimulated by a reaction to the seeming anarchy of democracy and partly by fears, real and imagined, about the likely impact of untrammelled religious diversity on the security of the new political and social order. Such arguments are sometimes closely linked with suggestions that what is needed is not so much political control, but a proper regulatory framework within which all religious organisations can operate under the broad umbrella of the law.

- Finally, there are more explicitly nationalist arguments, sometimes couched in negative terms and utilising chauvinistic anti-foreigner rhetoric, and sometimes in more positive ways that stress the uniqueness of the country concerned and the need to develop one's own model of religion–state relations. In many of the newly democratising countries this is the most potent line of argument, and it has emerged especially powerfully in Greece and Russia where processes of Westernisation and the external promotion of individualistic norms of conduct have aroused particular resentment amongst some sections of the population and political elite. Here we find arguments for privilege or restriction most clearly expressed in terms of the 'nation in danger.'[12]

In each of our cases the actors and the emphasis differ but in most of them, with the partial exception of Spain, some version of all four have been voiced. Clearly in many cases the motivations are not specifically religious, and have more to do with visions of the country's future and with broader political objectives. Even when voiced by churchmen it is often difficult to distinguish in any meaningful way between ideological claims and the pursuit of institutional or power interests. In rational choice terms, whatever the doctrinal objectives of religious institutions, they also as institutions have 'revenue maximisation' goals – increasing adherents, institutions and income – that require them to operate in the political as well as the spiritual realm, and therefore to make political alliances with forces whose motives are not always clear.[13] In such cases religious leaders have to adapt their own rhetoric so as to combine the voicing of genuine religious concerns with the need to acquire support within the broader political society.

4. IN WHAT WAYS MIGHT ONE EXPLAIN THE DIFFERENTIAL EXPERIENCES UNDER REVIEW?

Finding an all-embracing explanation for the ways in which transitional societies handle the issue of religious diversity is virtually impossible, but we can point to various types of explanation that might shed some light on developments in transitional societies. These might focus on prior regime type and the nature of the transition, on the impact of confessional difference, on socio-economic factors, or on the role of nationalism in promoting particular visions of how the new political community should be shaped and who belongs within it.

Regime type and the nature of transition

One might expect the nature of the authoritarian system to have some impact, given that in three of our major cases the old regime was explicitly committed to the *elimination* of religion whilst the two Southern European dictatorships saw one of their tasks as the *rescue* of Christian civilisation. Alfred Stepan and Juan Linz have suggested that the tasks of democratic consolidation might be easier in post-authoritarian states such as Spain – where there existed a developed civil society, a reasonably strong legal culture, a well-organised state bureaucracy and institutionalised economic society – than in a post-communist society where many of these features were absent.[14] In relation to our study one might also predict the transition from state control of religion to a religious free market to be a more problematic process in communist countries where extensive bureaucracies had dealt with religious issues and the state's predisposition was interventionist. Though the actual position varied from country to country – with the Polish state permitting, however reluctantly at times, a considerable degree of space for religious life, whilst the Russian and Bulgarian regimes promoted a tightly controlled Orthodox Church as a quasi-national institution – all of these regimes explicitly rejected religious participation in the public sphere. In consequence, a reasonable expectation would be that finding new models of church–state relations and evolving responses to the question of religious pluralism would be more problematic within post-communist than post-authoritarian polities, and in turn more difficult in Russia and Bulgaria than in Poland.

The nature of the transition process and the distance that the new polity has travelled on the road to a democratic order might also be of significance. Broadly speaking, we would expect that in those countries where democratisation has resulted from a process of negotiation and compromise, the resolution of religion–state issues might be more consensual in nature than elsewhere. Thus, in the cases of Spain and Poland where democratisation came about as a result of negotiation one might find key actors inclined to a search for policy compromises rather than attempts to achieve all of their desired objectives. In our other cases the nature of the transition was essentially 'accidental': in Greece a consequence of a botched military operation by a disliked regime, in Bulgaria a product of the knock-on effect from other East European changes, and in Russia and the successor states a consequence of imperial collapse. Unlike the first two cases, the churches here made little contribution to democratisation and thus lacked moral authority to participate in political transformation. Here the absence of any experience in facilitating the transition process in general meant that they lacked first-hand acquaintance with the negotiation and compromise that are an essential part of the policy process when mature democracies tackle policy issues, including those affecting religion.

In addition, the cultural context in the countries undergoing transition may be important to determining outcomes in the religious sphere. Most studies of societies undergoing transition in a liberal or democratic direction suggest that in the long term the evolution of a democratic mind-set or democratic political culture is important. In the first instance this may simply require that elites agree to play by the new 'rules of the game' and that they accept the legitimacy of the emerging system, but in the longer term it is argued that stability requires some form of mass acceptance of the political system and, if the democracy is to be truly 'liberal', the emergence of mass values accepting of difference and tolerant of alternative viewpoints. Such arguments usually make use of the concept of political culture which is based upon the assumption that 'every political system is embedded in a particular pattern of orientations to political action', encompassing beliefs, values and sentiments about the most appropriate way to manage political life.[15] Critics have charged that the concept is too deterministic and pessimistic insofar as it appears to suggest that without elite or mass acceptance of an appropriate political culture, change – especially in a democratic direction – is unlikely in certain countries. Yet despite new approaches to political research many scholars remain committed to the view that cultural context does matter and that at the very least the peculiar traditions of a country help to shape the way in which politicians and the wider population respond to specific political issues.[16] This very point is made by Monsma and Soper in their study of church and state in established democracies. Here they note that it is primarily such factors that serve to make a German-style church tax or English-style establishment impossible in the American context, even though neither could today be described as seriously encroaching on the population's religious liberty in their respective countries.[17]

It is difficult to see how political culture would impact upon the 'recognition' issue, though clearly in countries such as Greece, the constitutional and legal privileging of the Orthodox Church does not greatly disturb the majority of the population who view the Church as part of the nation's institutional structure. Where one might expect societal values and attitudes to have a greater impact is in relation to minority issues. Here the rather crude expectation would be that laws restricting religious liberty or minority rights were more likely to appear, and be more acceptable, in those countries where the levels of tolerance of 'otherness' or acceptance of social pluralism are low, and where authoritarian solutions to political problems are more readily accepted. Without pre-judging this issue we would expect laws restricting religious minority rights to be more acceptable in those countries such as Russia and Bulgaria where public opinion surveys indicate a continuing suspicion of diversity, especially amongst the generations brought up under the old order.

Confessional difference

A country's political culture is shaped in part by its religious traditions and, even though religious belief and adherence may have declined in the modern era, the legacy of past religious structures and practices may continue to affect the way in which social and political systems operate. Such linkages are, however, extremely difficult to document, for though social scientists can investigate aspects of religious influence such as the link between regular church attendance and voting behaviour – though even here causation is difficult to assess – the longer-term impact of religious traditions remains harder to gauge. Various writers have seen connections between religious traditions and socio-political outcomes, most notably Max Weber in his studies of the impact of the 'Protestant ethic' on the development of capitalism. This is not the place to explore his particular thesis but it is worth pointing out that Weber did not posit a deterministic set of relationships that would emerge in every circumstance, but simply made connections between religious and economic change at a particular time in history.

Of more relevance to those interested in democratisation processes of the last thirty years are the arguments put forward by Samuel Huntington regarding the impact of religious tradition on the 'third wave'. Noting a strong correlation between Western Christianity and democratisation and the fact that many of the third wave countries are Roman Catholic, Huntington suggested that many recent democratisation processes had been made possible in part by developments within that Church. In particular the impact of Vatican II and the increasing activism of the Church as a transnational actor has led national churches that hitherto passively accepted authoritarian polities to adopt a more critical, pro-democratic orientation. This in turn reinforced other challenges to these regimes and helped to modify the traditionally paternalistic nature of Iberian and Latin American political culture.[18] At the same time, Huntington suggests that the Protestant effect can still be felt in places such as Korea where growing campaigns for liberalisation paralleled substantial growth in Protestant numbers. He is not suggesting that religious factors are determining – though the later 'clash of civilisations' argument comes close to this – but that religious change has a longer-term impact upon the possibility of democratisation taking place. In particular, he argues that certain traditions (notably Protestant and Catholic) are, or historically have been, more conducive to successful democratic political change than others (Orthodoxy, Islam).[19]

A cursory look at the experience of the 'fourth wave' sweeping through Eastern Europe and the USSR from the late 1980s onwards might appear to offer some confirmation of this thesis. Broadly speaking the countries with Protestant and Catholic traditions have made more progress towards democratisation than countries with an Orthodox and Muslim inheritance, and we have to ask whether there is any causal relationship at work here. That is, are elements of the political tradition in these countries shaped by past religious allegiances that in turn serve to inhibit the development of democratic institutions or of pluralistic values amongst the elites and the wider population? There is also an argument that focuses on the national nature of the Orthodox churches, something that renders them weaker in relation to the state than the transnational Catholic Church. In this context the Orthodox churches have fewer resources with which to combat the authoritarian state and have developed a mentality rooted in subservience to the state. Thus Linz and Stepan suggest that whilst Orthodox churches may well support or live with democratic governments, they are more likely to follow the lead of dominant political elites than initiate any action in this area.[20]

If religious tradition is important, the link is essentially indirect and has little to do with current levels of religious adherence and practice. It is also not a simple question of religious determinism suggesting that certain religious traditions are simply incompatible with democracy – or more precisely, with a Western created model of 'liberal democracy'. Huntington's argument suggests that political cultural changes can follow amendments of religious teachings, and more recently Alfred Stepan and others have stressed the multivocal character of religious teachings in this area. Thus Islamic and Orthodox democrats can find elements within their traditions that might prove supportive of democratisation, for example in their understanding of the role of consultation in political society.[21] Nonetheless, though no religious tradition alone must of necessity promote or inhibit the building of a pluralist society, there remain currents in some traditions that do appear problematic. Religious traditions are multivocal but at any one point in time it may be that the dominant voice in those traditions works for or against the development of a pluralistic vision of the polity and the place of religion within it. For that reason our hypothesis here would be that in Orthodox and Islamic cultural contexts there is more likely to be a de facto if not de jure privileging of traditionally dominant religious groups. Equally there is more likely to be some restriction of minority rights than in countries where Catholic and Protestant traditions prevail.

Modernisation, secularisation and religious economics

The basic assumption of secularisation theory is not that as we become more 'modern' religious belief will decline, but that attendant upon processes of modernisation will be a decline in the public role of religion. In Bruce's words the social significance of religion diminishes in response to 'the fragmentation of societies and of social life, the disappearance of the community and the growth of massive bureaucracies (national and international), and increasing rationalization'.[22] Despite occasional periods of what Casanova calls the 'deprivatisation' of religion and others speak of as religious 'resurgence', proponents of the secularisation thesis argue that it continues to hold – at least in the industrialised world – except in societies undergoing rapid change or where religion can provide a 'cultural defence' against the onslaughts of modernity.[23] One by-product of secularisation and modernisation is the growth of religious liberty and the tolerance of different forms of religious practice. Some theorists suggested that religion needed to occupy a monopoly position, to erect what Berger called a 'sacred canopy' under which all worshipped and accepted a specific vision of truth.[24] Once this was fractured and people began to branch off into a variety of religious communities, religious claims became increasingly a matter of opinion and religious influence declined. Religious competition weakened the public role of religious organisation by undermining any concept of absolute truth that could be accepted by all. In consequence religious liberty emerged, not as a product of choice but from necessity, from the very processes of modernisation that in most countries undermined universal acceptance of a monopolistic religious vision. One of the consequences of this was a gradual trend towards the separation of church and state, the assumption being that true religious liberty was impossible where there was a state church – though the differential treatment of religious minorities in countries such as Greece and Denmark suggests that in the present era this assumption is too simplistic. What this might lead one to expect in the context of our study is that as one moves politically 'eastwards' towards the less developed post-communist world the degree of religious liberty would decline and the traditionally dominant religious institutions would seek to regain, preserve or create a monopoly position. In relation to our five major cases we might then expect religious liberty to be most advanced in Spain, followed by Greece, Poland, Bulgaria and Russia, whilst it would be in the latter countries that traditional churches might be most likely to lay claim to legal and institutional 'recognition'. The picture is complicated, however, by the fact that Bulgaria and Russia, though less 'modern' than the Western states, had experienced a peculiar brand of state-sponsored secularisation that had not been without impact upon public attitudes towards religion.

Not all those focusing on socio-economic aspects of religious developments are convinced by these arguments. Rational choice theorists, for example, tend to argue that religious revitalisation and decline are more cyclical in nature and shaped by changes in the levels of religious competition and by the regulatory framework within which religious groups operate. Here the basic assumptions are that (a) religious institutions should be treated much as firms operating in a market and seeking ways of maximising their 'revenue' (i.e. membership and financial resources); (b) where there is a religious monopoly participation and enthusiasm will decline in the protected church; and (c) where there is a relatively unregulated free market religious groups will become more 'efficient' and more will prosper because of the need to find ways of getting one up on competitors.[25] A further consequence of all this would be that in situations where there is a high level of regulation the level of religious competition is likely to be low and conversely, as the levels of monopoly and restrictive legislation decline religious competition will increase.

Anthony Gill has offered some thoughts on how the approach might be used to explain the origins of religious liberty. Starting from the assumption that variations in religiosity are determined by variations in religious liberty, he asks how one explains the evolution of differing levels of religious liberty. Rejecting the interpretations that see religious freedom as primarily a product of Enlightenment ideas or modernisation processes, he prefers to explore the issue of institutional design and the impact of government regulation on religious freedom. To this end he focuses on the question of why specific laws are developed at particular times, and suggests that we need to look at the preferences of political elites and churchmen in specific contexts. Religious liberty does not happen because of the triumph of liberal ideas, but because of specific choices made by politicians, on the basis of analysis of the costs or benefits involved in making political use of these issues, at certain points in history.[26]

In terms of our study rational choice approaches might predict that all our traditionally dominant churches will seek to maintain their near-monopoly situation by encouraging political elites to give them legal 'recognition', 'protection' or 'advantage'. Such an approach would also suggest that politicians will support the dominant churches so long as they see some advantage in doing so, whether electoral or in terms of utilising religious norms and values to reinforce citizen compliance.[27] But in time pressure may grow for deregulation – whether from internal religious and political competitors, or from external agencies such as the European Union in the case of Greece – and this when enacted will in turn reduce the cost of entry for others and lead to growing religious competition. Yet as we shall see, in two of the countries where religious competition was already extensive at the point of transition and became more so later, there has been resistance to genuine deregulation. Indeed, in Russia and elsewhere, we witnessed the emergence of new and more restrictive legislation because, as we shall suggest in the next section, there were other incentives encouraging the political support of national churches.

Nationalism and civil religion

One of the theses put forward by defenders of the secularisation theory is that religious resurgence takes place primarily in contexts of cultural defence and cultural transition.[28] Applied to our European cases the basic argument would be that in many cases the discussions about church–state relations and minority rights have less to do with religion, and are in fact informed primarily by wider concerns and located in a broader discourse about the nature of the new political and social order being built in these transitional societies. Writing about the debates over the 1997 Russian law on religion, John Witte quotes the Orthodox Ecumenical Patriarch who on a visit to America suggested that if anything the differences between the Western and Orthodox traditions was growing, and argued that 'the manner in which we exist has become ontologically different'. According to the Patriarch the West had been shaped under the shadow of the Enlightenment, which provided too little room for faith and too much for freedom. Witte goes on to note how arguments of this type reverberated in Russian Orthodox Church circles during the 1990s and how debates about legislation reflected more fundamental differences of understanding about what was acceptable in the religious marketplace. For example, proselytism, seen from a Western perspective as a consequence of freedom of religion, could also be seen as an illegitimate intrusion into the life of another community and a violation of their freedom of conscience.[29]

As we shall see, much of the public discourse over the public status of religion has made reference to the national or traditional status of the majority religion, and has been located in a much wider discussion about national identity, especially in the Orthodox countries. Though the attention of the churches has often focused on questions of their distinctive values and beliefs and their potential contribution to the tasks of transition, secular politicians have often been just as involved in raising religious questions in the context of the wider debates about national or state identity. Such arguments have had two separate but overlapping dimensions, one domestic and one international. Internally the debate has focused on the potential contribution of religious values to the stabilisation of the political order, whilst externally the emphasis has been on the need to do things 'our way' and on resisting the attempts of outside powers to impose 'alien' models on countries about which they know little. If the positive side of these debates is an attempt to preserve traditional cultures and ways of life against an encroaching, globalising world, the downside is a defensive mentality that sees threats all around.[30] In consequence one might expect to find churchmen and politicians seeking to privilege religious institutions seen as 'traditional' and restrict the rights of groups 'threatening' the country's national and spiritual inheritance in those of our countries where the issue of identity remains unresolved, notably Russia, and to some extent Greece – where

European Union membership has raised anew questions about what it is to be Greek.

Those politicians involved in these debates and in shaping religious policies do so in a context shaped by legacies from the past and inherited, if modified, patterns of opinion about how such issues are best handled. In seeking to resolve questions of 'recognition' and religious pluralism key actors might refer back, consciously or otherwise, to earlier relationships between church and state. Inevitably the same conditions rarely apply and the world has often changed in ways that make a simple copying of the past impossible, though in Greece it sometimes appears that time has stood still – albeit the Orthodox Church now has a greater degree of internal independence and freedom from state control. In Russia, though here the break has been longer, one might expect politicians and churchmen to refer back to the late Tsarist period when the Orthodox Church enjoyed a degree of social and cultural pre-eminence and when its representatives enjoyed a respect and public place later destroyed by the Soviet experiment. Equally, however, a more nuanced reading of history might make religious elites wary of a re-creation of a prominence that came at the cost of an unparalleled degree of subservience to state officials.

Many of the same dilemmas seemed likely to arise in the Catholic countries, as in Poland during the early 1990s where many churchmen appeared to believe that their role in opposing the old communist system gave them the right to restore a religious guardianship over the future development of the nation. By way of contrast, the Spanish Church, keen to promote its own values and teachings, was simultaneously aware of the dangers of re-awakening the polarisation around religious issues that had contributed to the bloody nature of the civil war. In other words, whilst both secular and religious politicians could not escape the institutional legacies of the past, contemporary considerations make it unlikely that there could be any simple 'return' to historical relationships between church and state, or an overarching religious hegemony. And in the Catholic world it is not just the outside world that has moved on but also the institution, which, under the impact of Vatican II, has formally rejected claims to any enforced religious monopoly.

It may also be the case that political elites lacking confidence in their country's prospects and direction may seek to promote the dominant religious tradition as a 'civil religion' that will provide a set of 'consensual values' capable of filling a perceived ideological or spiritual vacuum. The idea of 'civil religion' has its roots in the nineteenth-century comments of Alexis de Tocqueville on the importance of religion in civilising democracy, and in the fuller twentieth-century elaboration of the notion by Robert Bellah and others.[31] In particular the concept has been used with reference to the American experience, where it points not to the dominance of a single religious denomination or community, but to certain values said to transcend theological differences and arguably inclusive enough to encompass those Americans of other, little or no faith. Thus despite the formal 'wall of separation' between church and state, we have popular conceptions of the USA as a chosen nation, according to the Pledge of Allegiance's 'one nation under God'. This civil religion is reinforced on national occasions, whether the inauguration or funerals of presidents, the rituals accorded those servicemen who die overseas, or in the celebration of Thanksgiving. In Kenneth Wald's words:

A civil religion is neither the religion of a particular church nor, at the other extreme, a full articulated religion that competes with existing denominations. Rather, it is a code subscribed to, in varying degrees, by all religions in the nation . . . By imparting a sacred character to the nation, civil religion enables peoples of diverse faiths to harmonise their religious and political beliefs.[32]

At the heart of this idea is the notion that a political community needs what Monsma and Soper describe as a set of 'consensual religious beliefs and traditions' that provide a bedrock of common values that 'hold society together'.[33] Their reference is to mature democratic societies, but arguably even in contexts where political unity is maintained by coercion some form of value consensus may be necessary to maintain a regime in power over the long term.

Arguably, the need for some form of value cement is even greater in transitional societies, where the old ideologies have been thrown out but have not been replaced in the seeming chaos of democracy by any overarching belief system. This in turn might explain why politicians with apparently little religious conviction or belief take up religious issues in promoting their own careers or political programmes. At first sight, however, the promotion of a dominant 'national' religion seems at odds with the notion of civil religion in its American manifestation, for in the former case an exclusivist case is being made for a single or several religious traditions. In practice many national religious communities have in effect evolved along the lines of civil religion, in which the content of belief is less important than the social cohesion provided by the tradition. The political arguments for the promotion of a civil religion might be expected to be especially prominent in the post-communist states where transition is more recent and where a totalising ideological perspective has been undermined by political change. Here values and beliefs are in flux and the political elites are in constant search for mechanisms by which they might not just legitimise their own positions but also provide some form of value cement capable of holding their countries together. In such circumstances, it is often easier to build on existing religious and cultural traditions than to create civic traditions afresh. Occasionally, as in the reported revival of secular coming-of-age celebrations in the former East Germany, this may involve drawing on the socialist tradition, but in most cases this has been discredited and thus provides limited scope for revitalisation. Hence, the common response is to make use of the country's existing religious tradition. In the Orthodox countries this could involve the promotion and protection of the national churches, not primarily as believing communities with all the spiritual and critical challenges this might raise, but as a resource to be used on national occasions or in the rhetoric of politicians. For the churches this raises new dilemmas, as state protection has its value – both in institutional and even spiritual terms – but also has certain costs.

Finally, one has to ask whether is it possible to find any general patterns or explanatory models, or whether the most important factors are contingent, dependent upon the day-to-day needs of politicians and a product of circumstances that are peculiar to each country. Why did Boris Yeltsin veto the draft law on religion in late July 1997 and then approve virtually the same law two months later, and was the mellowing of the Bulgarian 'anti-sect' campaign towards the end of 1997 unrelated to the election of a new government? Here, too, one should perhaps make some reference to the international relations of the churches concerned, for it is arguable that the impact of Vatican II on a transnational church as well as John Paul II's promotion of human rights helps to explain why the Catholic Church in neither Spain nor Poland has made a serious case for a restriction of minority rights – though this has not of course stopped the same Pope from attacking Protestantism's 'ravening wolves' in Latin America or prevented some Catholic hierarchies in the same continent from doing just this.[34] In seeking to assess these approaches the concluding chapter will address all these questions, and offer comments as to which of the approaches are more useful in helping us to explain and understand the political response to religious diversity in these countries. At the same time it will raise the wider question of what a study of this nature in general, and in relation to these countries in particular, tells us about the evolution of a democratic mentality in these societies that is accepting of pluralism without having to deny their national traditions and distinctiveness.

Notes

1. A term used by Vaclav Havel to describe late communist societies which may have had 'totalist aspirations', but lacked the means or capacity to realise them. See his essay 'The power of the powerless', in V. Havel, *Living in Truth* (London: Faber & Faber, 1986), especially pp. 36–41.
2. On these distinctions see A. Przeworski, 'Democracy as a contingent outcome of conflicts', in J. Elster and R. Slagstad (eds.), *Constitutionalism and Democracy* (Cambridge: Cambridge University Press, 1988), pp. 61–3.
3. Figures from S. White, *Russia's New Politics: The Management of a Postcommunist Society* (Cambridge: Cambridge University Press, 2000), pp. 269–76.
4. M. Wyman, *Public Opinion in Post-Communist Russia* (London: Macmillan, 1997), pp. 134–41.
5. According to an unpublished survey on Bulgarian attitudes whose results have yet to be published. I am grateful to Emil Cohen of the Bulgarian Tolerance Foundation for giving me a broad outline of these results. Interview in Sofia, June 2000.
6. See the discussions in Guiseppe di Palma, *To Craft Democracies* (Berkeley: California University Press, 1990); J. Linz and A. Stepan, *Problems of Democratic Transition and Consolidation* (Baltimore: Johns Hopkins University Press, 1996); A. Leftwich, 'From democratization to democratic consolidation', in D. Potter (ed.), *Democratization* (Cambridge: Polity, 1997), pp. 517–36.
7. 'European' is used advisedly here because there is considerable discussion over the question of whether Russia is really part of Europe.
8. M. Fleet and B. Smith, *The Catholic Church and Democracy in Chile and Peru* (Notre Dame: University of Notre Dame Press, 1997), p. 179.
9. M. Chaves and D. Cann, 'Regulation, pluralism and religious market structure', *Rationality and Society*, 4: 3, 1992, pp. 272–90.
10. Michael Minkenburg has suggested that in Western Catholic countries there is no clear relationship between church–state ties and policy outcomes. For example, in the case of abortion the separation of church and state has resulted in less liberal abortion regimes than in states where the ties are closer, which suggests that the Catholic Church retains an independent role regardless of its formal relationship with the state. M. Minkenburg, 'Religion and policy effects: church, state and party configurations in the policy making process', paper presented at ECPR Joint Sessions, Workshop on 'Church and State in Europe', Copenhagen, 14–19 April 2000.
11. This is an argument used by Central Asian rulers who refer to the need to combat 'Islamic fundamentalism' in justifying their own authoritarian styles of rule.
12. A phrase used in G. Mavrogordatas, 'Church and State Greece', paper presented at the ECPR Workshop on 'Church and State in Europe', Copenhagen, 14–19 April 2000.
13. For an overview of the pros and cons of applying rational choice theory to religion see L. Young (ed.), *Rational Choice Theory and Religion* (London: Routledge, 1996).
14. Linz and Stepan, *Problems of Democratic Transition and Consolidation*, chapter 4.

15. G. Almond, 'Comparing political systems', *The Journal of Politics*, 18, 1956, p. 396; the 'classic' development of the concept can be found reprinted in G. Almond and S. Verba, *The Civic Culture* (Princeton: Princeton University Press, 1963).

16. For a wider discussion of these debates see R. Eatwell, 'Introduction: the importance of the political culture approach', in R. Eatwell (ed.), *European Political Cultures: Conflict or Convergence* (London: Routledge, 1997), pp. 1–12; L. Diamond, 'Introduction: political culture and democracy', in L. Diamond (ed.), *Political Culture and Democracy in Developing Countries* (London: Lynne Reinner, 1994), pp. 1–27.

17. S. Monsma and J. Soper, *The Challenge of Pluralism: Church and State in Five Democracies* (Oxford and New York: Rowman & Littlefield, 1997), p. 200.

18. Though this does not explain why differing national hierarchies in Latin America responded in different ways to Vatican II, with the Argentine hierarchy largely appearing to ignore the commitment to human rights and the Chilean and Brazilian bishops taking a much more prominent role in defence of the abused.

19. S. Huntington, *The Third Wave: Democratization in the Late Twentieth Century* (Norman: University of Oklohoma Press, 1993), pp. 72–85.

20. Linz and Stepan, *Problems of Democratic Transition and Consolidation*, p. 453.

21. A. Stepan, 'Religion, democracy, and the "twin tolerations"', *Journal of Democracy*, 11: 4, 2000, pp. 37–57.

22. S. Bruce, *Religion in the Modern World* (Oxford: Oxford University Press, 1996), pp. 38–9; for a more extensive discussion of this debate in relation to the European and American models see the essays in S. Bruce (ed.), *Religion and Modernisation* (Oxford: Oxford University Press, 1992).

23. Bruce, *Religion in the Modern World*, chapter 5.

24. P. Berger, *The Sacred Canopy: Elements of a Sociological Theory of Religion* (New York: Archer Books, 1990).

25. For an overview of this literature see Young, *Rational Choice Theory and Religion*; for an extremely critical view see S. Bruce, *Choice and Religion* (Oxford: Oxford University Press, 1999).

26. A. Gill, 'The political origins of religious liberty: initial sketch of a general theory', paper presented at the ECPR Workshop on 'Church and State in Europe', Copenhagen, 14–19 April 2000.

27. A. Gill, *Rendering unto Caesar* (Chicago: Chicago University Press, 1998), pp. 50–4.

28. Bruce, *Religion in the Modern World*, chapter 5.

29. J. Witte, 'Introduction', in J. Witte and M. Bourdeaux (eds.), *Proselytism and Orthodoxy in Russia: The New War for Souls* (New York: Orbis, 1999), pp. 18–27.

30. Some Russian Orthodox churchmen have commented to me on the way in which it is the new converts, often from communist backgrounds, who are the most defensive and ideologically zealous on behalf of their new faith which they promote in the style of Dostoyevsky's Grand Inquisitor.

31. R. Bellah and P. Hammond (eds.), *Varieties of Civil Religion* (New York: Harper & Row, 1980).

32. K. Wald, *Religion and Politics in the United States* (Washington DC: CQ Press, 1997), p. 60.
33. Monsma and Soper, *The Challenge of Pluralism*, p. 5.
34. Quoted in P. Sigmund, 'Introduction', in P. Sigmund (ed.), *Religious Freedom and Evangelization in Latin America: The Challenge of Pluralism* (New York: Orbis, 1999), p. 2.

2   Southern Europe: Spain and Greece

Democratisation's 'third wave' started to roll in Southern Europe during the mid-1970s, in Portugal, Greece and Spain. Though this was a region with many differences, for outside commentators there was still a feeling that these countries were somehow separate from 'normal' Europe.[1] In particular these were 'late' modernisers, countries steeped in clientelistic politics and a social conservatism often, though not entirely accurately, seen to be rooted in the superstitious piety of the largely rural masses. Indeed in Spain at least it was arguably the bourgeoisie that provided the traditionalist bedrock of the system. In all three a dominant religious tradition claimed a monopoly of influence, and one that was broadly accepted by the state. Historically only in Spain had anti-clericalism become a serious political issue, though in all three many intellectuals despised religious institutions and the growing industrial sector of the workforce was increasingly alienated from organised religion. By the early 1970s each of these countries faced incipient crisis as ageing dictators or politically inept officers struggled to come to terms with a Europe unsympathetic to their particular political visions. And in the two countries examined in this study – Spain and Greece – political transition was hastened by the death of a dictator in the former and an inept military adventure in the latter. In response to these developments sections within the political elite seized control of the process of change and ensured that what followed was essentially 'democratisation from above', especially in Greece where the old conservative establishment largely oversaw the process of change. In Spain the process drew in most political forces and was rooted in a political and civil society that had been increasingly influential from the early 1960s onwards. This elite manipulation of change ensured a degree of stability that served to see the two countries through the transition process and permit the eventual peaceful turnover of power to others during the 1980s. At the same time the transition phase raised new problems for traditionally dominant religious institutions both in regard to their public role and their relationship to the social and religious pluralism that ensued.

Spain: From Catholic Nationalism to Religious Pluralism

Political context: the 'model transition'

The regime that emerged in Spain after the Nationalist triumph in 1939 was something of a hybrid. On the one hand looking to the Axis powers for inspiration, Franco's rule nonetheless lacked the coherence and ideological motivation that characterised the 'totalitarian' systems promoted by fascism. Instead the Caudillo set about creating what Raymond Carr has described as 'a conservative, Catholic, authoritarian system'.[2] Crucial to this regime was a sense of negation, a reaction to all the ills that had beset Spain under preceding governments. More specifically this was a government of the victors, dominated by those had fought the crusade against 'anti-Spain' and committed to institutionalising the Nationalist victory in the civil war. In practice this meant the emergence of several political 'families' all tied into the regime by the 'pact of blood' linking them together through complicity in the repressions that followed Franco's victory.[3] Amongst these were the Catholic Church, whose role we discuss below; the Falange with their commitment to a more ideological model of the Spanish future; landowners and capitalists seeking to promote their own economic interests unchallenged; monarchists hopeful of recreating an older form of rule through the medium of the *Movimiento*; and soldiers keen to preserve a political influence that had been enhanced by their victory in the civil war. Above all these groups sat Franco, who skilfully kept each group in its place by playing off one against the other and utilising their fears of the vanquished to preserve his own power over the victors.[4]

For the regime the challenge was to maintain political control whilst managing socio-economic change. In 1957 this task was handed over to the 'technocrats', many of whom were associated with the Opus Dei movement that sought to put key lay Catholics into prominent economic and political positions. Under their influence the economy began to boom as Spain became more integrated into the world economy, opened its beaches to foreign tourists, and sent its own people abroad as migrant workers to earn foreign currency. By the early 1970s the living standards of many Spaniards were beginning to approach those of their northern neighbours, yet they were all too aware of the political and social freedoms available elsewhere in Europe. Within Spain growing worker unrest led businessmen to bargain with illegal trade unions rather than the officially approved syndicates. Many of these unions were in turn connected to the increasingly active if still underground opposition parties. On top of this the Franco regime faced major regionalist challenges in

Catalonia and the Basque territory, with some activists in the latter region turning to terrorism and in 1973 claiming the life of government leader Admiral Carrero Blanco. Simultaneously political discourse amongst the younger generation of activists and administrators increasingly left the old division of Spain into the good and the bad behind. Instead their conversations revolved around notions of 'modernity', 'Europeanness' and 'liberalisation'.[5]

By the time of Franco's death in November 1975 many within the political elite had come to recognise the need for change if Spain were to be properly integrated into emerging European Community structures and rebuild legitimate government at home. By this time various key sectors, including the Catholic Church, much of the business community, and the educated classes had developed a more critical relationship with the state, and this in turn reflected wider changes taking place in Spanish society. On the one hand there was the 'rebirth of civil society' evident in the growth of social organisation, trade union movements and political parties; on the other the emerging regionalist challenge to Madrid's supremacy. All these factors stimulated far-sighted elements within the old regime to push for more substantial political change, whilst seeking to avoid any return to the polarisation that had characterised Spain in the past or to slide into the chaos evident in neighbouring Portugal. For these reasons Prime Minister Adolfo Suárez, supported by King Juan Carlos, sought to process the controversial Law on Political Reform through the firmly traditional Cortes. At the personal level these two served as links to the old regime, helping to reassure fearful conservatives that things would not get out of hand, but each pushed the process much further than 'the bunker' would have preferred.[6] Simultaneously the relative smoothness of the process was helped by what some called the 'maturity' of the opposition, in particular of the Communist Party (PCE) which often adopted more moderate positions than the Socialists (PSOE).

All of this culminated in the first free elections of June 1977 in which Suárez's Union of the Democratic Centre (UCD) took 34 per cent of the vote, to the PSOE's 28.5 per cent and the PCE's 9 per cent. In 1978 a democratic constitution was discussed and approved, and over the next few years parties and interest groups began to operate in more normal circumstances, whilst regional autonomy statutes gave some measure of self-government to the regions. Problems remained. ETA continued to challenge the power of the Spanish state in the Basque territory, and for some years elements within the military remained uneasy with the process of rapid social and political change sweeping the country. Yet once King Juan Carlos had faced down the February 1981 coup attempt of Lt. Colonel Tejero Molina, the time of military risings appeared to have passed. Finally the electoral victory of the PSOE in the 1982 elections showed that in Spain political power could be transferred peacefully from one section of the elite to another. What has often been described as a model democratisation had been successfully completed.[7]

Religious context: from state support to interest group

Historically, the links between the Spanish Crown and the Roman Catholic Church had always been strong, though these were increasingly being challenged by the late eighteenth and early nineteenth centuries. Periodically the state had made encroachments on church privileges and property, but it had rarely challenged the spiritual prerogatives of the ecclesiastical establishment. This position had been further reinforced in a Concordat of 1851 which stated that the 'Apostolic Roman Catholic religion, which to the exclusion of all other cults, continues to be the only one of the Spanish nation', and therefore should be protected by the Crown.[8] This promise was maintained with varying degrees of enthusiasm by the Spanish state over later decades, albeit interspersed with occasional anti-clerical outbursts, and in at least some respects it was this close relationship that Franco sought to restore when he achieved victory in the civil war. Having faced anti-clerical assaults under the Republican government, that culminated in the destruction of numerous church properties and cost the lives of over 7,000 priests, monks and nuns, it was hardly surprising that the church welcomed Franco as its saviour. Priests travelled with his armies and described their cause in terms of a religious crusade. Several bishops criticised the ideology of the Falange, and the church was not uniformly reactionary, but the events of 1931–6 ensured that the vast majority welcomed the Nationalist government and saw in its appearance a chance to restore the greatness of Catholic Spain. For his part Pope Pius XII greeted Franco on the occasion of his triumph in 1939 and congratulated him on this 'victory for Catholic Spain'.[9]

The church's commitment to the regime was reinforced during the latter part of the civil war as Franco repealed republican legislation and restored many of the privileges that had been taken by previous administrations. Freedom of worship for non-Catholics was abolished, Catholicism became the state religion, religious education was reinstated in all institutions, and the church effectively took control over marriage and family life. At the same time the state promised to restore the church's wealth and pay the salaries of the clergy, and gave it a major role in maintaining the moral standards of the new order via the right to censor certain types of printed material.[10] Many of these changes were recognised and strengthened further in the Concordat signed with the Vatican in

August 1953, though at the cost of ceding to Franco the effective right to control the appointment of diocesan bishops. Rome retained, however, the right to appoint auxiliary bishops, a right that was to be used more extensively in the 1960s and 1970s to encourage the forces of reform.[11]

Many within the church hoped that this new arrangement would create the conditions for a re-evangelisation of Spain and an extension of religious influence amongst the masses. Some pointed to the increase in religious participation evident in the early 1940s, though critics noted that increases in piety often followed on from war and conflict. Equally it was clear that many of the triumphalist religious celebrations during this period were primarily supported by the Catholic middle classes and small farmers who had sided with the Nationalists. In contrast the 'losers' remained unreconciled and the working class largely irreligious. In consequence, even within the church a growing number of priests came to recognise the importance of the social question for the future of both church and state alike.[12] Part of the problem stemmed from the processes of social change affecting Spain from the 1950s onwards, but the dilemma was compounded by the very nature of the National Catholicism promoted by the regime during the immediate post-civil war years. Essentially this was a backward-looking faith rooted in the most negative versions of Tridentine Catholicism and taking as its model the Spain of Philip II. It was rooted in a reaction to the martyrdom of the 1930s and based on a rigid confessionalism that allowed little space for other visions to develop.[13]

This was especially clear in the sphere of religious liberty. From the time of Ferdinand and Isabella persecution of religious minorities had been characteristic of the Spanish Catholic state. In 1492 Jews were given the option of conversion or emigration, and during the same period the Moors also faced expulsion.[14] When the first Protestants appeared in Spain they were subject to harsh penalties, with at least 200 facing the wrath of the Inquisition. Several constitutions promulgated in the nineteenth century under liberal influences offered freedom of worship to non-Catholics, though, as Hughey points out, much depended upon the interpretations of those in power. In consequence, Protestants and others tended to face petty harassment rather than outright persecution. This changed with Franco's victory as Catholicism was restored to its position as state religion, Protestant churches were closed, those holding worship in homes were fined, and the teaching of Catholicism became compulsory in schools.[15] Yet as we shall see, the teachings of Vatican II (1962–5) on religious liberty were to encourage more liberal Catholics to support minority demands for religious freedom during the later 1960s.

This changing attitude towards religious discrimination was symptomatic of wider changes affecting the Spanish Catholic Church from the mid-1950s onwards. A younger generation of priests emerged who had not been scarred by the experiences of the 1930s and who saw that the church was failing to make any serious impact on the growing working class. At the intellectual level Catholic religious and lay activists familiar with developments in the wider Catholic world began to argue for a more humane Catholicism open to modernity and committed to religious and political liberty. By the late 1950s many of these people had become active in workers' struggles and often proved willing to cooperate with socialist and communist union organisers.[16] Some of these concerns were taken up by the younger generation of bishops, men like Vicente Enrique y Tarancón of Solsona, who published a series of pastoral letters criticising the authorities over their lack of concern for the poor.[17] All of this discussion was given further impetus by the Second Vatican Council at which the church turned its back on many traditional positions and accepted the value of democracy, pluralism and religious liberty. Yet until the mid-1960s the majority of the Spanish hierarchy continued to resist change, and in this were firmly supported by the Francoist establishment.

As the decade progressed the church's official position became increasingly critical under the influence of the numerous auxiliary bishops appointed by the Vatican to evade Franco's control over episcopal appointments. Central here was Tarancón, by 1971 Cardinal Archbishop of Madrid and chairman of the Episcopal Conference. At a joint assembly of bishops and priests that he inaugurated, the majority, not entirely enthusiastically in some cases, asked the nation's forgiveness for their failure to act as agents of reconciliation 'in the heart of our people divided by a war amongst brothers'.[18] Simultaneously leading churchmen, encouraged by the papal nuncio, began to argue more explicitly for political liberalisation, the protection of human rights, and a renegotiation of the close relationship between church and state that many saw as restricting the church's ability to proclaim the Gospel. Not all the bishops were committed to this approach, and many within the Francoist establishment felt betrayed by the church's more critical stance. Increasingly, however, the church found itself taking a middle position between regime and political opposition, and even radical politicians such as Communist Party leader Santiago Carrillo came to accept that on occasions the church was capable of playing a 'progressive' role in society.[19]

For the church democratisation was to prove a mixed blessing. Having shed its all too onerous connections with the state, it found itself having to compete with an array of cultural and intellectual influences that contributed towards a further secularisation of Spanish society. Most of the surveys undertaken since the 1970s suggest that whilst still culturally a Catholic country, overt commitment to religious belief has fallen considerably. In the 1970s some 40 per cent of the population regularly took part in religious activity, but by the mid-1990s this had fallen to 15 per cent. Belief in traditional teachings also appeared to be falling, particularly on sexual matters where the vast majority ignored the church's teaching on contraception and over half accepted the permissibility of abortion in certain circumstances. Institutionally the church faced a potential crisis as less than half the population opted to pay the voluntary church tax and the number of clergy fell precipitously from 26,308 in 1968 to 20,933 twenty years later.[20] Simultaneously, spiritual challenges were posed by the new pluralism that allowed a variety of religious organisations, new and old, to emerge though in total practising members of religious minority communities made up no more than 1 per cent of the population. By the late 1990s there were reported to be around 350,000 Protestants worshipping in around 3,000 churches, of whom perhaps three-quarters were Pentecostals. The latter were especially successful in attracting members of the gypsy community whilst Protestants as a whole were successful in growing urban conurbations around Madrid and in Catalonia. In addition, there were small communities of Mormons and other 'imported' religious trends, perhaps 40,000 Jehovah's Witnesses, 200,000 Muslims, 15,000 Jews and representatives of a variety of 'new religious movements'.[21]

Privileging the majority religion?

Addressing the congregation at the coronation mass of King Juan Carlos in November 1975 Cardinal Tarancón set out his vision of the relationship between church and state. Though noting with pride the historical connection between throne and altar, he made it clear that the church accepted a diminution of its explicitly political role in the future. Commenting on this sermon later he suggested that 'the Church is ready to work with everyone, but in its own way; the Church can even criticise certain things in its desire to co-operate but on its own terms'.[22] More critical commentators pointed to the prelate's argument that the church had the moral duty to support legitimate authority so long as it worked for the common good, and noted the implicit suggestion that on moral issues in particular the Catholic Church would be the judge for all Spaniards.[23] Nonetheless, most Spaniards responded favourably to Tarancón's homily, viewing it as a sign that the Church accepted its limited role in the new democracy and that it had no desire to resurrect the old clerical–secular divisions.[24] This position was reinforced during the first free elections of 1977 when the church refused to offer formal institutional backing to any particular party, though its preference for the UCD was fairly obvious.[25] Even the embryonic Christian Democratic parties were refused formal backing, with Tarancón suggesting that anyone utilising the name of the church or Christianity in its title was 'blatantly usurping' the words, though this did not stop individual bishops and priests intervening on behalf of specific candidates.[26]

Nonetheless, the church made clear its view that it deserved to be taken seriously in the new Spain. Central to its position was the belief that as the vast majority of Spaniards were Catholic, their church should be treated in some sense as special. Whilst accepting pluralism and eschewing privilege Cardinal Tarancón and others adopted the position that sociological reality required politicians to listen to the religious representatives of the Spanish people, and this was an argument that surfaced repeatedly in various debates from the late 1970s onwards, including those relating to divorce, abortion, education, church financing and the drafting of a new constitution.

The constitutional issue was potentially an area of great sensitivity, with the capacity to resurrect the tensions of the past. As already noted the Concordat of 1851 defined the special position of the Catholic Church, and this was reinforced in the constitution of 1876, which stated that 'the apostolic and Roman Catholic religion is that of the State...The nation is obliged to maintain the Church and its ministries.' In a context of growing anti-clericalism, however, the fundamental law promulgated by the Second Republic in 1931, in tandem with the abrogation of the various privileges of the church by decree, had helped to polarise Spanish society and thus contributed to the vicious civil war that followed at the end of the decade. Moderate republican ministers protested that anti-clerical measures would only unite the forces of reaction, and as we have seen the religious issue did indeed serve to exacerbate the hostilities of this period. For this reason churchmen and politicians alike entered the constitutional debates of the 1970s with one eye over their shoulders and an acute awareness of the need to avoid reopening old wounds.[27]

Despite this, at a gathering of bishops in mid-November 1977 Cardinal Tarancón repeated his argument that there had to be some recognition of the church's position in the political reorganisation of the country. The church was a 'social reality' encompassing the vast majority of Spaniards and for this reason it could not be treated as simply one religion amongst many, and had to be given some formal recognition in the new constitution. Whilst critics spoke of the Cardinal as advocating 'camouflaged confessionality', conservative Catholic fears were confirmed when one day after his speech, part of the draft constitution was leaked to the press and was seen to lack any explicit reference to the church.[28] As the debates progressed through late 1977 and then into 1978 other issues surfaced, particularly relating to questions of family life and religious education. On the latter Suárez's UCD insisted that there be some reference to the right to religious education, though critics felt that this would be another step towards establishing the spiritual hegemony of a single philosophical perspective. In the end the document opted to grant parents the right to 'ensure that their children receive moral and religious instruction', but remained ambiguous on issues such as divorce and abortion which were made the subject of separate legislation.[29]

Though the church continued to lobby hard on the question of constitutional recognition it remained wary of making a public issue of confessionality. From its historical experience it was acutely conscious of the need to avoid acting in ways that might encourage the reassertion of an aggressive anti-clericalism or secularism. Thus it preferred to lobby and argue within the corridors of power and was willing to accept the first two clauses of the proposed Article 16, which guaranteed freedom of religious belief to all citizens, and stated that no one should be obliged to declare their religious beliefs. It did, however, continue to argue for a formal recognition of the Catholic Church's special position to be inserted in the third clause whose first draft simply stated that there would be no state church in Spain. A radical minority suggested that the bishops were too fearful, with one priest describing the church's anxiety about a lay state as 'a betrayal of the Gospel' and motivated by the fear that 'if there is genuine religious freedom in Spain, many Spaniards will simply cease to be Catholics'.[30] But most within the church wanted the bishops to adopt a more assertive position that gave firm recognition to its place in society, an argument supported by conservative deputies.

In the political arena the major parties by and large adopted predictable positions, with the UCD and the Popular Alliance favouring some recognition of the position of the church and rejecting liberalisation on issues such as divorce and abortion. The PSOE took a far more aggressively anti-clerical line, advocating total separation of church and state, the ending of subsidies to religious schools, and constitutional provisions for the introduction of divorce and abortion laws. Perhaps more surprising was the communist position, with Carrillo describing his party's shifting position as that of a 'spectator' on religious issues and explaining his party's moderation in terms of the need to avoid polarising society.[31] In consequence, his party joined with the centre right in reaching a compromise solution, which left the third section of Article 16 reading:

There shall be no state religion. The public powers shall take into account the religious beliefs of Spanish society and will maintain consequent relations of co-operation with the Catholic Church and other confessions.[32]

Many within the church were content with this formulation that committed the new state to respect its structures and added authority to its attempt to influence the public on moral issues.[33] When the constitution was put to the people in a referendum at the end of 1978 the bishops collectively suggested that Catholics should vote as they saw fit on the document, though nine bishops and some priests urged their flocks to reject it. Cardinal González Martín argued that this was essential since the text made no mention of God and represented an attempt to foist an agnostic constitution on 'a nation of the baptised'.[34] There was also some suggestion that the new Polish Pope, John Paul II, shared the views of the more traditionalist bishops that the Spanish hierarchy should have fought harder for some reference to God in the constitution, and that they should have taken a tougher line on family issues. Nonetheless, despite some clerical opposition, on 6 December 1978 the document was ratified by a vast majority of the population.[35]

After the signing of an agreement between the Spanish state and the Vatican in 1976 the papal nuncio declared that 'the privileges have disappeared and we have begun a new epoch'.[36] Three years later the Spanish government and the Vatican signed the 'partial agreements' which replaced the 1963 Concordat and provided guarantees relating to the legal status of the church, the right of parents to choose religious education for their children, religious service in the armed forces, and collaboration between church and state in finding new ways of financing the former.[37] For some this document undermined the nuncio's comments that the era of privilege had disappeared, and over the next decade or so the issue of religious privilege, actual or perceived, was to rear its head in a number of areas: in matters relating to marriage, the family and reproduction; in education; and in terms of the continued state subsidy to religious institutions. Of these the first was the most hotly disputed, perhaps not surprisingly given Catholic teaching in these areas which it could hardly be expected to jettison at the whim of the secular power. Here the bishops followed the line of the Pope, arguing that the liberal state could not simply privatise matters that of their very nature had to be regulated by some sense of natural law. Perhaps energised by the moral 'conservatism' of John Paul II, the bishops took a much tougher line when the UCD proposed a liberalisation of divorce legislation permitting separation on the basis of mutual consent. Though Tarancón had recognised that the church could not impose its view of divorce on non-Catholics, several bishops argued that any relaxation of the law would lead to a destruction of family life in Spain.[38] Eventually the law was passed, but conflict became more acute under the PSOE government elected in 1982, especially when it introduced a law decriminalising abortion. Backed by the bishops, the conservative politician Fraga Iribarne took the draft law to the Constitutional Court on the grounds that it was in breach of Article 15 of the constitution guaranteeing the right to life. This had the effect of halting the law temporarily, but three years later a redrafted version decriminalising abortion in certain cases was passed by parliament.[39]

A second area where the church sought a continued formal recognition of its position – and some said, privilege – was in the sphere of education.[40] The 1978 constitution had provided a guarantee of the right to private education, and the right of parents to have their children given moral and religious education, though many Catholic spokesmen felt the text had been insufficiently supportive of religion in this area. In practice, 95 per cent of private schools were Catholic, and in the early 1980s the church controlled something like 23 per cent of all primary schools, 21 per cent of secondary schools and four universities. Under agreements signed with the Vatican in 1979 the state educational system would respect the rights of parents with regard to religious and moral matters, and all teaching would be respectful of Catholic and Christian values. Yet with the advent of a socialist government new tensions emerged following the publication of a draft law on education in 1983 that proposed greater state control over curriculum content in exchange for a continuation of public funding of private (mainly church) schools. As the law came to the vote some 250,000 Catholics took to the streets in Madrid, yet the law went through and in practice its impact upon the religious identity of church schools has reportedly been very limited. In general, the education system has remained pluralistic, though there have been some objections raised to the fact that the state pays the salaries of the teachers who teach Catholic education in private and public schools.[41]

The third issue that aroused controversy related to financial matters. Under the 1953 Concordat the Spanish state had agreed to finance the activities of the church and pay the salaries of its clergy, and this was continued during the early stages of the transition. Under the terms of the 1979 agreement the state would continue to pay the subsidy for a further three years after which a new system would be introduced. Under this the taxpayer would be given the option of deciding whether they wanted a proportion of their existing tax bill to go to funding the church or to other good works, though the state would also make up any shortfall in income and in practice continued to offer an additional subsidy to the church from general tax revenues. The percentage of tax income allocated to the church would be handed over to the bishops who could choose how best to use it. In practice, the system was slow to take off, and was opposed by some legal commentators and religious minorities. The former feared that its provisions contradicted Article 16 of the constitution, which promised that no one should have to declare their religious allegiance; the latter resented the linkage of church and state implied by the deal and felt that effectively it discriminated against those religious groups who did not receive a subsidy.[42] By the 1990s less than half of those in the regions where the tax was applied chose to donate money to the church.

In all these areas it is often difficult to distinguish between what might be described as legitimate democratic lobbying in pursuit of group interests and claims that the state privilege a particular institution or set of ideas. On moral and theological issues one would not expect the church to compromise, whereas in areas such as constitutional change, education and finance some degree of bargaining and compromise is always possible. For all this it might be suggested that during the early stages of the transition the Spanish Catholic Church did seek some form of formal 'recognition' within the new order. Its arguments for so doing were essentially sociological and nationalistic, i.e., we are the church of the majority and of historical Spain. Yet this was an increasingly difficult position to maintain when opinion surveys demonstrated that on matters of 'private morality' much of the Spanish population rejected the church's teaching, especially on contraception and divorce.[43] There were also elements of inconsistency in positions adopted by the hierarchy, evident, for example, in the tension between the 'sociological reality' approach and the argument that democratic majorities could not decide issues where natural law applied. By and large, however, by the mid-1980s the question of the formal position of the Roman Catholic Church in the new order had been resolved and since then there have been no serious attempts to renegotiate that position.[44]

On the road to religious liberty

Compared with some of the issues discussed above the question of granting formal and legal religious liberty to minorities has proved less problematic for the Spanish Catholic Church. It has expressed unease about new religious movements and the proselytising activities of some Protestant groups, and in some areas there are reports that such groups face a range of petty harassment from the clergy or 'Catholic public opinion'.

As an institution, however, the church has not publicly challenged the fundamental principle that in a democratic state all should be free to worship as they choose.

Things were not always thus. In the years before the civil war the position of religious minorities was often precarious, though the 1869 constitution did offer some protection for the private observation of their religious practices. Under Franco, however, such groups found themselves in a difficult position as church and state promoted the idea that being a good Spaniard and being a good Catholic was one and the same thing. For a brief period in the aftermath of the Second World War Spanish Protestants enjoyed something of a respite, and the Charter of the Spanish People issued in 1945 promised that whilst Catholicism enjoyed official protection as the religion of the state, freedom of 'private' worship was available to all. Yet the two decades from 1948 onwards were very difficult for religious minorities in general and Protestants in particular. The media frequently published material suggesting that such people were the enemies of Spain on a par with the Nationalists' opponents in the civil war. Protestant churches were closed and believers forced to meet in private homes, in some areas at considerable personal risk. In 1950 the Protestant churches petitioned Franco for change but met with a frosty response, though during the early 1950s foreign pressure, notably from US President Truman expressed through his ambassador to Madrid, led to at least some formal toning down of official rhetoric about Protestants. Nonetheless, harassment, the breaking up of meetings and disruption of Protestant funerals appear to have remained common.[45]

During the early 1960s, as part of the wider spread of liberal demands in Spanish society, but also stimulated by new trends in Catholic thought expressed most clearly in the Vatican Council's Declaration on Religious Liberty, there was discussion in more enlightened official circles of the possibility of passing a new Law on Religious Liberty. These discussions involving at various points the Spanish Foreign Minister, officials at the Vatican and a small group of Catholic intellectuals and politicians – were opposed by many within the church hierarchy. Eventually the law passed through the Cortes on 26 June 1967 and was approved by a substantial majority. Under its terms all Spaniards were assured of legal equality regardless of religious belief, and the right to practise their religion in private or public so long as this did not entail the expression of disrespect for Catholicism as the national religion. It left unclear the status of the active promotion of alternative religious visions, and Catholic bishops continued to express disquiet at the possibility of 'proselytisation' aimed at their flock. The Protestants, whilst welcoming the new law, remained wary about aspects of its implementation, in particular a registration process that entailed providing government bodies with extensive details about the community prior to legal recognition being granted. In practice, however, the formal closure of minority churches came to an end with this law, though the daily life of minority communities depended to a considerable extent on the attitude of officials and public opinion in the areas where they were situated. One other issue that remained unresolved at the time of Franco's death was the question of conscientious objection to military service, something that affected the small Protestant groups less than the Jehovah's Witnesses of whom several hundred were then in prison.[46]

After Franco's death considerable discussion revolved around how best to extend the legal guarantees available to religious minorities, and the first move in this direction was evident in the wording of Article 16 in the constitution adopted in 1978:

(i) Freedom of ideology, religion and worship of individuals and communities is guaranteed with no more restriction on their expression than may be necessary in order to maintain public order under the law;
(ii) Nobody may be compelled to make declarations regarding their religion, belief or ideologies.

At the same time, discussion began on creating further legal protection and this time government agencies held extensive consultations with religious representatives and their lawyers. A new Law on Religious Liberty came into effect in 1980, and this provided for the right to profess any religion, to pass it on to one's children, to manifest and propagate one's beliefs, to observe religious holidays, to perform marriages and funerals according to one's own rites, and to maintain relations with co-religionists abroad. Broadly speaking the Catholic hierarchy raised no serious objections to this law, though some Protestants remained uneasy about the necessity of legal registration as a prerequisite to the gaining of juridical status and indeed some saw no need for a new law given the guarantees provided by the constitution.[47]

Under the terms of the law religious organisations have to be entered in the Register of Religious Entities maintained by a religious affairs directorate at the Ministry of Justice, and the basic demand is that they submit documentation showing that they are 'religions'. Should they fail to meet this requirement they have the option of being registered as private associations. Under this law the Catholic Church as such does not have to register, though over 11,000 individual Catholic organisations had done so by the end of the 1990s. Alongside these some 899 non-Catholic churches, confessions or communities had registered, of which nearly 80 per cent were Protestant entities representing over 3,000 places of worship; followed by a range of other groups such as the Jehovah's Witnesses, registered as one entity but with nearly 900 places of worship, and representatives of many of the major religious faiths.[48]

At the same time, some observers pointed to problematic aspects arising from the phrasing of this law that, according to Gloria Moran, formally offered equality but in fact created several categories of religious groups enjoying differential legal positions. First came the Catholic Church, singled out in the constitution and having particular rights stemming from agreements between the state and the Vatican, and also with the church in Spain. These provided considerable guarantees for the rights of the church in education, in public institutions such as prisons, hospitals and the military, and regulated the financial situation of the church. Secondly come those churches 'with evidence of establishment', that have the right to sign agreements with the state similar to those developed with the Catholic Church. Then come other churches without 'evident establishment' status, but recognised as having a 'religious purpose' and thus enjoying certain rights, tax exemptions and the possibility of registration. Finally, come a range of groups not recognised as religious communities by the state's directorate of religious affairs, who may have the possibility of registration as private organisations. Such groups can appeal official decisions through the courts and at least one traditionalist Catholic group opposed by the official hierarchy has successfully gained registration in this way.[49]

A further problem alluded to by Moran and others stems from the law's rather vague requirements for registration, with the provision that a community provide proof of a 'religious purpose' giving ample scope for legal discussion and debate, though Article 3.2 does attempt to exclude those groups whose activities revolve around humanist or psychic phenomena. Even more difficult is the phrase 'evidence of establishment' used in Article 7, a term applied to those groups which may seek to make special agreements with the Spanish state. Here the requirement seems to be that such groups have both a historical presence and sufficient numbers to warrant special treatment, though nowhere is it spelt out what it means for a group to have 'deep roots in Spain' or what numbers are sufficient.[50] In practice three groups have effectively been recognised in this way and in the early 1990s signed a series of agreements with the state: the Jewish and Muslim communities, and members of the Federation of Evangelical Communities of Spain. These finally gave them the same legal status as the Catholic Church, with state recognition of their marriages as civil, some tax exemptions, and provision for instruction in the faith within the public school system. At this time, however, these three groups refused the offer of participation in the religious tax system.[51]

Despite these textual ambiguities, by the 1990s religious minorities probably enjoyed greater freedom than they had ever experienced in Spain, and there was little to suggest that the state or the Catholic hierarchy had any serious intention of restricting their legal rights. This is not to say that no problems remained, and in specific areas some religious groups felt that they were being treated differently from the dominant religious community. In particular there is a feeling that all groups do not have the same access to the media and that some decisions taken in the late 1990s adversely affected Protestant minorities. For example, the question of the licensing of their radio and television stations became an issue when nine of their sixteen stations were closed down in 1998 alone. Officially this was because there were insufficient wave bands, but Protestant leaders noted that this did not appear to prevent the licensing of Catholic stations and some suggested that this new policy turn was a product of the conservative Popular Alliance government's lack of sympathy for non-Catholic groups.[52] Yet such difficulties have also affected the Catholic Church, as in Catalonia where the regional government failed to renew the licences of three Catholic radio channels in mid-1999.[53] Some Protestant groups and the Muslims have also changed their position on the tax issue, and now argue that their members should have the option currently enjoyed by Catholics of opting for part of their tax to go to the religious institution, and in 2000 taxpayers were given the option of donating part of their tax revenue to the Muslim and certain Protestant communities.[54] Less amicable have been relations with the Islamic community over the issue of clothing, with one Muslim leader claiming discrimination when thirty Muslim girls in Granada were required to remove their head coverings for identity card photographs whilst Catholic nuns were not.[55]

Whilst the more established minorities have seen their rights increase in recent years, newer religious movements continue to face occasional restrictions on their activities, stemming in some cases from the legal requirement to prove a 'religious purpose'. In 1989, for example, a group of people attending a Scientology meeting in Madrid were arrested and charged with breaching various civil laws, and in 1990 members of 'The Family' were arrested at the orders of a Barcelona judge though this decision was later overturned in the courts. In both cases the formal charges related to breaches of civil law, though in the former those arrested were given no documentation showing what they had done wrong and in the latter the charges related in part to accusations that the children of the group had been deprived of proper care and education.[56] In general the state's directorate has been restrictive in its attitude to the registration of 'new religious movements', but there have also been tensions between the authorities and the legally recognised Jehovah's Witnesses over the question of blood transfusions, though in most cases doctors have accepted the wishes of adult patients even where this has led to their deaths.

More controversial has been the work of a special unit set up in line with parliamentary regulations approved in 1989 to monitor 'destructive cults'. According to its figures there were alleged to be as many as 200 such groups in the country and these had drawn in around 100,000 people. During 1995 the Penal Code was amended so as to provide punishment for those organisations that 'even if they have lawful aims, employ violent means which attempt to change or control people', and in May 1999 the Spanish Cortes passed a resolution calling on the government to tighten up control over such groups.[57] In consequence, human rights groups have expressed concern that as in France and some other European countries the development of 'anti-sect' activity by the state may develop in ways that threaten the rights of religious minorities in general. These fears were reinforced in the late 1990s when the government of the Canary Islands refused permission for the Salvation Army to open a centre for needy children on the grounds that it was a 'destructive sect'.[58]

For all this, there can be little doubt that the democratisation of Spain has greatly enlarged the area of religious freedom and undermined the arguments of those who would seek to restrict pluralism. Though in some areas public opinion may occasionally lead to the harassments of converts from Catholicism, the era when belonging to a religious minority could lead to an extensive juridical denial of rights appears to have passed. As we have seen, the legal situation was already changing prior to 1975, but the collapse of the Francoist regime and changing attitudes within some sections of the Catholic Church created an atmosphere in which the realisation of legal equality could be hastened.

Greece: two steps forward, one step back?

Political context: from the colonels to 'new democracy'

The political transition which took place in Greece in the mid-1970s differed in many respects from those political changes taking place at the same time in the Iberian peninsula. The duration of the rule of the colonels had been considerably shorter than that of Franco in Spain or Salazar in Portugal. True, Greek democracy prior to the military intervention of 1967 had been far from conforming to standard liberal democratic norms. In particular, the traumas of the civil war in the 1940s had led to a domination of political life by the political right, who had operated through what some called a 'para-constitution' to separate the 'nationally minded' Greeks from those whose loyalty was questionable. Yet the election victories of the Centre Union in 1963 and 1964 suggested that the post-war settlement was unlikely to last, and in part the military intervened to forestall a more thoroughgoing democratisation of the political system. A second difference, particularly from the Spanish case, stemmed from the nature of the regime, for unlike their Francoist counterparts the Greek junta had no real roots in society or clear constituency of support. Coming from the middle ranks of the army the plotters of 1967 enjoyed very lukewarm backing from senior army leaders, and from representatives of the navy and airforce, whilst most of the traditional right whom they might have expected to be grateful firmly rejected their actions.[59]

The situation of the middle-ranking officers who seized power in 1967 was further complicated by their lack of clear ideas about the sort of regime they hoped to establish. In the first instance their rhetoric revolved around bringing order to society and then returning to the barracks, but under Colonel Papadopoulos there quickly emerged a rhetoric focusing on the rejuvenation of Greece. Under this process corrupting influences emanating from the West would be eliminated and a purer 'Hellenic Christian civilisation' would be rebuilt. In order to achieve this the military would have to remain in power far longer than originally intended. With this in mind the colonels sought to build legitimacy in the armed forces by pensioning off the established military elites and encourage loyalty amongst the middle ranks by introducing rapid promotion processes that challenged traditional hierarchical notions. In the autumn of 1967 a counter-coup backed by the king was seen off and the monarch forced to flee the country. During the following year a plebiscite saw the approval of a new constitution that excluded any reference to civil rights and referred explicitly to the role of the army in safeguarding the integrity of the new political order.[60]

By 1973 the military regime faced growing difficulties. In May of that year a group of naval officers loyal to the king led an abortive coup attempt, and during November there were major student disturbances at the National Polytechnic in Athens. In between these two events Papadopolous declared the king deposed and held a further plebiscite, under conditions of martial law, to elect himself as president. Increasingly, however, he seemed out of touch with both public opinion and that of his peers, and at the end of November was deposed by hard line officers who installed General Phaedon Gizikis as president. In the following July these same officers were behind a plot to eliminate President Makarios of Cyprus, a move that was to lead to a Turkish invasion of part of the island and, more important for our purposes, a final undermining of regime credibility. Almost immediately senior military officials led by the president deposed the junta and set about creating the conditions for a return to civilian government.

The man chosen to head this process was conservative leader Constantine Karamanlis, the leader of the political right prior to 1967. Under his guidance the transitional government pursued a gradualist and incremental policy, one that sought to distance itself from the old order and push for a greater democratisation of Greek public life. It dealt slowly with the issue of punishing members of the military and though death sentences were later handed out these were soon commuted to life imprisonment. Simultaneously many of the civil-war era laws restricting civil liberties which Karamanlis had previously supported were abolished – though, as we shall see later, not all – and the communists legalised. Following elections in 1974 Karamanlis became accountable to parliament and in 1980 he became president of the republic. The whole process of democratic consolidation was relatively rapid, with all the key actors coming to accept that democracy was 'the only game in town' and developing an ability to compromise that had been sadly lacking prior to 1967. This process of stabilisation was further reinforced when a PASOK government came to power and its socialist prime minister found it possible to cohabit with a conservative president.[61] Unlike our other cases this was not such a clear-cut transition process following a lengthy period of authoritarian rule, and there remained continuities with the past, not least in the persistently clientelistic style of Greek political life. Nonetheless, the new regime instituted by Karamanlis in 1974 did represent a qualitative change with the past in many respects and was to preside over a far more thoroughgoing pluralisation of Greek public life.

Religious context: religion as pillar of the nation

Though much is made of the Orthodox Church's contribution to the protection and creation of Greek national identity, in practice the relationship between religious and national leaders was often ambiguous. One of the consequences of the Ottoman *millet* system was to turn the ecclesiastical administration into an instrument of alien rule, and for many church leaders Turkic rule had proved preferable to that of the Western Christian states whose attacks on Byzantium had helped to weaken her during the middle ages.[62] For that reason the church had never been inclined to promote rebellion, instead preferring to use its tenuous position as a recognised religion within the Ottoman Empire to promote Greek cultural and religious interests. When independence came it was largely a product of the activities of secular nationalists, though some leading clerics did support the campaign. Success in this did not, however, bring true freedom to the church for it very quickly became apparent that the new authorities were just as keen to maintain political control over ecclesiastical institutions.

A national church independent of the Patriarchate of Constantinople was created in 1833, and the constitution of 1844 proclaimed Orthodoxy the national religion, but subordinated the church to the king, himself a Bavarian Roman Catholic, who ruled it through a hand-picked synod. Over subsequent years the church faced a series of depredations as nominally Orthodox governments closed monasteries and confiscated property, reduced the number of bishops, and constantly interfered in the daily life of religious administration. Various attempts were made throughout the nineteenth century to reassert the independence of the church but most represented little more than fine-tuning of the existing situation in which the nationalist government viewed church leaders primarily as servants of the state. In 1923 the church was finally granted a significant degree of internal autonomy, but this proved short-lived and relations between church and state remained strained in many areas.[63] Throughout this period the Orthodox Church retained the status of a national institution and it was assumed by most that to be Greek was to be Orthodox. Yet this very assumption meant that the process of national integration remained potentially incomplete for, as Diamondouros points out, the identification of hellenicity with Orthodoxy continued to make it difficult for religious minorities to become fully integrated into modern Greek culture.[64]

During the Second World War the church took control of its own affairs again, but with the end of hostilities problems began to emerge as civil war split the nation. Many priests and bishops had joined the communist-dominated National Liberation Front in the struggle against the Nazis. In the new situation, however, such collaboration became problematic as the church leadership increasingly came to support the right. Political anti-clericalism had never been as strong a force in Greece as Spain, and the communist party programme published during the civil war made little reference to religion. Yet with Archbishop Damaskinos formally condemning the rebels in 1947 and communist bands in the north committing atrocities against priests, tensions increased. And after the civil war the church faced major tasks of reconstruction in those areas hitherto in rebel control. This encouraged its leadership to identify more clearly with conservative politicians who in turn gave the church a major role in controlling family life and education.[65]

Throughout the rule of the colonels the church remained largely a passive observer. In part this stemmed from a traditional acquiescence to the powers that be, but it was further encouraged by the interventions of the military in church affairs. The existing Holy Synod was dissolved and a new nine-member body made up of bishops believed to be sympathetic to the colonels was created. Over this presided Archbishop Ieronymous, a political conservative but someone committed to reform within the church. The junta also created new governing structures for the church in which local councils of priests and laity were given more power in relation to the bishops. At the same time much of the rhetoric of the regime revolved around the need to preserve Greece's Christian civilisation, a goal that many religious leaders could clearly identify with. In consequence, most of the hierarchs supported the new government or at least stayed quiet, though a few priests offered criticisms and Bishop Panteleimon of Salonika reportedly refused to officiate at services attended by junta members.[66]

The collapse of the military regime brought far less immediate change to the religious scene in Greece than was the case in some of the countries we are considering. On the one hand, the period of dictatorship had been relatively short, but more important was the fact that the vast majority of the population retained some degree of identification with Orthodoxy if only as part of their cultural heritage. By the early 1990s some 97 per cent still thought of themselves as Orthodox, and only about 250,000 adhered to other religious communities. Of these nearly half were Muslim Turks mainly situated in Western Thrace. These were mostly the descendants of those Turks, Pomaks and Romas who had been allowed to stay in Greece following the population exchanges with Turkey in the 1920s. There were also about 50,000 Roman Catholics – as well as many foreign Catholics – mostly located in the Athens area and on some of the Ionian and Cycladic islands. The 20–30,000 Protestants were mainly the descendants of Greeks who were converted as a result of missionary activity in the nineteenth century. Since the 1970s these communities have been more active in evangelistic work and have been supported by Evangelical and Pentecostal groups from outside Greece, but it does not seem that the latter have stimulated substantial growth. In addition, there are perhaps as many as 50,000 Jehovah's Witnesses, a group that has faced particular difficulties with both the secular and religious authorities; around 5,000 Jews; and a host of new religious movements with an unknown but relatively small number of adherents.[67] We shall say more about these communities later, but simply note here that in many respects the legislative acts in force, which largely favour the Orthodox and discriminate to some degree against minorities, have not been the subject of substantial change since redemocratisation.

For the Orthodox Church the period since the junta has been essentially a period of consolidation, presided over from 1974–98 by Archbishop Serafion. In 1977 he masterminded the approval of a new church constitution that sought to remove the possibility of state intervention in church life and which, perhaps more importantly, created the mechanism under which his successor would be elected by all the serving metropolitan bishops. In consequence, it was under this procedure that a new archbishop was elected in April 1998, though the choice of Metropolitan Christodoulos of Dimitriados was to prove a controversial one. Over the following years this intellectually gifted prelate was to prove a thorn in the side of many politicians as he used his undoubted media skills to advance the position of the church, challenge the impact of globalisation and Europeanisation on Greek culture, and offer outspoken comment on political affairs.[68]

Constitutional, legal and institutional 'privileging' of the Greek Orthodox Church

Though the role of the church in the constitutional structure was the subject of some debate in the new democracy during the mid-1970s, the issue lacked the emotional resonance of the Spanish debates. At the same time the Greek Orthodox Church was less constrained by its civil war experiences in seeking to maintain its privileged position. Since the 1844 constitution all Greek founding documents had made special reference to the dominant role of the church and latterly had included express prohibitions on proselytism by non-Orthodox religious groups.[69] Following the defeat of the military junta there were some on the left of Greek politics who saw separation of church and state as an essential prerequisite for the successful modernisation and democratisation of the country, but few were willing to make this a first-order issue. Whilst a few sought to remove the document's opening invocation to the Trinity and omit any proscription of proselytism, there was no real desire to challenge the sociological 'fact' that the overwhelming majority of the population identified itself with the Orthodox Church or that in some sense Christianity was essential to the nation's very identity. The Orthodox hierarchy was rather less accommodating, opposing any dilution of the constitutional recognition of its public role.[70]

In its final version the constitution met many, though not all, of the church's demands and, following the opening invocation to the Trinity, the key articles read as follows:

Article 3:
1. The prevailing religion in Greece is that of the Eastern Orthodox Church of Christ. The Orthodox Church of Greece, acknowledging our Lord Jesus Christ as its head, is inseparably united in doctrine with the Great Church of Christ in Constantinople and with every other Church of Christ of the same doctrine, observing unwaveringly, as they do, the holy apostolic and synodal canons and sacred traditions. It is autocephalous and is administered by the Holy Synod of serving Bishops and the Permanent Holy Synod originating thereof and assembled as specified by the Statutory Charter of the Church in compliance with the provisions of the Patriarchal Tome of June 29, 1850 and the Synodal Act of September 4, 1928.
2. The ecclesiastical regime existing in certain districts of the state shall not be deemed contrary to the provisions of the preceding paragraph.
3. The text of the Holy Scripture shall be maintained unaltered. Official translation of the text into any other form of language, without prior sanction by the Autocephalous Church of Greece and the Great Church of Christ in Constantinople, is prohibited.

Article 13:
1. Freedom of religious conscience is inviolable. The enjoyment of civil rights and liberties does not depend upon the individual's religious beliefs.
2. All known religions shall be free and their rites of worship shall be performed unhindered and under the protection of the law. The practice of rites of worship is not allowed to offend public order or the good usages. Proselytism is prohibited.
3. The ministers of all known religions shall be subject to the same supervision by the State and to the same obligations as those of the prevailing religion.
4. No person shall be exempt from discharging his obligations to the State or may refuse to comply with the laws by reason of his religious convictions.
5. No oath shall be imposed or administered except as specified by law and in the form determined by law.

Article 14 (on the media):
4. The seizure of newspapers and other publications before or after publication is prohibited. Seizure by order of the public prosecutor shall be allowed exceptionally after circulation and in the cases of (a) an offence against the Christian or any other known religion.

Article 16 (on education):
2. Education constitutes a basic mission for the State and shall aim at the moral, intellectual, professional and physical training of Greeks, the development of national and religious consciousness and at their formation as free and responsible citizens.[71]

Though some within the church were unhappy about the partial equality granted to all known religions and the removal of the requirement that the head of state be Orthodox – though he or she does have to swear a Trinitarian oath (Article 33.2) – in most respects this document confirmed the de facto dominance of the church in many spheres of life. Moreover, it went much further than any other European constitution in protecting the established doctrines and practices of the church and, together with other acts in force, gave the state considerable powers to regulate the religious life of the country.[72]

This constitutional recognition was further reinforced by a series of 'para-constitutional' regulations. We shall discuss these again in dealing with religious minorities, but a few comments need to be made here. The so-called 'Necessity Acts' passed during the Metaxas dictatorship in 1938–9 remain in force alongside the constitution and are seen by many as reinforcing the privileges of the dominant church. In particular, they ban proselytism and, of more importance to this section, give the Orthodox Church considerable power with regard to the opening of places of worship. Thus Act 1672/1939 requires that non-Orthodox religious groups gain a government permit before they open a place of worship. To gain this, fifty families have to make an application to the local authorities and they in turn require the approval of the local Orthodox bishop prior to granting permission. Though in theory this is simply a consultative process, until recently many Orthodox hierarchs treated this as an opportunity to restrict the growth of minority communities in their ecclesiastical territories. Though government officials claim that this requirement has effectively lapsed, there are still occasional reports of hierarchs offering stiff resistance to the opening of non-Orthodox places of worship.[73] In the same way, privileging is implicit in Act 1784/1939 that severely limited the functioning of private schools based on non-Orthodox foundations.[74]

Much discussion of the 1975 constitution had focused around the concept of 'known' religions – defined elsewhere as those with no secret doctrines who do not worship in secret – though as with the notion of 'traditional' religions in some of the post-Soviet states, no definitions are offered in the text of the document. Leaving aside the Orthodox, clearly the dominant known religion and effectively a state church, much depended upon the interpretations offered by the state and the courts and, as Pollis pointed out, on the vagaries of time, place and individual preference.[75] The 'known' religions are also further subdivided into corporations under public law, such as the Orthodox, Muslims and Jews – though this seeming 'plural establishment' does not imply equal treatment – and corporations under private law, which include most of the Protestants, Adventists, Old Calendarists, Buddhists, Mormons, Baha'is and Jehovah's Witnesses, though some of the latter groups have an often doubtful status as 'known' religions. For those coming clearly within this category the constitutional provisions of freedom of religion apply, though the Orthodox Church is in a class of its own with clergy salaries paid by the state and the maintenance of church buildings through the tax system. Equally, those who are not 'known' lack the same degree of constitutional protection, for example, the prosecutor would not seize papers that satirised or offended groups in this category.[76]

Though formally the church is not established, it is frequently described as the prevailing religion and in effect enjoys considerable constitutional privileging, a fact recognised by the European Court in the Kokkinakis vs. Greece case. Here the judges stated that 'according to Greek conceptions, it (the Church) represents de jure and de facto the religion of the State itself, a good number of whose administrative functions...it carries out'.[77] In arguing for the legitimacy of this position Orthodox sources also point to the Treaty of Amsterdam, which includes a supplementary statement that the EU recognised the local status of recognised religions in member states – though this has a purely declaratory function and cannot be used to justify breaches of European human rights regulations.[78] This status is reinforced through the Ministry of National Education and Religions whose task it is to regulate religious life in consultation with the church and to ensure that education is carried out in ways that strengthen the Orthodox identity of the nation. In early 1998 some sixty prominent public figures signed a petition calling for separation of church and state. In this they argued that the constitutional privileging of one group was inconsistent with the constitution and international agreements, and suggested that policies such as the mention of religion on identity cards and the hanging of icons in school classrooms was inappropriate in a modern society.[79] Yet despite such petitions this issue only occasionally reaches the political agenda, something that perhaps indicates a general popular acceptance of the close ties between nation and religion. Of course, de facto establishment does not always guarantee that the church lives in perfect harmony with the state and clashes take place at both the central level and in the local context. For example, one might point to the conflict that developed in Thessaloniki during the mid-1990s when religious leaders clashed with officials of the Ministry of Culture over the use of the fourth-century Rotonda, a national monument in which the church was permitted to hold several services a year but which was also used for cultural events.[80] And as already noted, at the central level there have been some strong exchanges between government and church since the selection of Christodoulos as Archbishop of Athens in 1998.

This historical link between church and nation lies at the heart of the justifications offered for the privileged position granted to the Orthodox Church (see chapter 5), for the size of the minorities hardly justifies this legal protection in terms of an explicitly religious threat to Orthodoxy. Article 25 of the constitution points to the state's right to ensure that all citizens 'shall fulfil the duty of social and national solidarity', a phrase which according to Pollis assumes a transcendant, holistic notion of Greek identity in which Orthodoxy plays a vital role.[81] This approach has also been evident in the speeches of politicians, as in 1989 when Prime Minister Mitosakis stressed that whilst Greece respected the rights of all, '*Orthodoxia*... constitutes the support of the nation.' Even the sceptical PASOK leader Andreas Papandreou was not above appropriating Orthodox symbols and language, as when he declared the Virgin Mary patron of the armed forces or sought religious recognition for his second marriage.[82] For all this, public opinion surveys dealing with the church often produced ambiguous results, with suggestions that whilst two-thirds felt the link between nation and religion to be important, amongst urban Greeks respect for the institution itself was declining. Moreover, many operated a 'pick and mix' approach in responding to the church's teachings on morality and sexual matters, and perhaps as many as half the urban population supported a formal separation of church and state.[83]

These changing attitudes did little to prevent the church seeking to preserve or be granted spheres of privileges in other areas and as in Spain these tended to revolve around three areas: family and sexual morality, education and finance. When democracy was restored the church retained considerable rights in the realm of divorce, with the local bishop's approval of a spiritual divorce essential before remarriage could be considered.[84] It was unable, however, to prevent the socialist government elected in 1981 from pushing through divorce reform that provided for civil marriage, easier divorce with no punishment for adultery, and the abolition of the dowry. The church also resisted attempts to liberalise abortion laws, though Halkias has noted that in much of the press debate over this issue nationalist considerations often took precedence over theological argumentation. Thus some priests were to be found stating that, yes abortion was a sin, but one primarily against the nation carried out by the assumed Orthodox citizen who had a duty to propagate so that Orthodox Greece could be defended against the faster-growing population of the Turkic world.[85] Yet the fear of the Turkic world has not prevented a degree of formal status being granted to the Muslim community. Their state-appointed muftis have the right to regulate family law practices amongst their own people, though since 1991 they cannot act in ways that might be seen as contravening the Greek constitution; for example, its clauses relating to the equality of women.[86]

Whereas the attempt to ensure Orthodox moral standards could not in itself be seen as the pursuit of privilege, the situation in the educational sphere continued to offer considerable advantages to the church. In the words of A. Tvitsis, one-time Minister of National Education and Religions, the 1975 constitution for the first time provided for 'the development of a religious consciousness which must be carried out in accordance with the theology of our Eastern Orthodox Church'.[87] The consequence of this approach was to give Orthodox clergy open access to schools and a considerable role in the training of those teaching religion, though some of the more derogatory texts relating to other religious communities have become less common in schools during the 1990s. Equally, the state has generally backed the right of individuals who are not Orthodox to absent themselves from religious education, though this has not prevented the public humiliation of such children in some places. For example, in September 2001 a teacher in the Thessaloniki region showed a class including a young boy from the Jehovah's Witnesses a video attacking his community and purporting to demonstrate the links between their beliefs and Satanism.[88] De facto privileging is also evident in the fact that until 1988 primary school teachers were required to be Orthodox and the fact that even in the 1990s there have been several cases of people being refused teaching posts because they adhere to minority religious communities.[89] More recently the issue of religious education has hit the headlines in the context of a 1998 decision of the Council of State ruling unconstitutional any reduction in the number of hours given over to religious instruction in schools.[90]

Financially the Orthodox Church also enjoys certain privilege, with clergy salaries, and the construction and maintenance of church properties paid for by the state, using income tax paid by all, whether Orthodox or not.[91] A challenge to this position was mounted by the PASOK government in 1987, not through a reduction of subsidies, but via a proposal to confiscate over 80 per cent of the church's agricultural land and around 50,000 acres of its urban property. The formal aim was to grant land to poor farmers, with the political side-effect of increasing support for PASOK, but many within the church saw this as discriminatory, and for a while threatened to excommunicate the relevant ministers. They also took several specific cases to the European Court which found against the state as compensation had not been paid in these cases, though somewhat ironically the government spokesmen used the traditional links between church and state to argue that this was effectively state land anyway and it was now to be used for social purposes. In the end a compromise solution was found and the proposal to take the land was substantially modified, but the issue illustrated the way in which the close ties of church to state could sometimes work against the interests of the church.[92]

As the Greek state entered the new millennium, constitutional and legal texts continued to protect the church's 'prevailing religion' status and offer it a degree of formal 'recognition' and public prominence unparalleled in modern Europe. Orthodox spokesmen persistently denied that this amounted to any 'privilege', arguing that the constitution's use of the word 'prevailing' simply represented a statement of sociological fact.[93] Though a minority of the political and social elite argued for change, the new Archbishop of Athens chosen in April 1998 remained implacably opposed to the separation of church and state. In early 2000 the issue returned to the fore in various contexts but, as George Mavrogordatas points out, by and large the pressure for change was external rather than internal, and this was evident in the fact that it was the Foreign Ministry that in 1999 set up a committee to review church–state relations. By that time, however, the issue had been removed from the agenda of constitutional reform due to be discussed in the new parliament elected in the spring of that year, with the result that major constitutional changes in this area during the next decade had been rendered unlikely.[94] The difficulty of introducing change was also made apparent in May 2000 when a government announcement of its intentions to implement an earlier decision to remove the section in Greek identity cards asking for religious affiliation provoked considerable hostility from sections of the religious and conservative elite.[95]

Restricting religious minorities?

The democratisation process in Greece did not throw up any law explicitly devoted to religious liberty, and critics suggest that in this sphere Greece retains the distinction of having the most restrictive legislation (and practice) in Western Europe – though church and government agencies sometimes suggest that minorities exaggerate their difficulties.[96] Though the 1975 constitution guaranteed freedom of worship and belief to all citizens, in practice ambiguities in the text as well other legislative or administrative acts have created a situation where religious liberty has been severely compromised on occasions, though arguably the situation has gradually improved since the early 1990s.[97]

Under Article 13 religious freedom was offered, but only to an undefined category of 'known' religions, a term that as we have already noted has been much debated within Greece and commented on adversely by various international bodies. This conception has several consequences. Firstly, it effectively divides religious groups into three, if not four, categories each with differential rights. Sitting on top of the pile is the Orthodox Church, which is considered the prevailing religion of the Greeks and as we saw accorded a special status in Article 3 of the constitution. The de facto recognition of a state church need not in principle be at the expense of other religious groups, but in this context it is difficult to see how this cannot be so. Under the terms of the constitution the dominant church is a legal person incorporated under public law, and as such some believe that it enjoys all the privileges accruing to the state whilst simultaneously remaining a distinct legal entity. Then come the Muslim and Jewish communities, whose central organisations are recognised by state law as public corporations. Other religious communities enjoy a lesser status, either as religious or voluntary corporations under private law.[98] One of the consequences of this is that non-Orthodox churches cannot own property as churches but have to form other legal entities to acquire property and consequently surmount further legal and bureaucratic hurdles in setting up their places of worship.[99]

In defining the category of 'known' religion much seems to depend upon the decision of the Ministry of National Education and Religions or the Ministry of Justice, or of the Council of State when the government brings a court case against a particular group. Often the attitudes of local authorities or administrative bodies are more important, as in the case of the Seventh Day Adventist ministers whom the Ministry of Defence denied the right to exemption from military service on the grounds that their faith was not a 'known' religion. Though this decision was overruled by the Council of State, it illustrates the oft-repeated necessity for religious minorities to take their cases to court in order to gain recognition, a problem that has affected the Jehovah's Witnesses more than any other group. For a long period their status has been open to debate within the Greek legal system. Prior to adoption of the 1975 constitution a local court had ruled that they were a 'sect of the Christian faith' with the right to freedom of worship in Greece, but since then this recognition has been challenged by various administrative bodies.[100] Since the mid-1980s the Council of State has consistently taken the view that they represent a 'known' religion, but civil courts and local authorities have taken the opposite view in many cases. Equally, the leaders of the Orthodox Church have failed to accept this recognition and a circular from the Holy Synod in late 1997 disputed their recognition as 'known' and the use of the word 'Christian' in front of their official designation.[101]

This question of being a 'known' religion is closely tied to the questioning of opening places of worship. As we saw earlier, the 1938/9 Necessity

Acts gave considerable latitude in this matter to the local authorities and Orthodox bishop, and these requirements remain in place and are still referred to on occasions by Orthodox bishops seeking to prevent the opening of minority places of worship. For example, in December 1997 the police in Thessaloniki opened a case against Reverend George Goudas, pastor of the Greek Evangelical Church, claiming that he was operating a church without the appropriate 'House of Prayer' licence required under the 1939 legislation. A similar case was reported in late 1999 when the pastor of a Pentecostal Church that had been recognised in Greece for over fifty years was prosecuted by the attorney general of Thessaloniki for organising a prayer house without the permission of the local Orthodox bishop.[102] In December 2000 these cases came to court along with those of several other Protestant and Catholic churches in Thessaloniki who were charged with 'unauthorised operation of a house of worship'. Though the judge acquitted those charged with the offence and the district attorney suggested the need for some modernisation of the Metaxas legislation, the court avoided making any precedent-setting statements about the 1930s legislation.[103] As already noted most of these cases are resolved after appeal to the Council of State, but they continue to lengthen the bureaucratic processes facing those seeking to open a church or other religious building.

Roman Catholics are also reported to have experienced some difficulties in this area, with the legal status of some Catholic organisations still unclear even after a parliamentary resolution of July 1999 confirmed the legal status of all those Catholic organisations existing prior to 1946.[104] Though many groups face problems in this area, it is the Jehovah's Witnesses who have experienced the greatest difficulty in opening places of worship. Viewed as an un-Christian sect by the Orthodox Church, in many cases religious activists and local authorities work closely together to prevent the creation of new churches. Several of these cases eventually reached the European Court. For example, in 1987 a local group of Witnesses in a village on Crete were subject to vilification in the preaching of an Orthodox priest, who also asked the security police to close down their place of worship. Having been charged with breach of the 1939 laws, four members of the community were brought to trial but acquitted in the criminal court in Heraklion, on the grounds that all religious believers were free to hold meetings. The cases dragged on as the prosecutor appealed and got the decision reversed and the Supreme Court intervened to back the local authorities. The Witnesses in turn appealed to the European Commission on Human Rights which in May 1995 took the case to the European Court who found against the Greek government, and suggested it was imposing 'rigid, or indeed prohibitive, conditions on the practice of religious beliefs of certain non-Orthodox movements'.[105] There are also occasions reported when the police and local authorities appear willing to turn a blind eye to the resolution of property issues by illegal means, as when in 1998 local Orthodox leaders in the Athens suburb of Galatsi encouraged the seizure and occupation of a property built and owned by the Old Calendarists.[106]

Perhaps the most controversial issue of all has related to the question of proselytism. The 1939 Necessity Act, which specifically banned proselytising activities aimed at the Orthodox Church and is still supported by that Church, defined the offence in terms of intrusion

on the religious beliefs of a person of a different religious persuasion, with the aim of undermining those beliefs, either by any kind of inducement or promise of an inducement or moral support or material assistance, or by fraudulent means, or by taking advantage of his inexperience, trust, need, low intellect or naivete.[107]

Penalties for the offence were severe, ranging from fines and police surveillance, to terms of imprisonment or expulsion from the country in the case of foreigners. Under the 1975 constitution the emphasis was changed slightly insofar as all religious groups were protected from prosleytism and in theory even the Orthodox were not allowed to engage in such activities.

In practice the cases that have come to court have been directed at smaller religious communities, including the Evangelicals, Pentecostals, Hare Krishnas, Buddhists and Jehovah's Witnesses. Of these the latter have suffered the harshest treatment, with some 20,000 having been arrested at various points since 1939. Nonetheless, the number of arrests has been declining in recent years, with some 2,000 prosecutions in 1983–8, 71 arrests in 1993, just 11 in 1998 and none in 1999, a trend that has much to do with the Kokkinakis case we discuss below. This has not, however, ended the dozens of cases of assault or harassment initiated by police, clergymen or laity when the Witnesses engage in evangelistic activities. Extreme, but not untypical of such, was the situation that developed in Kassandreia in the Halkidiki region during 1999 when the local mayor, citing the dangers posed by evangelisation, incited residents to impede the construction of a Witness prayer hall and organised pickets and blockades to prevent building work. Though the local planning office gave permission and the central media covered the story, the local mayor appears to have ignored all calls for moderation and encouraged assaults on two of the journalists covering the story.[108] Disruption of meetings is not uncommon in many parts of the country, as in August 1999 when a national gathering of Witnesses in Larisa in Central Greece was met by hostile shouting and the ringing of the mourning bell by local Orthodox

churches.[109] Other religious cases that have come to court include that
of a foreign Hare Krishna devotee sentenced in his absence to two years
by a court in Athens during 1997, and that of a schoolteacher unsuccessfully charged at the instigation of the local bishop with making frequent
references to Buddhism during a German language class.[110]

Several of these cases have eventually progressed to the European
Court, with mixed results for the Greek authorities and one turning into
a landmark case that may eventually lead to a fundamental shift in Greek
practice in this area and perhaps lead to the abrogation of the Necessity
Act. This latter case revolved around the activities of Minos Kokkinakis
(d.1999), a Witness who had been prosecuted some sixty times since the
late 1930s and served over six years in prison for proselytism. In this particular case the charges related to a conversation he had with the wife of
an Orthodox cantor, which led to charges that he had exerted undue pressure upon a poorly educated woman. This case eventually reached the
European Court of Human Rights that deliberated at length in an explicit
effort to balance the rights of Kokkinakis to propagate his beliefs and the
right of the state to protect citizens from unwanted pressures. Though
the judges adopted a variety of positions, the eventual outcome was that
the Court found against the Greek government in this case, though it offered little comment on the older legislation. In essence it suggested that
the acts of 1938/9 were not necessarily incompatible with religious freedom, but argued at the same time that they lacked specificity in defining
what constituted 'improper' pressure. They also questioned the Greek
state's right to arrogate to itself the decision as to whether an individual
was too weak to resist the importunities of the proselytiser.[111] In consequence of this decision, the Greek Ministry of Justice issued instructions to subordinate legal institutions at all levels to adapt their practice
accordingly,[112] though as we have noted such a ruling has not been accepted throughout the legal and administrative system.

A second case – Larissis and others vs. Greece – related to three
Pentecostal airforce officers who had been carrying out evangelistic activities between 1986 and 1989 both amongst civilians and amongst airmen
in their units. Charged with proselytising Orthodox Christians under the
act, they were tried and sentenced to suspended periods of twelve, thirteen and fourteen months. After a process of appeals through the Greek
courts they went to the European Commission on Human Rights and
then on to the European Court. Here the judges basically found that
their rights had been contravened to the extent that the charges related to
civilians, but found for the Greek government in the case of attempts
to proselytise those subordinate to the officers as here there might have
been undue pressure owing to the hierarchical nature of military units.

Nonetheless, the court expressed regret that the earlier ruling in the 1993 Kokkinakis case had not been followed by any serious attempt on the part of the Greek authorities to clarify the situation regarding legitimate propagation of one's beliefs.[113] In response to some of these developments, in 1998 a group of prominent Greeks proposed that these laws should be abrogated as a remnant of an out-of-date era, and that the constitution should be amended to remove the ban on proselytism.[114]

Further issues that have arisen regarding the treatment of religious minorities relate to the questions of identity cards, employment rights, conscientious objection, state surveillance of religious communities, and child custody in situations where divorcing parents have different faiths. Under a law of 1986 all Greeks were required to indicate their religion on their personal identity cards. In 1993 parliament rejected an amendment that would have made this reference optional, though, according to the Ministry of Justice, this requirement had no legal implications and simply made things easier when it came to issues relating to inheritance and funeral rites. The Orthodox Church also opposed the amendment, though perhaps ironically it seems to have led some non-Orthodox to declare themselves as adherents of the national church so as to avoid discrimination in certain professions and occupations. For the UN Rapporteur on Religious Tolerance this issue was problematic for, as he pointed out, the compulsory declaration of religious adherence would appear to violate various international conventions.[115] In 1997 parliament approved a law that would have removed this question from the list of questions referred to on personal ID documents, though nothing was done to implement the decision. Only after the elections of spring 2000 did the government make the announcement, perhaps rather tactlessly without warning the Archbishop of Athens and perhaps deliberately whilst he was out of the country, that the religious question was to be omitted from future documentation. This provoked an instant response from the outspoken church leader and a chorus of protest from many conservative politicians who saw the move as one more step on the road to the erosion of Greek identity (see chapter 5). For minority representatives, however, this was a welcome move that might serve to at least reduce the reality and perception that a failure to mention religious affiliation effectively denied them access to certain employment opportunities.[116]

Under legislation in force at the time of the transition there were no provisions for conscientious objection, though after 1975 ministers of 'known' religions were exempt from military service. Until very recently, however, the Greek state was reluctant to consider the possibility of alternative civilian service, citing Article 13 of the constitution which denied that religion could serve as a reason for not performing obligations to the state, or arguing that if there were different provisions for different people this would in effect undermine equality under the law. A draft law produced in the late 1980s was rejected, though a draft drawn up by the Ministry of Defence in 1991 permitted unarmed military service. At the same time the government rejected the more comprehensive exemption desired by the Jehovah's Witnesses, who refuse to wear a uniform, salute the flag or accept the proposed longer period of alternative service. Their commitment to this line was further reinforced by the fact that in total Witnesses had reportedly served some 5,000 years in military prisons between 1938 and 1992 for conscientious objection.[117] And even in the mid-1990s there were hundreds still imprisoned, serving sentences of up to four years. New legislation was eventually steered through parliament in 1997 that permitted civilian service in places such as homes for the disabled and the elderly, though those involved would have to spend twelve months longer in state service than the normal period for conscripts.[118]

In 1993 the Greek Intelligence Service issued a confidential report detailing its surveillance activities in the religious field. Here it was suggested that files were kept on all non-Orthodox communities in order that appropriate measures could be taken against non-genuine Greeks. This issue came to a head in the case of Tsavachidis vs. Greece, initially heard in the European Court but then subject to an out-of-court settlement in 1997. The case stemmed from the prosecution of Tsavachidis, a Jehovah's Witness who had opened a place of worship without the appropriate permit. When it eventually reached the courts there appeared on his file an anonymous document, presumed to have originated from the intelligence services, detailing the activities of his group. His argument, and one that was eventually accepted by the Greek authorities, was that anonymous files could not be used in court and that secret surveillance amounted to an infringement of his personal liberty.[119]

On the child custody issue the two cases that have been reported relate to situations where one parent was a member of the Jehovah's Witnesses, and the other has used this to gain custody over a child. Thus in September 1998 an Athens court gave parental rights to an Orthodox father on the grounds that the Witness attitude to blood transfusion might endanger the life of the child. Finally, one might point to the raid on the administrative offices of the 'Channel Station 2000' on 2 December 1999, which had been denounced for 'dangerous proselytism' by the church on the previous day. The authorities claimed that the radio station had no proper operating licence – something no private radio station has – but this follows a pattern, for in 1994 the police had closed down Greece's only evangelical television station. In this new case, however, the courts came to the defence of the minority community and at the end of December an Athens judge ruled they could begin broadcasting again.[120]

In addition to all these problems, which stem from ambiguous or restrictive legislation, one should also point to the specific problems affecting the Muslim community, predominantly located in Western Thrace, though here religious and ethnic issues are closely intertwined and solutions to this problem may well depend as much on Turkish–Greek relations as domestic administrative policies.[121] Under the terms of legislation approved in 1920 the Muslim community enjoyed the right to elect their own representatives, but the military dictatorship introduced a system – which continued to operate after 1974 and was confirmed by decree in 1990 – whereby the state maintained the right to oversee the appointment of muftis in this region, albeit from a list provided by a committee of prominent local Muslims. Equally, the Greek president retains the right to remove a mufti should he be rendered incapable of carrying out his task or commit criminal acts. In 1991 religious communities in Xanthi and Komotoni decided to elect their own muftis, a decision opposed by the state, which imposed its own candidates, and the courts, who sentenced the two elected muftis to short prison terms for usurping the titles. From the government's perspective the existing arrangement was both practically and constitutionally essential, for on the one hand they chose from a list provided by the Muslims and therefore they could not be said to have imposed unwanted candidates. Secondly, given that the muftis performed certain judicial functions in their territories, they could not be exempted from the constitutional provision that judges be appointed. Nonetheless this issue continues to cause problems as many within the communities only recognise the elected muftis. At the same time, the government shows no sign of backing down on this issue, and in early June 2000 Mehmet Emin Aga, the elected mufti of Xhanti, was sentenced to seven months' imprisonment for 'usurping the function of a religious minister'.[122] And though the official view was that the election of rival muftis was likely to stir up religious and ethnic tensions, the European Court for Human Rights saw no reason why a group of believers should not be able to elect their own leaders.[123]

Much of the state's dealings with the Muslim community has a political resonance that makes seemingly rational solutions problematic, and this led the UN Rapporteur on Religious Tolerance to point out that the state's treatment of Muslims in Thrace should not be subordinate to considerations concerning Turkey.[124] Problems persist, however, not just in Thrace but also in metropolitan Athens, which has acquired a larger Muslim population in recent years. During the mid-1990s the mayor had to postpone the building of a mosque for the local and migrant population of the Rouff district in the face of stiff protests from the Holy Synod, even though there were no other places of worship available to them,[125] whilst proposals to build an Islamic centre in Athens in time for the holding of the Olympic Games in 2004 have also aroused some debate, though on this occasion the church supports the decision if not the site chosen. In addition to these more formal difficulties, the Muslim community has to face occasional assaults from activists who daub anti-Islamic slogans on its buildings, and occasional anti-Islamic outbursts from Orthodox radicals. Insults do not always come from fringe actors, but from the Orthodox hierarchy, as in Western Thrace where in 1993 Orthodox leaders offered special payments to Greek families in the region who had a third child in order 'to fight the area's major demographic problem'.[126] In the face of such actions, the public affability of the first meeting between the head of the Orthodox Church and the leadership of the Thrace Muslims in September 1999 should not perhaps be taken at face value.[127]

Conclusion

Overall it is clear that post-military Greece has not made as much progress towards providing legal guarantees for religious minorities as its Spanish counterpart. Yet it should also be noted that in many areas the problems affecting minorities are increasingly not the product of state policies but of the failure of the centre to persuade lower local administrative agencies of the need to protect minority rights. Within the government elected in 2000 there is on the surface a broader commitment to the protection of minority rights, though, as already noted, much of the pressure for this is external rather than domestic. Symptomatic of this was the short-lived appearance of a committee on religious affairs within the Ministry of Foreign Affairs, a body that, unlike the Ministry of National Education and Religions over the previous four decades, has granted access to representatives of religious minorities.[128] On the issue of 'privilege' it has been suggested that despite its protests the Greek Orthodox Church's formal status goes beyond that of a simple recognition of sociological reality. How this might be justified is a question that we leave to a later chapter, but it might be noted here that there are some fundamental differences of approach at work in Spain and Greece. Though the historical patterns of church–state relations have some superficial similarities, the Spanish church has more immediate memories of persecution that may have increased its inclinations to seek a consensual solution to conflicts with the political order. Equally, it has opted, occasionally reluctantly, for the more individualistic approach to rights and privileges that characterises the majority of international treaties, whilst the Greek Orthodox Church has sought to preserve something of a communitarian heritage that sees religion as contributing fundamentally to the nation's sense of identity. As we shall see, this has had an impact on the types of arguments that have been utilised by the two churches in defending their position in democratising societies.

Notes

1. See the discussion of regional identity and distinctness in Salvador Giner, 'Political economy, legitimation and the state in Southern Europe', in Guillermo O'Donnell, Philippe C. Schmitter and Lawrence Whitehead (eds.), *Transitions from Authoritarian Rule: Southern Europe* (Baltimore and London: Johns Hopkins University Press, 1986), pp. 11–44.
2. R. Carr, *Modern Spain* (Oxford: Oxford University Press, 1986), p. 165.
3. P. Preston, *The Triumph of Democracy in Spain* (London: Methuen, 1986), p. 4.
4. Ibid., pp. 4–6; Carr, *Modern Spain*, pp. 165–7.
5. V. Perez-Diaz, *The Rebirth of Civil Society* (London: Harvard University Press, 1993), p. 28.
6. On the role of the king see J. Podolny, 'The role of Juan Carlos I in the consolidation of parliamentary democracy', in R. Gunther (ed.), *Politics, Society and Democracy: The Case of Spain* (Boulder: Westview, 1993), pp. 88–112.
7. Cf. Juan Linz and Alfred Stepan, *Problems of Democratic Transition and Consolidation* (Baltimore: Johns Hopkins University Press, 1996), pp. 87–115; R. Gunther, 'Spain: the very model of the modern elite settlement', in J. Higley and R. Gunther (eds.), *Elites and Democratic Consolidation in Latin America and Southern Europe* (Cambridge: Cambridge University Press, 1992), pp. 38–80.
8. D. Nichols, 'Religious liberty in Spain: a survey to 1968', *Iberian Studies*, 1: 1, 1972, p. 5.
9. J. Hooper, *The Spaniards* (London: Penguin, 1986), p. 172.
10. E. De Blaye, *Franco and the Politics of Spain* (London: Penguin, 1976), pp. 411–12.
11. A. Brassloff, *Religion and Politics in Spain: The Spanish Church in Transition, 1962–96* (London: Macmillan, 1998), p. 7.
12. Ibid., p. 11; W. Callahan, 'The evangelisation of Franco's "new Spain"', *Church History*, 56, 1987, pp. 491–503.
13. Perez-Diaz, *The Rebirth of Civil Society*, pp. 130–40.
14. S. Payne, *Spanish Catholicism* (London: University of Wisconsin Press, 1984), chapter 2.
15. J. Hughey, 'Church, state and religious liberty in Spain', *Journal of Church and State*, 23: 3, 1981, pp. 485–95; several Protestant clerics were killed in 1939–40, including two members of the Spanish Episcopal community. Electronic interview with Bishop Carlos Lopez Lozano, 21 July 2000.

16. See E. Mujal-Leon, 'The left and the Catholic question in Spain', *West European Politics*, 5: 2, 1982, pp. 32–54.

17. Frances Lannon, *Privilege, Persecution and Prophecy: The Catholic Church in Spain, 1875–1975* (Oxford: Clarendon Press, 1987), various sections but especially pp. 231–5.

18. N. Cooper, 'The church: from crusade to Christianity', in P. Preston (ed.), *Spain in Crisis* (London: Harvester, 1976), pp. 73–4.

19. S. Carillo, *Eurocommunism and the State* (London: Lawrence & Wishart, 1977), pp. 28–33.

20. Cf. Perez-Diaz, *The Rebirth of Civil Society*, pp. 173–4; T. Lawlor and M. Rigby, *Contemporary Spain* (London: Longman, 1998), pp. 323–6.

21. Report from Human Rights without Frontiers, 16 September 1999; Antonio Gómez Mouellán, *La iglesie católice y otras religious en la Españe da hoy* (Madrid, 1999), pp. 107–10.

22. Quoted in R. Graham, *Spain: Change of a Nation* (London: Michael Joseph, 1984), p. 214.

23. Brassloff, *Religion and Politics in Spain*, pp. 86–7.

24. This desire to calm the situation is viewed by some as commendable for the stability of the new democracy but also as having negative effects on the quality of participation after 1975 as the church failed to mobilise its flock in the direction of an 'active' support for the new system. P. McDonough et al., *The Cultural Dynamics of Democratisation in Spain* (Ithaca: Cornell University Press, 1998), pp. 14–15, 145.

25. W. Callahan, *The Catholic Church in Spain, 1875–1998* (Washington DC: Catholic University of America Press, 2000), pp. 560–65.

26. R. Gunther, G. Sani and G. Shabad (eds.), *Spain after Franco: The Making of a Competitive Party System* (Berkeley: University of California Press, 1988), p. 220; L. Edles, *Symbol and Ritual in the New Spain* (Cambridge: Cambridge University Press, 1998), p. 69.

27. For a detailed discussion of this debate and its historical context see R. Gunther and R. Blough, 'Religious conflict and consensus in Spain: a tale of two constitutions', *World Affairs*, 143: 4, 1981, pp. 366–412.

28. Brassloff, *Religion and Politics in Spain*, p. 95.

29. A. Bonimo-Blanc, *Spain's Transition to Democracy: The Politics of Constitution Making* (Boulder: Westview, 1987), pp. 95–7.

30. *The Tablet*, 4 March 1978.

31. Gunther et al., *Spain after Franco*, p. 221.

32. W. Callahan, 'Church and state in Spain, 1975–91', *Journal of Church and State*, 34: 3, 1992, p. 507; J. Linz, 'Church and state in Spain', in *Daedalus*, 120: 3, 1991, pp. 172–73.

33. P. Heywood, *The Government and Politics of Spain* (London: Macmillan, 1995), pp. 49–51.

34. *The Tablet*, 9 December 1978.

35. Brassloff, *Religion and Politics in Spain*, pp. 97–8.

36. Quoted in Hughey, 'Church, state and religious liberty in Spain', p. 491.

37. Ibid., pp. 100–1.

38. *The Tablet*, 21 February 1981.

39. Brassloff, *Religion and Politics in Spain*, pp. 123–4.
40. For a brief overview of the role of the Church in Spanish education see J. McNair, *Education for a Changing Spain* (Manchester: Manchester University Press, 1984), pp. 139–50.
41. Callahan, 'Church and state in Spain', pp. 506–7, 512–17; Mouellán, *La iglesie católice y otras religious en la Españe da hoy*, p. 118.
42. Cf. Hooper, *The Spaniards*, p. 180; 'Notes on church–state affairs', *Journal of Church and State*, 26: 1, 1984, pp. 154–5, 34: 2, 1992, p. 424 and 34: 4, 1992, p. 911; Brassloff, *Religion and Politics in Spain*, p. 134.
43. S. Ashford and N. Timms, *What Europe Thinks: A Study of West European Values* (Aldershot: Dartmouth, 1992), pp. 34, 61.
44. Mouellán (*La iglesie católice y otras religious en la Españe da hoy*, p. 124) comments on the continued artificial maintenance of the church's position through state protection.
45. P. Preston, *Franco: A Biography* (London: HarperCollins, 1993), pp. 609–10, 617.
46. The next two paragraphs are largely based on J. Hughey, 'Church, state and religious liberty in Spain', and *Protestants in Modern Spain* (South Pasadena: William Carey Library, 1973), pp. 25–53.
47. Hughey, 'Church, state and religious liberty in Spain', pp. 491–4; see discussion in 'Debate VN: la libertad religiosa hoy', *Vide Nueva*, No. 1240, 2–9 August 1980, pp. 29–38.
48. US State Department, *Annual Report in International Religious Freedom for 1999: Spain*; an English translation of the law can be found at http://www.mju.es/ar_n02_i.thm.
49. Cf. G. Moran, 'S ispanskoi tochki zrenoya: beseda s prof. Gloria Moran', in S. Filatov et al., *Religiya i prava cheloveka: na puti svobode sovesti III* (Moscow: Nauka, 1996), pp. 89–97; G. Moran, 'The legal status of religious minorities in Spain', *Journal of Church and State*, 36: 3, 1994, pp. 578–95.
50. Moran, 'The legal status of religious minorities in Spain', pp. 578–80; Alberto de la Hera, 'Relations with religious minorities: the Spanish model', *Brigham Young University Law Review*, 2, 1998, pp. 387–400.
51. See 'Notes on church–state affairs', *Journal of Church and State*, 34: 2, 1992, p. 424, 34: 4, 1992, p. 911.
52. Report from *Human Rights without Frontiers*, 16 September 1999.
53. *Annual Report on Religious Freedom for 1999: Spain.*
54. *Annual Report on International Religious Freedom: Spain* (US State Department, 5 September 2000).
55. Ibid.
56. 'Notes on church and state', *Journal of Church and State*, 31: 2, 1989, p. 341; K. Boyle and J. Sheen (eds.), *Freedom of Religion and Belief: A World Report* (London: Routledge, 1997), p. 385.
57. *Annual Report on Religious Freedom for 1999: Spain.*
58. US State Department, *International Religious Freedom Report, 2001*, http://www.state.gov/g/drl/rls/irf/2001/5666.thm.
59. P. Nikiforos Diamondouros, 'Regime change and prospects for democracy in Greece: 1974–83', in O'Donnell et al., *Transitions from Authoritarian Rule*,

pp. 139–47; for a general political history of Greece see C. M. Woodhouse, *Modern Greece: A Short History* (London, Faber, 1998), or R. Clogg, *A Concise History of Greece* (Cambridge: Cambridge University Press, 1992).

60. T. Veremis, *The Military in Greek Politics: From Independence to Democracy* (London: Hurst, 1997), pp. 159–65; A. Papandreou, *Democracy at Gunpoint* (London: Penguin, 1970).

61. Diamanorous, 'Regime change and prospects for democracy', pp. 155–64; Linz and Stepan, *Problems of Democratic Transition and Consolidation*, pp. 130–8.

62. Woodhouse, *Modern Greece*, pp. 103, 126–7.

63. This section relies heavily on C. Frazee, 'Church and state in Greece', in J. T. Koumoulidis (ed.), *Greece in Transition: Essays in Modern Greek History, 1821–1974* (London: Zeno Publishers, 1977), pp. 128–44; see also A. Papadakis, 'The historical tradition of church–state relations under Orthodoxy', in P. Ramet (ed.), *Eastern Christianity and Politics in the Twentieth Century* (Durham: Duke University Press, 1988), pp. 41–2.

64. P. Nikiforos Diamondouros, 'Greek political culture in transition', in R. Clogg (ed.), *Greece in the 1980s* (London: Macmillan, 1983), p. 55.

65. Clogg (ed.), *Greece in the 1980s*, pp. 144–6; D. Close (ed.), *The Greek Civil War, 1943–50: Studies of Polarisation* (London: Routledge, 1993), pp. 16–17, 158.

66. Frazee, 'Church and state in Greece', pp. 149–51; Papandreou, *Democracy at Gunpoint*, p. 348; P. Scwab and G. Frangos (eds.), *Greece under the Junta* (New York: Facts on File, 1970), pp. 29–30.

67. For statistical data see Boyle and Sheen, *Freedom of Religion and Belief*, p. 331; *Greece 1999*, Country Report on Human Rights Practices, issued by US State Department on 25 February 2000.

68. See the comments on his election in *Athens News*, 29 April 1998.

69. Frazee, 'Church and state in Greece', pp. 128–53.

70. T. Stavrou, 'The Orthodox Church and political culture in modern Greece', in D. Costa and T. Stavrou (eds.), *Greece Prepares for the Twenty First Century* (Baltimore: Johns Hopkins University Press, 1995), pp. 47–8.

71. Extracted from http://www.hri.org/MFA/syntagma/artcl125.html#P1.

72. For a general discussion of the constitutional provisions see Boyle and Sheen, *Freedom of Religion and Belief*, pp. 332–4.

73. Report of the UN Special Rapporteur on Religious Tolerance, 7 November 1996, Sections 20–22 (henceforth cited as Amor Report); there is debate as to the extent to which this provision still applies, and officials of the Ministry of National Education and Religions report that they no longer seek the views of the local bishops, though in some areas local officials may still do so. US State Department, *Annual Report on International Religious Freedom for 1999: Greece*, 9 September.

74. S. Stavros, 'The legal status of minorities in Greece today: the adequacy of their protection in the light of current human rights perceptions', *Journal of Modern Greek Studies*, 13: 1, 1995, pp. 12–15.

75. A. Pollis, 'Greek national identity: religious minorities, rights and European norms', *Journal of Modern Greek Studies*, 10: 2, 1992, p. 181.

76. Amor Report, Sections 7–10; Report from Human Rights without Frontiers (HRWF), 7 June 1997, found at http://www.hrwf.net.
77. Quoted in Boyle and Sheen, *Freedom of Religion and Belief*, p. 333.
78. *Athens News*, 13 September 1998.
79. Ibid., 5 May 1998.
80. See the useful analysis of this clash in C. Stewart, 'Who owns the Rotonda: church vs. state in Greece', *Anthropology Today*, 14: 4, October 1998, pp. 3–9; I am grateful to Ruth Macrides for drawing my attention to this article.
81. Pollis, 'Greek national identity', p. 176.
82. N. Kokoslakis, 'Greek Orthodoxy and modern socio-economic change', in R. Roberts (ed.), *Religion and the Transformations of Capitalism* (London: Routledge, 1996), p. 260.
83. P. Dmitros, 'Changes in public attitudes', in K. Featherstone and D. Katsoudas (eds.), *Political Change in Greece: Before and After the Colonels* (London: Croom Helm, 1987), pp. 72–5; N. Alivizatos, 'A new role for the Greek Church?', *Journal of Modern Greek Studies*, 17: 1, 1999, pp. 23–40; yet such figures should not be overstated, because surveys taken during the conflict over the identity card issue in mid-2000 suggested that over half the population favoured the maintenance of the religious identification. *Athens News*, 30 May 2000.
84. Hooper, 'Notes on church and state', *Journal of Church and State*, 22: 3, 1980, p. 553.
85. Ibid., 26: 2, 1984, pp. 365–6; A. Halkias, 'Give birth for Greece: abortion and nation in letters to the editors of the mainstream Greek press', *Journal of Modern Greek Studies*, 16: 1, 1998, pp. 111–38.
86. Stavros, 'The legal status of minorities in Greece today', pp. 22–3.
87. Stavrou, 'The Orthodox Church and political culture', pp. 36–7.
88. Letter from the local community to the Ministry of Education and Religions, http://groups.yahoo.co./group/balkanhr/message/2885; see also the case of the boy of undisclosed philosophical beliefs who was expelled from a central Greek school after he refused to participate in his village's celebration of its patron saint. *Athens News*, 1 June 2000.
89. Boyle and Sheen, *Freedom of Religion and Belief*, p. 337.
90. G. Mavrogordatas, 'Church–state relations in the Greek Orthodox Case', paper presented to the ECPR Joint Sessions on 'Church and State in Europe', Copenhagen, 14–19 April 2000, p. 3; C. Papastathis, 'Church and state in Greece in 1998', *European Journal of Church and State*, 6: 1, 1999, pp. 65–6; in the summer of 2000 the government excluded religion from the nationwide exam schedule that all would-be students are required to sit.
91. *HRWF*, 99.
92. Cf. 'Notes on church and state', *Journal of Church and State*, 29: 3, 1987, p. 584; J. Pettifer, *The Greeks: Land and People since the War* (London: Viking, 1993), p. 54; S. Stavros, 'Human rights in Greece: twelve years of supervision from Strasbourg', *Journal of Modern Greek Studies*, 17: 1, 1999, pp. 10–11.
93. Interview with Vassile Feidas, Professor of Canon Law at Athens University, 31 May 2000.

94. Mavrogordatas, 'Church–state relations in the Greek Orthodox case', p. 2; reportedly this committee was short-lived and in 2000 was wound up under pressure from the Orthodox hierarchy. Communication with Maria Koutatzi, Communications Officer of the Catholic Bishops Conference in Greece, 26 September 2000.

95. See the reports in *Athens News*, 9, 11, 12, 16 and 17 May 2000.

96. Amor Report, Section 80.

97. According to several Protestant spokesmen interviewed in early June 2000.

98. S. Stavros, 'Citizenship and the protection of minorities', in K. Featherstone and K. Ifantis (eds.), *Greece in a Changing Europe* (Manchester: Manchester University Press, 1996), pp. 120–1.

99. US State Department, *Annual Report on International Religious Freedom for 1999: Greece.*

100. 'Notes on church and state', *Journal of Church and State*, 15: 1, 1973, p. 155.

101. Papastathis, 'Church and state in Greece in 1998', pp. 68–9.

102. Human Rights without Frontiers, quoting a statement from the Greek Evangelical Alliance, 20 October 1999; report of Greek Helsinki Group, http://222.greekhelsinki.gr/englsih/reports/ihf-greece98.html.

103. News Release from Greek Evangelical Alliance, 12 December 2000.

104. IHF Report, *Annual Country Report on Human Rights*, 1 June 2000 (http/:///www.hrwf.net); Communication with Maria Koutatzi, 26 September 2000.

105. http:///religioustolerance.org/rt_greec.htm.

106. *Human Rights in Greece 1999*, Greek Helsinki Monitor, 1999; the Old Calendarists broke with the Orthodox Church in 1924 when the latter adopted the Gregorian Calendar.

107. Stavros, 'The legal status of minorities in Greece today', p. 15.

108. *Human Rights in Greece 1999*, Greek Helsinki Monitor, 1999.

109. IHF Report, *Annual Country Report on Human Rights*.

110. Human Rights Without Frontiers, 7 June 1999.

111. Cf. Boyle and Sheen, *Freedom of Religion and Belief*, pp. 335–6; Malcolm Evans, *Religious Liberty and International Law in Europe* (Cambridge: Cambridge University Press, 1997), pp. 282–5, 332–4; D. Robertson, 'The legal protection of religious values in Europe', in *Religious Liberty and Secularism* (Vatican, 1998), p. 185.

112. Amor Report, section 136.

113. Human Rights Without Frontiers, 1998 Report.

114. Human Rights Without Frontiers, 2 June 1998.

115. Ibid.; Amor Report, sections 26–30.

116. See the persistent reports that Catholics and others could not get high-ranking posts in the army, police or diplomatic service. Amor Report, Section 65.

117. Boyle and Sheen, *Freedom of Religion and Belief*, p. 338.

118. Amor Report, section 137; US State Department, *Annual Report on International Religious Freedom for 1999: Greece.*

119. It has been reported that in several European countries intelligence services have become involved in monitoring new religious movements and groups designated as 'cults'. On the Tsavachidis case see the press statement of the European Court Registry issued on 21 January 1999, at http://www.dhcour.coe.fr/eng/PRESS/New%20Court/Tsavachidis%20epress.html.

120. Mavrogordatas, 'Church–state relations in the Greek Orthodox case', p. 3; Human Rights Without Frontiers, 18 February 2000.

121. On the wider problem see H. Poulton, 'Changing notions of national identity among Muslims in Thrace and Macedonia: Turks, Pomaks and Roma', in H. Poulton and S. Taji-Farouki (eds.), *Muslim Identity and the Balkan State* (London: Hurst & Co, 1997), pp. 82–92.

122. Human Rights Without Frontiers, 2 June 2000.

123. Amnesty International Report on Turkish minorities in Greece, January 2000.

124. Stavros, 'The legal status of minorities in Greece today', pp. 22–3; Amor Report, sections 41–51, 105–21, 140.

125. *Athens News*, 10 July 1997.

126. Report on Greece produced by the International Helsinki Federation for Human Rights, 22 March 1999.

127. A brief factual report can be found in the church-sponsored Ecclesia website, 28 September 1999.

128. Interview with Fotis Romeos, General Secretary of the Greek Evangelical Alliance, June 2000; Catholic spokesperson Maria Koutatzi reports that in 1999 the Archbishop of Athens tried unsuccessfully for six months to get a meeting with the minister.

3   Central and Eastern Europe: Poland and Bulgaria

The impact of democratisation on religious life in Central–Eastern Europe after 1989 was far greater than in Southern Europe, for the simple reason that here dictatorship had been accompanied by an active hostility to religious ideas and institutions. In Poland and Bulgaria the party-states maintained a formal commitment to atheism until the end, though in the former this had effectively been rendered meaningless by the late 1970s and in the latter it was pursued with only intermittent, although sometimes brutal, bursts of enthusiasm during the later Zhivkov years. More importantly, the response of the churches in the two states had been very different, with the Polish Catholic Church gradually carving out a position for itself as defender of the nation and human rights, whilst the Bulgarian Orthodox Church retreated into a liturgical role that offered no challenge to the state and its policies. This in turn had much to do with the nature of the regimes – with the Polish leadership reluctant to opt for the full Sovietisation that was required of, or chosen by, the Bulgarian elite – but also with the religious traditions of the country. Whilst the Bulgarian church had in the nineteenth century been as committed to national defence as its Polish counterpart, the fact remained that the Polish church came to play in the twentieth century a much more prominent role as protector of the nation and this may have owed at least something to the cultural differences between the religious traditions of the Russian oppressor and the oppressed, differences that were absent in the Bulgarian case.[1] And this leads us to suggest, rather tentatively at this stage, that whilst previous regime type may be a major influence on later developments in the areas we are considering, religious traditions may be equally important in determining state and church policies in the field of 'recognition' and minority rights.

Poland: rebuilding a Catholic society?

The political context: transition via negotiation

Poland has always seemed different.[2] With a tradition of independent political existence and some historical experience of constitutional politics, the country represented nothing but trouble to the surrounding absolutist states. More importantly Poland saw itself as special. After all it was Jan Sobieski (ruler from 1674–96) who had saved the West from the Turks threatening the gates of Vienna. Yet for the best part of 200 years Poland was to find itself subject to successive partitions and dominated by alien powers, whether Teutonic or Slavic. This in turn created a suspicion of both Germany and, more lastingly, Russia. In such circumstances it was hardly surprising that Poles developed what Karen Dawisha describes as a 'deep and abiding Russophobia',[3] a mentality reinforced by the Molotov–Ribbentrop Pact, the Katyn massacres, the passivity of the Red Army during the Warsaw uprising, and the eventual imposition of Soviet rule after 1945.

In January 1947, rigged elections confirmed communist rule, though Wladyslaw Gomulka recognised the need to create some form of popular legitimacy for the new regime. Soon, however, he was replaced by the Moscow-oriented Boleslav Bierut who embarked upon the imposition of one-party rule and the collectivisation of a very unwilling agricultural sector. Following substantial labour unrest in 1956 Gomulka was to make a triumphant return and Polish political life was never again to experience the same degree of restriction as the neighbouring peoples' democracies. Most sources attribute this to two factors: the strong position of the Roman Catholic Church, to be discussed below, and the failure to collectivise agricultural production. At the same time, the political elite proved unwilling to push Sovietisation too far and permitted a degree of intellectual and cultural space to emerge that would have been unthinkable in the rest of the Soviet bloc. At the same time the failure of Gomulka to deliver on the promise of 1956 contributed to the final alienation of the working class from the political system and led to successive outbursts of unrest in 1970 and 1976.

At the end of 1970, the announcement of food price rises of up to 30 per cent or more triggered off a new wave of labour unrest and those involved adopted a rhetoric highly critical of the regime. Under the impact of this militancy Gomulka was replaced by Gierek, who promised a rising standard of living to all but sought to achieve this goal by mortgaging Poland's economic future. He too faced labour unrest after introducing price rises in 1976, but when the workers took to the streets again they met with a brutal police response. More importantly, the events of 1976 helped to bring together the various streams of resistance within Polish society. Hitherto the gap between workers and intellectuals, as well as that between the latter and the Catholic Church had seemed impossible to bridge, but after 1976 these three key sectors of society began to develop a close, if occasionally uneasy, working relationship. One sign of this was the creation of the Workers' Defence Committee, a body that sought to defend the victims of police and bureaucratic persecution.[4] In this task the Committee was increasingly joined by the Catholic Church, which issued numerous pronouncements on the need for the regime to respect human rights in general. This gradual evolution of societal resistance was given a further fillip by the election of Karol Wojtyla as Pope in 1978 and by his visit to Poland in 1979 where millions flocked to hear him preaching the necessity for individuals and states to respect human dignity.

All of these strands came together in the events of 1980–1 and the rise of the Solidarity movement.[5] Though the movement was temporarily crushed by the imposition of martial law in December 1981, the authorities never fully regained control of Polish society. Economic problems, continued societal resistance embodying what Adam Michnik was to call the 'new evolutionism' – a gradual reclaiming of public space by society rather than overt confrontation[6] – and changes in the international environment all combined to undermine the legitimacy of the Polish regime. Of the latter the most important was the selection of Mikhail Gorbachev as leader of the USSR in 1985 and his gradual acceptance of the need for the East European states to create their own legitimacy and find their own paths of political development. During early 1988 price rises were attempted once more but met with resistance from a younger generation of activists less willing to accept the caution advocated by Lech Wałęsa and church leaders. More importantly strikers now made much more explicitly political demands, of which the most significant was for the relegalisation of Solidarity. In response to growing pressures round-table talks were held at the beginning of 1989, and in April Solidarity was relegalised, the media liberalised and elections scheduled for the summer. And though these did not allow for completely free and fair elections, the result was a clear victory for the opposition, with Solidarity winning nearly all the seats in which they were permitted to stand. In consequence, President Jaruzelski asked the Catholic intellectual Tadeusz Mazowiecki to form a government.

Since then Poland, despite slow progress in some areas, has advanced considerably in terms of democratic consolidation. On the one hand, as the first Central European state to opt for change, it was also the first to elect a government dominated by the successor parties to those of the communist period. Against this one might note that it was also amongst the last to adopt a post-communist constitution, and during the first half of the 1990s persistently failed to develop a stable party system. Instead numerous groups have emerged, fragmented, reappeared in new guises, and then disappeared once more. Party identification remained weaker than is 'normal' in democratic societies, and under Wałęsa there were persistent tensions between president and parliament. According to Linz and Stepan, at least part of the problem stemmed from the very nature of the opposition in Poland, that was rooted in an ethical critique which counterposed 'truth' to falsehood. Whilst this was useful in opposition, it was less helpful in a process of democratic consolidation where politics is about compromise and negotiation rather than the pursuit of truth and certainty.[7] Nonetheless, the peaceful transfer of power following successive parliamentary and presidential elections, as well as the country's entry into NATO, might be seen as signs that the outside world recognises Poland's progress and readiness for reintegration into modern, democratic Europe.

The religious context: reclaiming God's playground

Though Poland prides itself on its long Catholic heritage, for much of the eighteenth and nineteenth centuries the church had a somewhat ambiguous attitude towards Polish nationalism, though the weakness of other cultural institutions meant that it could not but play a role in preserving a sense of national identity.[8] Only in the twentieth century did that link come to be stressed more explicitly by some within the nationalist camp, and only under the impact of Nazi and Soviet threats to national integrity did the connection come to appear central. During the early years of communist domination the church's prime concern was with defending its own position against the assaults of an explicitly atheist regime, but from the mid-1950s the doughty Cardinal Wyszynski increasingly came to be seen by many as a spokesman for the 'true' interests of the 'real' Poland. Crucial here was the fact that in Poland much of the working class, newly arrived from the more religious villages, retained some degree of religiosity – though this should not be overstated – and that by the 1970s many within the intelligentsia were questioning their view of the church as an essentially reactionary force.[9]

Though Wyszynski remained cautious in his dealings with the regime, and never rejected the view that the church's interests came first, from the early 1970s onwards the bishops became increasingly vocal in their defence of human rights. A pastoral letter of 1971 stressed the need for freedom of conscience, social justice and freedom of expression, whilst in a series of sermons during 1974 Wyszynski rejected any attempt to impose a rigid political framework on society. In January 1976 intellectuals and the church joined hands in opposing amendments to the constitution which linked the rights of citizens to fulfilment of their duties to the motherland and, implicitly, to their acceptance of the close ties with the USSR.[10] This growing rapprochement between church, intelligentsia and workers was given a further stimulus by the repression of working-class protest in 1976. Increasingly the church moved beyond protesting repression to concrete defence of the repressed, with a number of priests involved in the Workers' Defence Committee and many churches providing a haven for meetings, discussions and alternative activities of various types.[11] All of this was encouraged by a long-term process of religious and social renewal promoted by activist hierarchs such as Archbishop Wojtyła who sought to restore links with the creative intelligentsia, and reach out to the masses by updating the style of religious education. Above all these religious leaders stressed the role of the church in the 'strengthening of optimism . . . and working to raise national morale'.[12]

This process of religious and national reassertion was given a major boost by the election of Karol Wojtyła as Pope in October 1978 and then by his first visit to the country in June 1979. In Szajkowski's words the latter represented a 'psychological earthquake, because he expressed in public what had been hidden for so long, the peoples' private hopes and longings for uncensored truth, for dignity, and demonstrated that the vast majority of the people viewed the Church as the main organisation standing up to the regime'.[13] During this visit, John Paul II told one congregation that 'the future of Poland will depend upon how many people are mature enough to be non-conformists', and during the following year it was to appear that the vast majority of the population had been reinvigorated by this message. In the months following the visit and leading up to the creation of Solidarity, the bishops published ever sharper critiques of the mendacity which lay at the heart of the system, and in a pastoral letter of February 1980 called on all Poles to exhibit civil courage and witness openly to their convictions.[14] The immediate causes of the events of the 1980s were economic, with a wave of strikes in the summer of 1980 affecting the dockyards, in particular, but also other industrial sectors. Nonetheless, religious symbols came to dominate, with crosses erected in many workplaces, and early on the Gdańsk workers called on Fr Henryk Jankowski to organise daily masses in the shipyard.[15]

The imposition of martial law in December 1981 posed a problem for the church, now led by Cardinal Glemp. His first broadcast on 13 December appeared to justify the imposition of martial law as the lesser evil, and he urged self-restraint on all Poles. Though the church later issued stronger condemnations of the excesses of martial law, many even within its own ranks were unhappy about Glemp's cautious approach in dealing with the authorities.[16] Despite this, the church continued to offer support for those subject to repression, to provide aid for their families, and to make available church property for the creation of alternative visions of society. Alongside this, more outspoken priests emerged, most notably Fr Jerzy Popiełuszko who organised weekly masses for the nation that became the focus for outspoken criticism of the martial law regime and preached sermons calling on people 'to live in truth'. Though the hierarchy denounced his later murder, it remained cautious, arguing, according to Casanova, that 'Polish civil society had to be sacrificed for the sake of the nation' and all too aware that during the martial law period churches were fuller than ever and new ones were still being built.[17] John Paul II took a more forthright stand, condemning the banning of Solidarity as a breach of human rights, and during his 1983 visit to Poland preaching against demoralisation.

By the late 1980s it was becoming increasingly clear that Poland could not remain indifferent to the changes taking place in the Soviet Union. During the third papal visit to Poland in 1987 the pontiff called for the relegalisation of Solidarity, and over the next two years the church was to play a role in assisting the transition to a new political system. Simultaneously, growing labour unrest challenged the continued refusal of the regime to recognise free trade unions. Under pressure, talks began between Solidarity and the government, at first in secret and mediated by various clerics including the bishop of Gdańsk. These in turn led to the institution of more open round-table talks in April 1989 at which the church was represented though only as observer rather than formal participant. Yet in practice their role in mediation was sometimes crucial and their spokesmen generally adopted the same stance as Solidarity when dealing with contentious questions. The outcome of all this was the agreement to hold semi-free elections noted in the previous sections and the eventual transition to a new form of government where the prime minister's position was taken by the Catholic Tadeusz Mazowiecki.[18]

With the ending of the communist system the church faced new dilemmas. What would its role be in the new system, how would it cope with the transition from being a major voice of the people to being one pressure group amongst many, how would it react to the experience of social and religious pluralism, and how would it maintain its hold on popular opinion once it was no longer needed as a bastion of resistance? In the initial months of change church spokesmen made clear their commitment to democratisation but expressed fears about some of the implications of this process. They were especially concerned at what they saw as the moral decadence accompanying the advent of social and political pluralism. In

July 1991 the bishops issued a statement attacking the media for its promotion of permissiveness and pornography,[19] and later sought to insert a
clause in a media bill that would necessitate respect for Christian values
(see below). More important, the church hoped that in the new situation
it would be possible to prohibit or severely restrict the right to abortion.
To this end it encouraged those politicians keen to promote such a law
and eventually saw a triumph in the passing of restrictive legislation in
1993, though this was to be partially reliberalised later in the decade.
Problems also arose over the extent to which the church should get involved in election campaigns. During the first elections held in 1989
the church remained formally committed to neutrality, but in practice
clearly supported the Solidarity campaign. During later campaigns the
church as an institution preferred to step back from direct intervention,
though individual bishops and priests often made their views clear. Only
in 1995, when the former communists were on the verge of an electoral
comeback, did the church as an institution step more explicitly into the
fray, issuing in August 1995 a pastoral letter urging Catholics not to vote
for those who participated in the exercise of power 'under totalitarian
rule'.[20]

Adapting to democracy has proved something of a problem for the
church. Should it, as some seem to hope, seek to create a national-
Catholic state where the bishops could exercise a tutelary role over the
morality of the nation, or should it opt for the self-limitation that is characteristic of religious institutions in most established democracies? On
the one hand, it could not renounce John Paul II's belief that democracy
would not be successfully built on a foundation of moral indifference
as if all values were equally acceptable. On the other hand, how could
it promote this position in a way that did not simply appear as an attempt to privilege its own positions in a fashion unacceptable in a modern democracy?[21] There was also a practical side to this, for in seeking
to intervene vigorously in the political arena the church faced the risk of
alienating the Catholic majority it claimed to represent. Here, as in other
Catholic nations, the church experienced a growing divergence between
popular commitment to the institution and willingness to follow its teachings on certain issues. Opinion polls throughout the 1990s demonstrated
a very gradual decline of public confidence in the church that reflected an
unwillingness to see the dictatorship of the commissars replaced by that
of the bishops. Thus whilst surveys taken in the early 1990s showed that
up to 75 per cent of the population had confidence in the church, by the
mid-1990s this had dropped below 50 per cent – though it still remained
far more popular than most other institutions.[22]

Whilst the population remained wary of the church being granted a
pre-eminent position within the new Poland, there were also reservations

amongst members of religious minorities whose memories of 'Catholic Poland' had not always been happy ones. Historically Poland was more religiously diverse before 1939 than it is today, with sizeable Orthodox communities to the East and perhaps as many as 900,000 Protestants prior to the First World War. Amongst these were to be found representatives of the mainstream Reformation Churches – Lutherans, Calvinists – as well as Moravian Brethren, and a variety of small evangelical groups. After the Nazi occupation, Protestants of German extraction were often singled out for repression and the number of Protestants in the post-war years was significantly lower than hitherto. In consequence, remaining communities tended to keep their heads down during the communist era and sometimes benefited from the simple fact of not being the 'national church'. Indeed, at least one Baptist leader was to claim that they enjoyed more freedom under the communist regime than at any previous time.[23] With the collapse of the old regime some of these groups have become more active, though groups such as the Baptists are keen to point out that they have been present since the mid-nineteenth century and the Jehovah's Witnesses since early in the twentieth century. Some of these groups have received support from co-religionists abroad, though not always in the forms desired. At the same time, the country has experienced a slight expansion in the activities of new religious movements, though this has not been as extensive as in some former communist countries nor on the scale claimed by Polish anti-cult movements.

Recreating national Catholicism?

According to some commentators the leadership of the Roman Catholic Church in Poland hoped to use the situation emerging after the fall of communism to advance its own institutional interests, not merely as one lobby group amongst many, but as a central institutional pillar of the new Poland. Ray Taras suggests that during the 1989 round-table talks the episcopate effectively sought the role of king-maker in mediating between the government and Solidarity.[24] Sabrina Ramet goes further in arguing that the church had a precise game plan to restore its influence in the post-communist era and acquire the role of moral guardian of the Polish nation. To this end it went beyond the limits of what was acceptable in a democratic society by claiming a privileged legal and constitutional position on issues such as abortion, education and partial control over the media.[25] This anxiety was also voiced by liberal commentators in Poland who on various occasions expressed fears about what they described as attempts to create a theocratic state at the end of the twentieth century.

Some of these criticisms came from intellectuals of a deeply anti-clerical persuasion, but similar fears were expressed by sensitive and sympathetic observers such as Adam Michnik, who attacked the aggressive attitudes of both sides of the debate but also called on the church to decide whether its primary role was institutional defence or the promotion of freedom for all, Catholic and non-Catholic alike.[26] From the church's perspective such interpretations were a nonsense. Far from there emerging a theo-cratic state, the new Poland was turning into a secularised and liberal state modelled on Western lines, and one in which the values preached by the church were subject to constant ridicule. More importantly, this was a state being created on the basis of ideals alien to the majority of the Polish people whose church deserved formal recognition in the new institutional structures – though here as in Spain the appeal to majori-tarianism was selective and deemed inappropriate when applied to moral issues. In fact both sides of this argument probably overstated their cases, with the church finding it hard to cope with the new free-wheeling style of media debate and satirical programming, and the critics resorting to rhetorical excess when warning of the rise of theocracy. Nonetheless, the episcopate probably did hope that in the new order they would be able to exercise some form of what Casanova calls 'tutelary power over cer-tain reserved domains of policy-making, such as religion, education and family morality'.[27]

Most of the focus of this chapter will be on the constitutional issue, but before dealing with that we shall briefly visit some of the issues raised by Casanova to point to the ways in which the church may be seen as seeking a privileging of its own position, in particular in relation to the issues of education, the media and sexual morality – though as in the last chapter it is not always easy to distinguish between a legitimate lob-bying for one's position and a pursuit of unreasonable privilege. The first of these issues emerged almost immediately after the fall of commu-nism when the church called for a restoration of religious education in schools, and in June 1990 the Catholic Bishops' Conference argued that this should be compulsory so as to combat the distorted view of religion and morality promoted by the old regime. The government, however, remained cautious, wary of anything that might prove divisive in the new situation, especially after small public demonstrations in several towns protesting against the replacement of communist with national-Catholic totalitarianism.[28] Surveys carried out in 1991 showed that many young people opposed compulsory religious education as potentially leading to discrimination.[29]

Despite these reservations religious instruction began to be introduced in the 1990–1 school year, and at the end of that year instructions from the Education Ministry made education in religion or ethics compulsory for all children from April 1992 – though in theory parents could take their children out of explicitly Catholic classes. More controversially, the instruction allowed for the recording of grades and provided state funding for priests teaching religion. In early 1993 this instruction was challenged by the Ombudsman Tadeusz Zielinski who argued that it was unconstitutional because it required parents to state their religious preferences, awarded grades, and provided for state financing of the clergy involved. He also expressed concern about the placing of crosses in state schools, as this represented an implicit discrimination in favour of Christian believers. More fundamentally he criticised the fact that this instruction had been effectively introduced by administrative fiat and that on such a contentious issue it would have been more appropriate if parliament had been involved.[30] Zielinski's ruling was then challenged in the Constitutional Tribunal, which only partially supported his rulings. In particular, they accepted that it was illegal to force declarations from parents about their willingness to have their children given religious instruction (though it was not illegal to ask parents what they wished) and that grades should not be given for minority religious education classes taken outside schools. However, they did support the retention of crosses in schools and argued that religious education did not contradict the separation of church and state because the state was not actually administering religious education – though it was paying for it.[31] Following these decisions it was resolved that children should be offered the choice of religious education or ethics, but in practice schools could rarely afford to provide the latter whilst in many rural areas there were considerable social pressures for the majority to take the state-subsidised religious education classes provided by the church, or more rarely by representatives of recognised minority communities.[32]

A second issue that aroused some debate related to the media. From the beginning of the democratic experiment bishops expressed unease at the more garish face of the free press, in particular its perceived permissiveness and promotion of sexual license. For this reason, the bishops advocated the insertion into a media bill, discussed by parliament at the end of 1992 and beginning of 1993, of a clause requiring the media to respect Christian values and not to promote activities that conflicted with morality and the public good. At the same time, the law created a National Council to monitor the media, with 25 per cent of its membership made up of church representatives. Many within parliament opposed this clause, some fearing the influence it might give the church. Opposition was also forthcoming from the head of national television and radio, Marek Markiewicz, who feared that it might be utilised to impose censorship on the media and argued that defining what was meant by 'Christian values' in practical terms might be difficult.[33] Equally, minority representatives pointed to the public broadcasting of weekly masses and the granting to the church of the right to relicense radio and television stations to operate on church frequencies as further evidence of a creeping establishment.[34]

Not all of these issues can be explored here in any depth, but other concerns raised by minorities fearing that the Catholic Church was being granted a 'privileged' position related to the question of finance, and of access to prisons, military units and hospitals. On the financial front the Concordat approved in 1998 included a reference to the subsidisation of the Papal Theological Academy in Kraków and the Catholic University of Lublin, whilst the same document guaranteed access to military units, prisons, and education and welfare institutions. Critics also pointed to the 'soldiers' prayer book' issued in the Warsaw military district in early 1995 stating that members of a special honour guard who did not take part in military masses would be considered to be disobeying orders, though in practice no one has attempted to enforce this requirement, which has no legal status. Nonetheless, minorities saw such attempts as symptomatic of the Catholic Church's lack of respect for non-Catholic Poles.[35]

Perhaps inevitably, the most explosive issue to reach the political agenda was the question of abortion, where the church's position was very clear and uncompromising. As early as October 1990 the upper house of parliament introduced a bill that would have prohibited abortion in virtually all circumstances. In May 1991, fierce debates took place in the Sejm as both sides of the argument sought to push their agendas, whilst liberals within Solidarity's ranks tried to find a compromise solution. In the end, the bill was rejected but the episcopate made it clear that it would seek to resurrect the issue should later elections produce a more sympathetic parliamentary majority.[36] At the beginning of the following year the National Catholic Party, a member of the ruling coalition, stated that it would seek a near-total ban, except where the mother's life was in danger, and anti-abortion legislation was introduced in parliament in March 1992. After prolonged debate, this was eventually approved in amended form one year later, and though the church did not see it as sufficiently restrictive, Cardinal Glemp accepted the legislation as a step forward.[37] Yet with many political activists committed to changing the law one way or the other, it was clear that abortion would remain a political football, and indeed the return of the reformed communists to power in 1995 saw parliament approve a revision of the law which permitted social circumstances to be taken into account in deciding whether an abortion should be permitted, and this was approved by parliament in the summer of 1996 – though later facing further obstacles in the Constitutional Tribunal.[38] This did not of course deter the church from maintaining its campaign to protect human life from the moment of conception or from rejecting the view that moral issues could be decided by parliamentary votes.

As Mark Brzezinski notes, Poland has a rich constitutional history whose roots date back to the thirteenth century, and in 1791 it became only the second state in the world to adopt a written constitution. Though this first document did not usher in a democratic order, it did help to create some sense of the need for institutional constraints on the power of political institutions and leaders.[39] Under the communists such notions were clearly secondary to expediency in most cases, though when attempts were made to amend the constitution in 1976 so as to enshrine the leading role of the party and close ties to the USSR, protests were forthcoming from many intellectuals and from the leadership of the Catholic Church.[40] In spite of this tradition, however, and despite being amongst the first Central–East European states to break with the Soviet order, Poland was one of the last of them to adopt a complete post-communist constitution. It was perhaps the very lateness that made debates over constitutional definitions so intense, for whereas in Bulgaria hasty adoption in 1991 limited the extent to which a weakened Orthodox Church could make a serious contribution, in Poland the hierarchy had sufficient time to work out its own strategy in making a contribution to the creation of a new constitutional order.

Following the collapse of the communist system it was assumed that a new constitution would emerge quickly, but in fact its final adoption did not take place until 1997. During the early 1990s an increasingly fragmented political elite failed to build a consensus on a constitutional settlement, so a temporary compromise was reached whereby the so-called 'small constitution' was approved which provided the basis for government until a full constitution could be adopted. In relation to human rights the text largely followed that of its communist era predecessor, though, as Brzezinski points out, more reliable guarantees for their observance were provided by Article 1, defining the country's commitment to democracy, by the creation of a Constitutional Tribunal, by the work of the Ombudsman on human rights – a position that had been created as early as 1987 – and by Poland's decision in November 1992 to ratify the European Convention on Human Rights.[41] Article 82 of this small constitution read as follows on the religious issue:

The Republic of Poland shall guarantee freedom of conscience and religion to all citizens. The Church and other religious organisations shall freely exercise their religious functions. Citizens shall not be prevented from taking part in religious activities or rites. No one may be compelled to participate in religious activities. The Church shall be separate from the State. The principles of the relationship between Church and State, and the legal and property rights of religious organisations shall be defined by laws.

In practice, this rather neutral terminology was not entirely satisfactory from the church's viewpoint, but its temporary nature gave the episcopate time to rethink what it would want from any final constitutional settlement.

Discussion of a new text began almost as soon as the ink on the 'small constitution' was dry, though serious debate over the controversial issues only really became heated in the second half of 1995. In the meantime, the picture was clouded somewhat by the negotiations over a proposed new Concordat with the Vatican. Initially signed in July 1993, many commentators were unhappy about the way in which the document appeared to treat church and state as equal partners, and to privilege the Catholic Church in legal terms – for example by giving the church rights that could not be overturned by parliament. By early 1994, the Social Democratic successors to the communist party were making clear their opposition to the existing document, and suggesting that its ratification should be delayed until a new constitution had set out the proper relationship between church and state.[42] In July 1994 this argument seems to have been accepted by the Sejm whose members voted by a majority of twenty to refer the document back to a special commission for further discussion. For its part the Vatican stated that the text had been agreed and was not up for renegotiation, whilst President Wałęsa suggested that the Sejm allow him to ratify it and then commission parliament to adapt Polish law so that it conformed to the provisions of the text. This was rejected by the socialist-dominated assembly elected in 1995 which continued to maintain that ratification should await the approval of a constitution.[43]

By the middle of 1995 seven different drafts had been submitted to the Constitutional Commission, some from political parties, one from Solidarity, one from the Senate and one from the president. Informally, the church supported the proposals of the Solidarity draft that referred explicitly to the thousand-year link of the people to Christianity and to the 'heritage of Christian faith and culture'. In addition, it proposed support for the right to life from the moment of conception, and obligated the state to provide for the teaching of 'legally recognised religions at public schools'. Other versions appearing to lean in the church's direction included that of the Senate which started with an invocation to God, and

that of the Confederation of Independent Poland which argued for granting the Roman Catholic Church a 'leading position among denominations of equal rights'. By way of contrast the SLD draft described Poland
as a secular state in which no church could enjoy special privileges.[44] As
the debate unfolded in the mid-1990s three questions aroused particular
concern in church ranks: separation of church and state, the inclusion of
references to God and Christian values, and the issue of abortion.

For Bishop Tadeusz Pieronek, Secretary of the Bishops' Conference,
it remained true that the church and the state were separate bodies, but
nonetheless he argued that formal separation was unnecessary in any
new constitutional document, especially in the context of a country with
a strong Catholic tradition.[45] A similar argument was offered by Tadeusz
Mazowiecki who suggested that the traditional understanding of separation was inappropriate to Poland. He argued that the two institutions
had to find a 'third way to work together' and that 'this debate cannot
be resolved with a one sentence formula "the separation of Church and
state" '.[46] For their part the bishops gradually shifted their position, maintaining a rejection of separation and arguing for a definition that stressed
the autonomy and independence of the church. In particular, they were
worried about the implications of the word 'separation' given the experience of the recent past, and they opposed any wording that might be seen
as pushing the church exclusively into the private sphere of life. In Bishop
Pieronek's words, given the country's history and the role of Catholicism
in recent events, there was a need for some formal recognition of 'the
public and social life of the Church'.[47]

As the debate over the constitution quickened from 1995 onwards all
of these concerns were frequently expressed. At one point it seemed that
a compromise had been found on the vexed question of separation, with
the bishops seemingly divided on how far to push on this issue, but this
hope quickly foundered. In their attempts to gain formal recognition
of the Church's position they were supported by Lech Wałęsa, president until late 1995, who noted in his usual blunt style that 'communist bandits ruled this country for fifty years, but the Church for 1,000
years.... That is why you must not forget the roots of the nation. That
is why this should be recorded.'[48] In contrary vein, representatives of
several minority churches, including the Orthodox, Adventists, Pentecostals and Assemblies of God argued for a formal separation of church
and state.[49] In subsequent months, various revisions were proposed by
the Constitutional Commission in an effort to find a satisfactory solution
on the separation issue, with a proposal in April 1995 that the text refer
to the state's impartiality on religious and philosophical matters. Yet by
mid-1996 Archbishop Josef Michalik, chairman of the episcopate's own

constitutional affairs group, was stating that the church could not accept the constitution in the absence of any reference to God and the failure to mention natural law. The new socialist president Alexander Knasniewski pointed out that such a rigid stance was unwise given that the text was still open to discussion and amendment.[50]

The debate reached the floor of parliament in early 1997, and here Solidarity leader Marian Krzaklewski made an impassioned plea for the constitutional preamble to make explicit reference to religious values, and for the inclusion of a formal protection of the right to life. By late February some 482 amendments had been submitted of which a number referred to the religious issue, but the Democratic Left Alliance government continued to reject anything that formalised the role of the Catholic Church or made reference to natural law. Equally the church was unhappy with a new formulation of the preamble that referred to people's responsibility before God or conscience. Eventually, however, the Constitutional Commission opted for the rather awkward compromise wording proposed by former prime minister Tadeusz Mazowiecki which included the words

We the people of Poland – all the Polish citizens, both those who believe in God, who is the source of truth, justice, goodness and mercy, as well as those who do not share this faith and derive the values they recognise from other sources, equal in rights and obligations towards the common good – beholden to our ancestors for their labours, their struggle for independence achieved at great sacrifice, for our culture rooted in the Christian heritage of the Nation and rooted in universal human values ... recognising our responsibility before God or one's own conscience ... pass this constitution.

On the broader question of relations between church and state, the final version of Article 25 read as follows:

(1) Churches and other religious organizations shall have equal rights.
(2) Public authorities in the Republic of Poland shall be impartial in matters of personal conviction, whether religious or philosophical, or in relation to outlooks on life, and shall ensure their freedom of expression within public life.
(3) The relationship between the State and churches and other religious organizations shall be based on the principle of respect for their autonomy and the mutual independence of each in its own sphere, as well as on the principle of cooperation for the individual and the common good.
(4) The relations between the Republic of Poland and the Roman Catholic Church shall be determined by international treaty concluded with the Holy See, and by statute.
(5) The relations between the Republic of Poland and other churches and religious organizations shall be determined by statutes adopted pursuant to agreements concluded between their appropriate representatives and the Council of Ministers.[51]

On 22 March a joint session of parliament approved the constitution containing these words and proposed that it be put to a referendum.[52]

Many within the church remained unhappy about this formulation, which Cardinal Glemp described as not meeting the expectations of the majority of Catholic Poles, though he did suggest that people should vote according to their conscience. Others were more forthright in their condemnations, with Bishop Stanislav Napievala describing the document as morally unsound and Lech Wałęsa's favourite priest, Fr Jankowski, calling for a 'no' vote in the referendum. This argument was taken up by the conservative, and highly controversial, Catholic radio station Maryja. Official church spokesmen expressed unease about the aggressive tone of their broadcasting on this and other issues,[53] but the radio station aptly expressed the reservations held by many within the church, especially after the constitutional referendum during May 1997, in which only 40 per cent of the population voted, and in which the document gained the approval of only a small majority. For all this, most church leaders preferred not to seek further changes, preferring instead to turn their attention to the ratification of the long-delayed Concordat.

Although this document was first agreed between the Polish government and the Vatican in 1993, parliamentary ratification had been delayed by socialist and liberal suspicions of the privileges it granted the church and the feeling that approval should follow the creation of a new constitution. With the debates over the latter complete, negotiations began again. Under the terms of the Concordat Catholic marriages were made legally binding, certain religious feast days were made public holidays, provision was made for religious education to be provided by teachers authorised by their local bishops, subsidies were granted to certain Catholic educational establishments, and priests given access to those working in public institutions and the military or serving terms in prison. Critics charged that this institutionalised the position of the church in ways that might be detrimental to the interests of non-Catholics, especially with regard to religious education and the provision for parish cemeteries where local priests might be able to refuse burial to non-believers or suicides.[54] The church for its part defended the document as simply providing it with the freedom to carry out its mission, rather than entailing any illegitimate privilege. Eventually, in early 1998, the Polish parliament agreed to ratify the text[55] – a decision that, taken together with the finalisation of the constitution, appears to have taken the sting out of debates over the formal place of the church in Polish society. From this point on, the leading bishops began to adopt a more cautious and diplomatic approach in dealing with the political arena, though this did not hinder strong comments when they felt their values and interests to be threatened.[56]

The position of religious minorities

As in the Spanish case, the Polish Catholic Church has focused on the need for constitutional recognition, rather than on an attempt to restrict the rights of religious minorities. In the Polish case this stems in part from the impact of the Second Vatican Council with its acceptance of religious diversity, and partly from the fact that there are relatively few representatives of minority religious communities present in the country which pose only a limited threat to Catholic hegemony – though of course in Greece this has not stopped the Orthodox Church from seeking to restrict minority rights. Moreover, having spent much of the 1970s and 1980s promoting the importance of human rights it would be hard for the church as an institution, despite any qualms some may have, to take a proactive position in opposing the granting of rights to other religious groups.

As noted above, the number of those belonging to minority groups is relatively small – perhaps 3 per cent of a population of around 38 million – though they are organised in a wide range of religious communities. Amongst the most significant minority groups were the Orthodox (around 500,000 in the mid-1990s, of whom most were of Ukrainian or Belarussian origins), the Eastern-Rite Catholics (110,000), the Polish National Catholic Church (52,000), Lutherans (85,000), Baptists (5,000), Adventists (9,000), Pentecostals (18,000), Jehovah's Witnesses (over 100,000), Muslims (5,000), Jews (2,000) and a variety of small charismatic and evangelical groups. These were joined from the 1980s onwards by a small number of Hare Krishnas, Scientologists, 'Moonies' and other 'new religious movements'.[57]

General guarantees for religious freedom are set out in Article 53 of the Constitution, which defines religious liberty in terms of:

> the freedom to profess or accept a religion by personal choice as well as to manifest such religion, either individually or collectively, publicly or privately, by worshipping, praying, participating in ceremonies, performing of rites or teaching. Freedom of religion shall also include possession of sanctuaries and other places of worship for the satisfaction of the needs of believers as well as the rights of individuals, wherever they may be, to benefit from religious services.

The same article went on to guarantee parents the right to bring up children according to their own convictions, the teaching of legally recognised religions in schools, the right not to disclose one's philosophical convictions, and not to be compelled to participate in religious rites.[58]

Earlier the regulatory regime affecting religious communities had been set out in the Statute on Guarantees of Freedom of Conscience and

Creed (17 May 1989). This law, adopted when the transition process was just beginning, promised religious freedom to all Polish citizens and gave them the right to form churches and denominations, to preach their religion and raise children according to their beliefs. Article 9 of this document spoke of the separation of church and state, and prohibited state subsidies to religious organisations except under certain circumstances. At the same time, it spoke of the right of all communities to have equal access to the media, to teach religion in schools and universities – though it was rather imprecise as to how such rights could be exercised in practice. In terms of regulation, individual groups and religious denominations could register – and thus acquire legal personality – with the Office of Denominational Affairs, providing fifteen Polish citizens signed a document in support of this, with an outline of their doctrines and other information about their activities. The assumption was that subsequent registration would be more or less immediate, and this proved to be so in the vast majority of cases. The law also provided for the creation of special agreements between the state and individual denominations or faith communities registered by the state, and these have since been signed with some fifteen of the 120 or so recognised denominations, including Roman Catholics, Orthodox, Methodists, Baptists, Adventists, Muslims, Jews and Pentecostals – though not the 2,500-strong Church of Evangelical Christians.[59] These tend to be similar in wording and basically offered religious communities and their leaders the same rights to religious freedom, tax exemptions, access to schools and other public institutions, and in principle the ability to claim back property seized during the communist period.[60]

Despite this liberal regulatory regime, which had permitted the registration of over 100 non-Catholic religious denominations by the mid-1990s, a few problems still remained. In part these stemmed from local practice – where individual priests, officials or communities found it hard to accept religious diversity – but perhaps more important was the minority perception that Catholic attempts to promote their own position might have negative implications for genuine religious freedom. As we have already noted, two issues in particular raised concern: religious education in schools and the Concordat with the Vatican. On the former, anxieties were raised by the special position seemingly granted to Catholic priests in this process and the more subtle peer pressure that might be exerted on non-Catholic students, and the general Protestant preference was for voluntary classes on church premises.[61] Regarding the Concordat, the concern was that under its terms the Catholic Church would enjoy both psychological and legal advantages in relation to minority groups. In particular, its marriages would be equated with civil weddings, state subsidies would be provided for the main Catholic universities, its personnel would enjoy a special legal status, and the church could refuse burial in its cemeteries to non-Catholics.[62] For Reformed pastor Bogdan Tranda, writing in the early 1990s, it was important that the Catholic leadership try to understand Protestant anxieties, for though the dominant church might argue that its own search for influence implied no diminution of the rights of others, from a minority viewpoint things looked very different. Catholic bishops were to be found at major state occasions, masses were broadcast freely on state television, and Catholic religious instruction was being introduced into schools.[63] Insecurities were not helped by an awareness that many Catholic priests remained unconvinced about the changes in this area introduced in Vatican II, or the fact that Cardinal Glemp had in the past written sympathetically about the notion of a confessional state and had opposed religious freedom on the rather old-fashioned grounds that the church could not tolerate falsehood.[64] Then there was Radio Maryja whose Fr Tadeusz Rydzyk may have been extreme in his denunciations of 'sects', but who was not alone in categorising most non-traditional groups in this way.

As in some of the other countries discussed here, the 'sect' question was one that was frequently debated in the mid-1990s and the danger allegedly posed by some religious groups was used in campaigns to tighten up the legislative framework within which religious minorities operated. Figures differed as to how many 'sects' were active in Poland and which of them represented a real danger to Polish society. From quite early on the state security services appear to have devoted some attention to new religious movements, and a 1995 report from the National Security Service stated that there were some 300 sects operating in Poland of which a few were potentially dangerous. According to its authors the small number it characterised as 'destructive' were dangerous because of their use of 'sophisticated and immoral methods' in gaining new members whose minds they then sought to control. For that reason they called for a tightening of the registration requirements and closer monitoring of sect activity.[65] This growing concern with 'sects' or 'cults' appears to have had a limited impact upon state policy, though it met with a response in some areas. For example, in 1996 the governor of the Lublin region clamped down on the Niebo community, claiming that they did not send their children to school and refused to perform military service;[66] whilst during the second half of the decade there were reports that officials were taking longer to process registration requests in order to weed out 'destructive cults'.[67]

All of this contributed towards calls for firmer action against the 'sects' and a tightening of the legislative framework. In the autumn of 1995 the

Forum of Catholic Women called for a prohibition of all sectarian activity, though without making clear which groups were included, whilst Radio Maryja campaigned to limit registration to those who had been active in Poland for fifty years.[68] Alongside these appeals several Catholic-based anti-cult groups were created, though most have enjoyed little success and a number were brought to court by Hindu and Buddhist organisations, which successfully sued them for slander and misrepresentation of their religious activities.[69] In 1997 the government created an Inter-Ministerial Team for New Religious Movements, headed by Krzysztof Wiktor, who described his task in terms of coordinating analysis of such groups and only intervening where they 'violated fundamental human rights and caused destruction consciously and intentionally'.[70] One year later, in June 1998, the law on freedom of conscience was amended so as to require 100 signatures from those desiring legal recognition. At the official level the Catholic hierarchy has not endorsed calls for restrictions, and relations with the mainstream minority churches appear to have improved in recent years. Nonetheless, in some areas there have been reports of religious discrimination instigated by Catholic authorities – as in Silesia where a Lutheran pastor was denied access to a home for the elderly – and more conservative Catholic priests continue to rail against the 'sects'.[71] Moreover, representatives of several minority churches have expressed concern that anti-sect rhetoric has been used in such a way as to stigmatise many of the smaller religious communities. This led representatives of the 9,000-strong Adventist community to express alarm about new units set up by the police during 2000 to monitor new religious movements and to criticise one Education Ministry document that had described them as a 'threatening sect'.[72]

In conclusion it can be said that legally religious minorities in Poland enjoy considerable freedom of religion and that here the position is similar to that in Spain and better than the situation in Greece. Existing legislation does allow space for the free development of religious life, though practice may differ in some parts of the country – with several reports suggesting that not just smaller communities but also larger groups such as the Orthodox and the Eastern Rite Catholics have faced considerable obstacles from local religious and political authorities in acquiring places of worship.[73] By and large the state has preferred to stay out of religious matters and rely on civil or criminal law for dealing with any undesirable activities that might be promoted by a minority of religious groups. There remain, however, problems of perception, with a Catholic hierarchy still partially wedded to national-Catholic ideas that leave minorities feeling that they are not always accepted as genuine Poles. Here one cannot ignore the persistent strain of anti-Semitism, for though this is not simply a religious question, it does have negative implications for the country's few remaining practising Jews. Fr Henryk Jankowski of Gdańsk may be exceptional in his reported views on the Jewish question, but the ambiguous or tardy reaction of some leading churchmen and politicians to his occasional outbursts suggests the persistence of social and religious intolerance amongst both the elite and the public.[74]

Bulgaria: the half-hearted pursuit of privilege

The political context: a silent transition

The Bulgaria that started on the path of post-communist state building in 1989 had very few historical antecedents to build on in attempting to create a democratic order.[75] For the best part of 500 years it formed a part of the Ottoman Empire and was largely cut off from intellectual and political currents in Europe. Its emergence as a quasi-independent state towards the end of the nineteenth century sprang largely from the carving up of Balkan territories by Russia after its armies reached Istanbul in 1878, though the enlarged territory granted to it at San Stefano in that year was radically reduced by the other powers in the Treaty of Berlin. In subsequent Balkan wars the embryonic state saw its lands redefined and, after supporting Germany in 1914–18, Bulgaria found its territory reduced further still by the victorious nations. Following a coup in 1923 that overthrew Stambolski's Agrarian Union the country was dominated by a series of authoritarian governments, influenced by fascism though not following its tendencies to mass mobilisation and the encouragement of anti-Semitism until the country became subordinate to the German authorities in the early 1940s.

The communists dominated the Fatherland Front that took over the country in 1944, and their activists waged a campaign of intimidation and terror against representatives of the old order over the next three years before taking complete control in late 1947. After spending several more years dealing with real and imagined opponents within the country the Communist Party then followed the Stalinist example by turning on its own members. Unlike its Polish counterpart, the Bulgarian leadership faced no challenge from religious organisations and proved quite willing to force through collectivisation of agriculture. In 1954 the leadership fell to Todor Zhivkov who was to remain party leader until 1989, and who throughout sought to maintain close relations with the USSR. Even when it began to appear that Gorbachev's commitment to change in the USSR was more than rhetorical, Zhivkov refused to sanction genuine reform. Instead, in the mid-1980s, he embarked upon a quasi-Stalinist campaign aimed at the forcible assimilation of the Turkish minority. As Gorbachev embarked upon reform in the Soviet Union which encouraged the growth of civil society, the authoritarian nature of the Zhivkov regime and the public apathy engendered by forty years of conformity meant that there were no substantial social forces pushing for change comparable to those active in the Central European countries, the Baltic states or Russia.

In consequence, when political transition came it was initiated from within the regime and largely controlled by the party during the early stages. In effect there was an internal party coup in November 1989, led by Peter Mladenov and seemingly sanctioned by Moscow, which led Zhivkov to offer his resignation. Over the following months the regime continued to control the pace of change and oversee the round-table negotiations with the opposition that led to the first elections in June 1990. When these took place the renamed Bulgarian Socialist Party (BSP) was able to triumph, in part because of its ability to utilise its organisational assets and powers of patronage in the rural areas.[76] The experience of the early post-communist years gave little room for optimism about Bulgaria's democratic prospects. On the one hand, the newly elected BSP government showed few signs of breaking with the past, whilst much of the opposition Union of Democratic Forces (UDF) refused to accept the legitimacy of the new government. During the constitutional debates of 1991 many walked out of the National Assembly, angered by the refusal of the BSP to allow a serious reckoning of crimes committed by regime officials, though perhaps because many UDF deputies had worked within the old communist system the movement was divided on this issue. Following a scandal involving Mladenov, UDF leader Zhelyu Zhelev became president in the summer of 1990 and in October 1991 the hastily cobbled together opposition movement won new parliamentary elections. Subsequent elections in December 1994 returned the BSP to power, with the support of some disillusioned groups within the UDF, and then in 1997 a new coalition around the restructured UDF succeeded in taking power once more. In 2001 parliamentary elections gave power to a government dominated by the new political movement created by former King Simeon whose policies remained rather unclear.

In terms of democratic indicators, most notably electoral competition, by the end of the century Bulgaria appeared to meet the requirements for a consolidated democracy. Despite minor infringements, international observers rated the elections relatively fair, and they had produced the peaceful alternations of government that democracy is said to require. Nonetheless there remained problems. Linz and Stepan pointed to the rather 'flat' nature of civil and political society, which had failed to develop from the weak beginnings of 1989. They also noted opinion polls from the early 1990s onwards which showed nearly half of those polled agreeing with the proposition that it might be better to get rid of parliament and find a 'strong leader who can quickly get things done'.[77] Daskalov pointed to other flaws, noting that despite the electoral turnover, there is a considerable continuity of elites from the old regime, a proper sense of the rule of law is absent, and high levels of corruption have a negative impact upon public respect for democratic politics.[78] Though there is some evidence to suggest a growing institutionalisation of political life and a gradual increase in respect for the law since the 1990s, most commentators within the country would argue that this remains a 'democracy' that is far from mature or fully consolidated.

The religious context

Christianity in its Orthodox form came to Bulgaria in the ninth century when Boris I accepted the faith and imposed it on his subjects, but at this stage the Bulgarian church remained dependent upon Byzantium for its leadership, and not until the eleventh century did it acquire a measure of autonomy.[79] During the Ottoman period the imposition of the *millet* system meant that all 'Christians' were placed under the ecumenical patriarch in Istanbul, and during this time some Bulgarians converted to Islam – whether voluntarily or not remains a subject of academic and political controversy. All this began to change during the second half of the nineteenth century, with pressures from religious and national leaders eventually forcing a reluctant sultan to permit the creation of a Bulgarian exarchate in 1870. The achievement of Bulgarian independence in 1878 proved a mixed blessing for the church, with successive political leaders interpreting the Turnovo constitution of 1879 as giving them the green light to interfere in its affairs. For all this, it was not until the inter-war years that Boris III succeeded in creating a synodal church structured in similar ways to the Petrine model favoured in Russia.[80]

Prior to the communist takeover many other religious groups had been active in Bulgaria, encouraged to some extent by the recreation of a national state independent of the Ottoman Empire. As early as 1860, in a move partly designed to irritate Russia, Istanbul had formally recognised the existence of the Bulgarian Eastern-rite Catholic Church, and this body quickly established three sees in the new Bulgarian state.[81] Latin-rite Catholic activism also increased at the end of the century, reinforced by the arrival of members of religious orders and given protection by the selection of a Catholic Sax-Coburg family to rule the new state.[82] Protestant missionaries, especially from the United States, also came to Bulgaria during the second half of the nineteenth century. Though their work met with limited success and the number of Evangelical and Pentecostal communities remained small, the congregations they generated exhibited high levels of commitment.

Perhaps more significant, especially because of the ethnic question, was the Muslim community. When Bulgaria acquired independence the Turkic population retained its Islamic structures, with the preservation of Muslim courts and educational institutes, and the state initially abstaining from intervention in community affairs. The situation became more complicated in 1912–13 when the government launched a mass campaign to change the names and faith of Bulgarian Muslims, an assault joined enthusiastically by several Orthodox brotherhoods in the Rhodope mountain region. Though this failed, the inter-war years were marked by periodic bouts of anti-Islamic enthusiasm on the part of the state.[83]

The communist takeover inevitably brought new problems for religious organisations as the party initially adopted a tough stance in relation to religion. Several Orthodox leaders were imprisoned or murdered, and many hundreds of priests were sentenced to lengthy terms in labour camps. The constitution introduced in late 1947 formally separated church and state, but in practice the state increasingly established tight control over all aspects of religious life, including the appointment of religious leaders. In response those Orthodox hierarchs who survived the earlier onslaught opted for passivity and subservience to the regime. This new attitude was symbolised in the stance of Kirill of Plovdiv, elected Patriarch in 1953, and was continued by his successor Maksim appointed in 1971. The experience of other religious communities was similar, with periods of violent repression in the early communist period followed by persistent harassment and pressures to conform evident in the later years. In 1949, fifteen Protestant pastors were sentenced to lengthy prison terms on trumped-up charges, and in 1952 there was a major show trial in which fifty-five Catholics were accused of spying for Rome following which four were sentenced to death. For the Muslim community the early years of communist rule were marked by a vicious assault on Islamic institutions and the vast majority of mosques were closed. Later, as Bulgarian nationalism was increasingly exploited during the 1970s, campaigns were launched to assimilate the Turkic community, culminating in the 'revivalist' process of 1984–6 under which Turkic people had their names forcibly changed and public symbols of Muslim identity, including gravestones, were destroyed. In consequence several thousand resisters were imprisoned, several hundred were reportedly killed, and many thousands of Turks later fled the country.[84]

All of this happened as political reform was on the agenda in the USSR and beginning to affect other Soviet bloc states. Todor Zhivkov appeared to accept the need to be seen as a supporter of perestroika and at the end of 1988 gave a speech in which he called on religious organisations to play a greater role in the restructuring process. There was little evidence of a serious change in policy apart from a reduction in the sentences handed out to a number of Protestant activists. Nonetheless, within the tentatively emerging world of independent social organisation religious voices began to make themselves heard, most notably in the shape of the Independent Committee for the Defence of Religious Rights, Freedom of Conscience and Spiritual Values. Headed by the controversial Hristofor Subev, the Committee's declared aim was to end state interference in religious life and promote understanding between religious communities. In March 1989, the ever-subservient Holy Synod declared that the church already enjoyed full freedom and condemned the Committee's activities as divisive. Nonetheless, on 7 December 1989, several thousand participated in a demonstration for religious freedom, and when the UDF was formed Subev's committee was one of its constituent members.[85]

In consequence of the changes going on in Bulgarian society there were a series of public attacks on the Orthodox Church leadership that singled out its subservience under the old regime, and called for the resignation of Patriarch Maksim. In early 1992 a parliamentary committee on religious affairs headed by Subev declared that the selection of Maksim as patriarch had been uncanonical. This ruling was supported by the Directorate for Religious Affairs, which proceeded to offer support to the critics of the religious establishment. The details of what followed need not concern us here, but these events led to the establishment of rival leaderships within the church and the election of an alternative patriarch by Maksim's critics. The subsequent struggles for influence between the two synods then descended into farce as rival groups exchanged words and sometimes blows. Each denounced the other's bishops and both sides included men who had overtly collaborated with the communist security police, and accepted high levels of state intervention in the affairs of the church, though some of those in the rival group had offered a public repentance for their actions. In the autumn of 1998 a pan-Orthodox Council appeared to have resolved the issue and confirmed the elderly Maksim as patriarch, but the state directorate continued to support the rival synod which still enjoyed the support of a substantial minority of priests.[86]

A similar situation prevailed in the Muslim religious establishment where in 1992 the Directorate for Religious Affairs, backed by the Turkic Movement for Rights and Freedoms, pronounced the election of Mufti Gendzhev illegal and created an interim Islamic Council pending elections within the community. As in the Orthodox Church conflicts broke out between supporters of the two sides, though Gendzhev's position was not helped by his doubtful stance at the time of Zhivkov's revivalist process. Events were also partly dependent upon political developments, for in early 1995 the newly elected BSP government restored Gendzhev to power in the face of extensive protests from within the Muslim community. Finally, under the auspices of a UDF government, a Muslim unification congress was held in October 1997 and this body elected Mustafa-haji as Chief Mufti for Bulgaria, though once again it was alleged by Gendzhev's supporters that state officials had played a role in the selection of delegates to this gathering.[87] Eventually, at the end of 2000, following a case brought by the leadership deposed in favour of Gendzhev in 1995, the European Court of Human Rights issued a ruling critical of the Bulgarian government and thus raised further questions about the right of states to intervene in the appointment of religious leaders and the resolution of conflicts over the leadership of religious administrations.[88]

Whilst these two communities were struggling with division, other religious groups were active in seeking to extend their own freedom of action under the new political order or to enter the country for the first time. Roman Catholics, Methodists, Baptists, Adventists, Pentecostals and Jehovah's Witnesses had been present in Bulgaria for many decades, but these groups were now reinforced or joined by missionary groups from outside, including various charismatic and evangelical groups, Mormons, Hare Krishnas and others. As we shall see, the presence of such groups was to attract negative attention from both state authorities and the traditionally dominant religions as the 1990s progressed.

Defining the status of the Orthodox Church

Whereas in the other countries we have examined so far the constitutional position of the traditionally dominant church has been extensively discussed and has sometimes provoked political conflict, in Bulgaria, as indeed in Russia, debates over the fundamental law have rarely addressed the religious question. Instead, the question of 'recognition' emerged more prominently in the context of a discussion of a new law on religion that began in late 1998. This is not to say, however, that there were no groups in church and society seeking to acquire a position of formal privilege for the national church. Prior to communist rule the Turnovo constitution of 1879 had recognised the Bulgarian Orthodox Church as the 'prevailing religion' but had also promised, though not always delivered, freedom of religion to other faiths.[89] Under the communist government the authorities in effect recognised the Orthodox as the national church, albeit one fully subservient to the state. The 1949 Denominations Act – still partially in force in mid-2002 – spoke of the national church as 'the traditional religious denomination of the Bulgarian nation', which as such was 'a national, democratic church in structure, character and spirit'.[90]

The BSP-dominated parliament elected in mid-1990 almost immediately set about producing a new constitutional text, though the process was contentious and elements within the UDF contested the right of former communists to draft a democratic constitution. In practice the fact that parliament was not fragmented into many competing groups, as was the case in Poland, and that society was still too weak to make a major input, enabled a constitution to be produced relatively quickly. Indeed, when the assembly approved the document on 12 July 1991 Bulgaria, rather unexpectedly, became the first of the Soviet bloc countries to adopt a post-communist constitution.[91]

The Orthodox Church, weakened by internal squabbles and a lack of confidence engendered by its past subordination to the old regime, made little contribution to this debate, though in the end its position gained at least a partial recognition. Article 13 read:

(i) The practising of any religion is free.
(ii) Religious institutions shall be separate from the state.
(iii) Eastern Orthodox Christianity is considered the traditional religion in the Republic of Bulgaria.
(iv) Religious institutions and communities and religious beliefs shall not be used for political ends.

To reinforce this latter clause, Article 11 banned the creation of political parties formed on religious lines, though a later constitutional court ruling made it possible for the Muslim–Turkic-based Movements for Rights and Freedoms to organise. As originally approved, the constitutional text was felt merely to provide a recognition of historical fact, but since then parliamentary deputies have periodically attempted to revive discussion of the issue and push through legal drafts that might provide the Bulgarian Orthodox Church with a more privileged status.[92]

Whilst the early measures promoted by the post-1989 government did little to give the Orthodox formal privilege, it is probably also true to say that in this period the church gained less de facto advantages than in some of the other states covered in this study. True black-robed priests became a more common sight at public and state gatherings, and new institutions and buildings were often the object of clerical blessings. In the media press coverage was a mixed blessing, with many of the papers emerging in the early 1990s finding it hard to resist exploring the church's past relationship with the old regime or focusing on the divisions and scandals besetting the institution through most of the decade. The church may have benefited from the virulent media campaign against the 'sects' during the mid-1990s and in general found it easier to gain access to the state media than other religious groups, though the 1998 Radio and Television Act in theory gave all religious organisations the same rights of access.[93] It also received some financial support from the state budget, along with the Muslim and Jewish communities, though the extent of this subsidy was fairly limited in practice.

The one other area where it did appear that the Orthodox Church might acquire some privileges comparable to those of some of the other national churches we have examined was in the field of religious education. In April 1993 UDF deputy Stefan Stefanov introduced a bill to replace the 1949 Denominations Act that, amongst other things, would have ensured that only Orthodoxy could be discussed in schools or the media.[94] By 1997 religious education had been introduced into schools at the request of parents, with the formal possibility for non-Orthodox to gain teaching in their own traditions, but as most schools had few representatives of minorities it was hard to see how this might be realised in practice. Interviewed about the situation in schools in late 1997 deputy education minister Roumen Velchev argued that in most areas it was impossible to find qualified religion teachers, something made even harder for minorities when the law specified that only those trained in Bulgarian theological seminaries could engage in such teaching. He could not, however, answer charges that even in areas where non-Orthodox groups were sizeable it was proving difficult to find teachers, or the suggestion that virtually all the official textbooks supplied for religious studies only touched on Orthodoxy.[95] Many Protestants took the view that if they excluded their children from religion classes this would subject them to unacceptable pressures from their peers. The situation appears to have been less problematic in the Muslim areas, for in most cases the minority populations were concentrated in specific areas and thus sufficient teachers could be found, and in early 2000 the government introduced elective classes in Islam in elementary schools in twenty-two cities with large Muslim populations.[96] Here we might also note that Orthodox priests may be appointed as prison chaplains in Bulgaria, but that other minority religious communities have to apply for permission each time they make a visit to one of the country's thirteen prisons.[97]

For all this, until the late 1990s the search for a formal recognition of their special status by or for the Orthodox Church was less evident in Bulgaria than in Greece, Poland or Russia. In some respects the comparison might be with Spain insofar as the experience of the past made the respective national churches wary of pushing their claims too far. In the Spanish case there was the fear of revitalising old religious–anti-clerical polarisations, though they pushed far harder on the constitutional issue, whereas in the Bulgarian case the all too recent history of subservience and lack of resistance to the old regime weakened the church's moral case for recognition. Equally important was the institutional weakness of a church that, despite its claims to be national, found its priests out-numbered by Protestant pastors – some figures suggest a total of around 700–800 active priests to over 1,000 pastors.[98] Unlike its Russian coun-terpart, the Bulgarian Orthodox Church lacked any significant degree of public confidence. For example, where opinion polls in the aftermath of communist collapse suggested that around two-thirds or more of the population had confidence in the Russian Orthodox Church, in Bulgaria a 1992 survey showed that only 38 per cent of those polled trusted it, with much higher rates of confidence expressed in the army, presidency and police.[99] The church's ability to argue for advantage was also lessened by the continuing quarrels within its own ranks – by comparison internal church struggles in other countries were relatively minor – and the fact that the state authorities here, in the shape of the interventionist State Directorate, seemed less publicly supportive of the church's demands than in some other transitional states, though it was to back a formal 'recognition' in a proposed new law on religion.

Despite this, by the end of the 1990s there were a few signs that ele-ments within the church and the political elite might seek to strengthen the formal position of the Orthodox establishment. This was particu-larly apparent in three draft laws on religion circulating in the summer of 1999. That proposed by several UDF deputies, and reportedly drafted by the Directorate of Religious Affairs, reaffirmed the equality of all be-fore the law but in practice offered the Orthodox Church a special status. According to Article 8 of this proposed legislation:

(i) Eastern Orthodoxy is the traditional religious denomination of the Bulgarian nation. Its mouthpiece and its only representative is the Bulgarian Orthodox Church.
(ii) State institutions shall support and pay special attention to Eastern Ortho-doxy as the traditional religious denomination of the Bulgarian nation.

A supplementary clause gave the Bulgarian Orthodox Church the sole right to produce and sell church accessories and candles at prices set by the Holy Synod, a provision that might affect many other religious communities. Similar phrasing was evident in the version put forward by the Bulgarian Socialist Party (BSP), but a more radical text was proposed by the Internal Macedonian Revolutionary Organisation (IMRO). Here it was suggested that religious groups be divided into three categories. Under this scheme, Orthodoxy would be the state religion, followed by all those groups existing in Bulgaria prior to 1944, and finally all those registered since 1989 who would face a series of restrictive regulations that severely limited their rights.[100]

In November 1999 a more liberal draft law was sent to the parliamentary committee by several deputies belonging to the Union for National Rescue. Article 5 of this version guaranteed equality before the law for all religious groups, whilst Article 9(ii) stated clearly that 'the state has no right to give privileges to any religious organisation'.[101] This text was firmly rejected by the parliamentary commission on human rights and religious freedom, which took the decision to allow the first three to go forward for parliamentary discussion and in February 2000 the assembly voted to appoint a special committee that would synthesise the key features of these texts.[102] For religious minorities all of the versions were inadequate insofar as they offered symbolic and actual privileges to the Orthodox Church and entailed the restriction of minority rights. Whilst they had no necessary objection to a description of the majority church as 'traditional' they did oppose any reference to a church of the nation with its implication that those who did not belong were somehow not really Bulgarians. They also feared that a law resembling any of the three drafts under consideration might create the conditions for the re-emergence of some of the problems that they faced during the middle of the 1990s and which we outline below.

Restricting minority rights

The Bulgaria that broke with the communist system in 1989 contained a number of religious minorities, the largest of which was the Muslim population, representing 12 per cent of the population. In the census of 1992 a question was asked about 'traditional religious belonging', and this recorded 85 per cent of the population as Orthodox and around 1 per cent in total from the other Christian communities, though this may have overstated the Orthodox position as those with no belief were automatically assigned to that category. Of the non-Muslim minorities the largest group were the Catholics (both Latin and Eastern rite) numbering perhaps 70,000, the various Protestant groups (including Pentecostals, Baptists, Methodists and Adventists) with perhaps 30,000 members, around 5,000 Jews, and several thousand Jehovah's Witnesses.[103] With the advent of political and religious pluralism many of the existing Protestant groups were able to revitalise their activities and gain some converts. More importantly, from the viewpoint of the media and to some extent the public, they were joined by, and often confused with, a vast array of preachers and organisations coming from the outside world to sell their spiritual wares.

Thus a report produced by the Centre for Ethnic Conflicts and Regional Security at the beginning of 1996 pointed out that in Sofia alone there were some 250–300 active evangelists, with many more in other parts of the country. Leaving aside those connected to the existing Protestant groups, these included a wide variety of 'wealth and prosperity' Pentecostals, the Word of Life movement, members of the Unification Church, Mormons, Baha'is, the Family, Hare Krishnas and others. In addition, the report pointed to, or alleged, the growth of Islamic organisations of a 'fundamentalist' inclination.[104] Numerically all of these groups remained small, but this did not prevent the emergence of an often virulent and generally misinformed wave of media attacks on 'non-traditional' religions during the mid-1990s, an assault often joined by politicians of a nationalist persuasion.

During the 1990s the life of religious organisations was regulated by a variety of legal documents and institutions.[105] Article 37 of the constitution adopted in 1991 guaranteed religious freedom to all:

(i) Freedom of conscience, freedom of thought and the choice of religion and of religious or atheist views are inviolable. The state shall assist the maintenance of tolerance and respect among believers from different denominations, and among believers and non-believers.
(ii) Freedom of conscience and religion shall not be practised to the detriment of national security, public order, public health and morals, or the rights and freedoms of others.[106]

True, there was a clause suggesting that religious freedom could be curtailed if it threatened an undefined concept of national security, but broadly speaking the text assigned the state no role in defining the philosophical or religious beliefs of its citizens. On a daily basis the life of religious communities was subject in theory to a series of other regulatory acts, some pre-dating the new political system and others emerging in the early 1990s.

At the centre was the 1949 Denominations Act that remained in force throughout the decade despite several attempts to replace it. This act required that all religious denominations or churches register with the Council of Ministers, whilst their local communities registered with regional or municipal administrations, and included a wide variety of restrictions on the life of religious communities. For example, it prohibited religious work amongst children and young people, severely limited the activities of groups whose religious centre was outside of Bulgaria – a provision specifically aimed at the Catholics – and granted the government's Directorate for Religious Affairs considerable powers to interfere in and control the life of religious communities. Some aspects of the Act were undermined by a Constitutional Court decision of June 1992 that sought to bring its interpretation into line with international agreements. Soon after this the president tried unsuccessfully to persuade the Court to scrap the whole Act. In 1995, however, it did state that certain articles were indeed unconstitutional, including Article 12, which gave the state the right to dismiss priests.[107] There were also criticisms of the work of the state Directorate during the 1990s as successive governments used it to intervene directly in the affairs of the Orthodox and Muslim communities by imposing politically acceptable leaders upon them and thus maintain some degree of control over their internal affairs.

In the wake of the press campaign against 'sects' that gathered pace during 1993, parliament also amended the existing Persons and the Family Act. Under the version approved on 3 February 1994 a new article 133-A was introduced which read: 'juridical persons with a non-profit purpose, performing activities connected with religious faith or dealing with religion and religious education, should be registered according to conditions here mentioned after the approval of the Council of Ministers'. A further provision required the re-registration of all such existing organisations within a three-month period. Following this the government set up a special commission under the leadership of the head of the Directorate of Religious Affairs to supervise the activities of religious organisations and to oversee the re-registration process. In the past, registration under this Act had been preferred to recognition under the Denominations Act for it did not place religious organisations under the control of the government, but as a result of this amendment a number of organisations were deprived of their registration and local authorities often used the act as a pretext for harassing minority groups they disliked. Though a formal appeals procedure was envisaged, during the mid-1990s many felt unwilling to protest publicly at a time when the media was attempting to stir up mass anger at 'sect' activity.[108]

In addition to the civil law, the Bulgarian Penal Code contains a number of clauses that could be used to restrict, or indeed protect, minority rights, though there is little evidence to suggest that they have been used in recent years. Article 164 forbids the instigation of religious hatred, Article 165 penalises the disruption of religious meetings, and Article 166 prohibits the creation of religious-based political parties.[109] Arguably the first two of these could have been used against opponents of the 'sects' who in the media and some parts of the country persistently stirred up hostility against minority groups and against individuals who on several occasions desecrated their places of worship or private homes. Whilst many of these acts were enforced by the police or through local administrative agencies, there have also been persistent reports suggesting the existence of what might be called a religious police. This was confirmed in 1997 by the Acting Director of the National Security Service, who stated that their primary task was to monitor the activities of unregistered religious groups and ensure that they did not act unconstitutionally, whilst other sources suggested that this unit recruited informers from within the ranks of new religious movements.[110]

In practice, during the mid-1990s the legal and political context created considerable problems for many religious minority groups. Specific difficulties arose over the question of registration, the opening of places of worship, the disruption of meetings, discrimination in the workplace, media assaults on their integrity, and the question of conscientious objection. On the question of registration, many groups have faced constraints on their activities stemming from the requirement to re-register under the 1994 amendment of the Persons and the Family Act. In particular, problems have arisen over Article 133-A's failure to define what are activities of a 'religious or related' nature and the lack of clarity over the procedures to be followed by those applying for registration. In consequence, whilst some thirty denominations and twenty-two associations were re-registered, another twenty or so were denied registration on the grounds that their statutes infringed Bulgarian law. These included the White Brotherhood, various Pentecostal groups, the Jehovah's Witnesses and Gideon's International (they regained registration in 1997).[111] In many cases the denial of registration appeared to rely on spurious arguments. Thus the Swedish-based 'Word of Life' movement had its loss of registration confirmed by the Supreme Court on the grounds that its beliefs were 'vague',[112] whilst local authorities in the Plovdiv region deprived a Pentecostal community of registration after it changed its name, though the group concerned had been legally recognised since 1935 and had over 1,000 members.[113] In 1997 the Unification Church, with some 400 members, was also denied registration because, according to the head of the State Directorate, 'there are some things in its activity which are contrary to the country's constitutional and legislative base'.[114] Since then this group, along with the Church of the Nazarene and several Gypsy Protestant communities, have found it hard to gain registration.[115]

    In this sphere, the Jehovah's Witnesses have faced particular problems, being denied registration in 1994 though present in the country for a century or more. Official objections were couched in terms of their refusal to undertake military service, whilst their resistance to blood transfusions was said to represent a threat to public health. There were also frequent charges in the more sensationalist media that Witnesses engaged in the kidnapping of children. As early as 1995, the Jehovah's Witnesses took their position to the European Court of Human Rights, which ruled that they had a case, and this led the government to settle the issue, as well as that relating to the registration of a number of Protestant organisations. In 1998, the Witnesses were officially registered with the Council of Ministers, but at the local level they continued to face many problems with at least one local mayor publicly expressing his unhappiness at the government's decision to recognise them.[116]

Closely related to the problem of registration was the issue of opening church buildings, a process very much dependent upon the attitude of local authorities. Most minority groups, and not just the more controversial ones, have faced official obstructionism at one time or another. Thus, Baptists, Adventists, Pentecostals and Methodists, some having a presence in Bulgaria dating to the nineteenth century and all pre-dating the Denominations Act, have all on occasion faced difficulties in building or developing their premises. For example, the Evangelical Methodist Episcopal Church in Varna had their building taken away in the 1970s and turned into a puppet theatre. After the fall of communism an agreement was reached whereby an alternative site would be found, but this allegedly generated local complaints on the grounds that it was too close to a school and might lead to the corruption of the children. In consequence, the local authorities started to stall, and building work was halted for some time before being resumed in 1999. In a similar vein the Baptist headquarters in Sofia faced difficulties in the mid-1990s when the local authorities threatened to confiscate land that had already been partially developed as a school, orphanage and church complex. Again the argument voiced by local administrators turned on the proximity of the centre to a school, and again the project was delayed for several years until, perhaps under the pressure of the central government as well as the threat of legal action, the city authorities relented.[117] There have also been extensive inconsistencies in relation to church property confiscated under the communist system. For example, a law on the restitution of Catholic properties was passed as early as December 1992, but at least half of the property claimed is yet to be returned and there have been cases where the Catholics sometimes have to pay taxes on buildings formally restored to them but in fact still utilised by other agencies.[118]

Alongside obstructionism several minority groups have faced persistent disruption of their activities, sometimes in ways that clearly contravene the articles of the Penal Code cited earlier. In many cases during the mid-1990s these attacks were incited by representatives of small nationalist organisations such as the Bulgarian National Radical Party and the Internal Macedonian Revolutionary Organisation (IMRO), but on occasions representatives of the local police or security services were involved. During the course of 1997 police officials were responsible for the arrest of numerous Jehovah's Witnesses distributing literature, beat up several Adventist evangelists, raided alleged Muslim fundamentalist study groups, and were used by local authorities to 'protect' those demonstrating against the 'sects'. During May 1998 police in Burgas and Kyustendil broke up Jehovah's Witnesses meetings in private apartments and fined those involved.[119] Such problems were especially acute where IMRO was well organised, as in the Plovdiv region where their members have sought to prevent the registration of Pentecostal communities and where they disrupted several services.[120] Though such cases could be seen as the work of extremists, the frequency with which they affected religious minorities in some areas during the mid-1990s and the lack of serious official response suggest that the authorities are unwilling to deal with discrimination, or perhaps are unable to alter rapidly a political culture which remains suspicious of minorities. Moreover, harassment was not always the product of nationalist agitation, for there were repeated cases in 1999 and 2000 when the police were involved in breaking up Mormon meetings or fining Jehovah's Witnesses for holding meetings without having official permission.[121]

There were also continued reports during the mid-1990s of discrimination against members of religious minorities. On several occasions mothers were denied parental rights over their children on the grounds that the group to which they belonged represented a danger to the infants. In February 1995 the Supreme Court upheld a lower court decision against a woman who belonged to the 'Warriors of Christ' on the grounds that her 'behaviour threatened the interests of the child', though the decision made no reference to whether she was a good mother or not. In similar vein the Plovdiv regional court confirmed the decision to take an eight-year-old from a member of the Jehovah's Witnesses who had told the local monastery that she no longer wished to be considered Orthodox. Another case to attract some legal attention was that of two would-be students at the Sofia University Theological Faculty. Both had been refused entry, one for not showing his Orthodox baptismal certificate and the second for showing one issued by the Bulgarian Church of God, a Pentecostal group. In court, their lawyer argued that given this was a state institution, religious tests were inappropriate, and with some qualifications the judge did accept their case. Yet after the event the university reportedly changed its rules so as to allow their exclusion.[122] In another case a Pentecostal schoolteacher was intimidated and forced to leave her work as a result of her religious adherence.[123]

A further issue that has disproportionately affected religious minorities has been the question of conscientious objection, with several Jehovah's

Witnesses being subject to imprisonment in the years after 1993. Under the communist regime there was no provision for alternative service and for most of the 1990s refusal to take an oath to the flag remained a criminal offence.[124] During the course of 1997, however, a draft law on alternative military service was under discussion that enabled conscientious objectors to undertake unarmed service, though this law was still deemed inadequate by many. In particular it appeared to restrict the grounds for objection to religious beliefs alone, defined annual quotas for such alternative service, and provided that alternative service would be twice as long as military service.[125] This law was confirmed by the National Assembly at the end of October 1998, though its provisions appear not to have altered the fate of those imprisoned prior to its approval, and the one religious prisoner still detained in Bulgaria in early-1999 was a conscientious objector from the Jehovah's Witnesses.[126]

For the Muslim community the collapse of communism brought an end to attempts at enforced assimilation and, despite state interference in the affairs of the religious leadership, an opportunity to rebuild their religious life. Though perhaps only around 15 per cent of the Turkic population regularly involved themselves in religious practices, attempts were made to familiarise the younger generation with the tenets of Islam. One consequence of this, however, was a growing fear on the part of the state that the increasingly active Islamic teaching fraternity would encourage a growth of 'fundamentalism' amongst Bulgarian Muslims.[127] This led to growing pressure on Islamicists from the police who utilised national security fears to justify breaking up study circles and Muslim schools. For example, in July 1999 Daruish al-Narif was expelled from the country for teaching Islam to under-age children in the town of Smolyan, despite the fact that his activity had the approval of the Bulgarian muftiate and that though stateless he had two children with Bulgarian citizenship. In early 2000, another six Islamic preachers were expelled from the Shumen region for preaching without a permit from the Directorate of Religious Affairs, though the permit requirement of the 1949 Denominations Act had been invalidated by the 1992 Constitutional Court judgement.[128]

In addition to these legal and semi-legal infringements of minority group rights, religious communities in the mid-1990s often faced a virulent media and political campaign that reinforced negative public images of their activities. From 1993 onwards numerous articles denounced the foreign sects making inroads into the country who were alleged to bribe officials, buy converts, corrupt the young and destroy families. This campaign reached such a pitch that even leaders of the more established Protestant communities, who generally preferred a low political profile, began to protest publicly.[129] Such articles became ever more lurid in their descriptions of 'sectarian' activities, accusing them of kidnapping, drug trafficking, causing suicides, and sexual deviance. Not untypical of the hysterical campaigns were the events that surrounded the community of Jehovah's Witnesses in the Black Sea port of Burgas in 1997–8. It all started in December of 1997 when papers reported the disappearance of a fourteen-year-old boy who was rumoured to have been seen distributing religious literature. Over the next two months the local media waged a virulent campaign against sectarians, focusing in particular on the Witnesses as a 'clandestine' group who corrupted the young and prohibited them from leading normal lives. In response, representatives of the local community set up an unofficial committee whose aim was to include anti-sect clauses in the Penal Code. According to journalist Katia Kasabova, this group was joined by local citizens, journalists, police officers, the military and even the manager of a local security firm who offered them free guns to chase the sects out of town. In fact the later police report indicated that the boy whose disappearance started this whole furore had run away from home after a row with his parents, and following these events the government Directorate organised a meeting with local officials and media representatives aimed at discouraging such sensationalist approaches to religious questions in the future.[130]

This seemingly concerted media campaign died away after the UDF election victory in 1997, though anti-sect articles continued to appear on a more occasional basis, generally accompanied by a 'something needs to be done' message. Towards the end of that year the government proposed a new law on religion whose *declared* aim would be to bring order into this sphere. Early versions of this law failed to satisfy human rights commentators who noted that it continued to assume a government right to control religious life and proposed restrictive requirements for the legal recognition of religious groups.[131] Pressures also came from other sources, with the Sofia town council in early 1999 adopting new restrictions on the activities of religious groups. These were criticised by minority representatives, with the Bulgarian Evangelical Alliance expressing unease about the wording of clauses on the participation of children under sixteen in religious services and the advertising of religious events, whilst the Catholics were wary of a proposal that only Bulgarian citizens could preach in Sofia.[132] Around the same time, it was reported that the nationalist IMRO had produced a draft law that would have only recognised those religions present in Bulgaria in 1908.[133]

Finally, in July 1999 several deputies from the ruling UDF placed a draft law on religion before the National Assembly. At a meeting held on 18 July forty representatives of minority religious communities rejected this draft, broadly supporting the critique offered by human rights groups.

Commenting on this text the Bulgarian Tolerance Foundation noted that whilst the text had some positive features that enhanced religious liberty, there remained major deficiencies, including:

- the preservation of a major role for state agencies in supervising religious life, with all religious activities effectively requiring the permission of the state;
- the requirement that only one religious community be formed on the basis of one system of beliefs. The draft prevents the natural divergence of religious groups, for example preventing the emergence of two denominational groupings describing themselves as Baptists;
- the creation of new commissions at local level to decide whether the rules have been broken and with the power to fine, a development effectively creating religious courts;
- the centralisation of permission for the construction of church buildings, previously the preserve of local authorities, a move that might particularly affect the Muslim communities who often control their own local administrations;
- the fact that registration can be denied to a group on the grounds that it had practised religion publicly prior to registration;
- Article 8's granting of special privileges to the Orthodox Church (see the wording in the previous section).

In addition, the law (Article 42) made it plain that without registration no religious activity could take place, not simply that the community involved in such was denied legal personality.[134] American legal expert Cole Durham also pointed out the dangers of the politicisation of registration decisions likely to stem from the failure to grant the final decision to the courts, and the provision of undue discretion to administrative officials.[135]

In response to this document the Tolerance Foundation and the Bulgarian Helsinki Committee commissioned Plamen Bogoev to draw up a new and much simpler draft law that laid the foundations for what they saw as a genuine realisation of religious freedom. This relatively brief text promised religious equality to all, prohibited the state from privileging any religion, made the registration of religious communities simply a process of recognition requiring minimal bureaucratic procedures, denied the state any right to intervene in the daily life of religious communities, banned religious groups from supporting political parties, and elaborated a broad range of rights for all religious communities in the country – including the right to create educational institutions, carry out charitable work, have equal access to the state media, and to receive tax-free donations. At the same time the draft proposed to replace the Denominations Act and Article 133-A of the Persons and the Family Act. This text was in turn proposed in parliament by several deputies from the opposition Union for National Rescue but swiftly turned down by the committee on human rights and religion, whose chairman Ivan Sungarski (the son of an Orthodox priest) has been unrelenting in expressing hostility to minority religious communities.[136]

As noted earlier, in early February 2000 three drafts were put before the National Assembly, given their first reading and then sent to a special committee for harmonisation. For those opposed to the drafts this was a disappointing decision, not simply because of the contents of the three texts that all shared the failings outlined above, but also because in the period since July 1999 there had been no serious consultation with minority religious groups. In addition, they expressed unease at the fact that the three drafts proposed yet another registration process, even of those groups already registered, and the fact that vagueness in terminology would give considerable freedom to local officials to apply the law harshly to religious groups they disliked.[137] During May 2000 the parliamentary committee began to go through the laws clause by clause. Around the same time a new draft was put forward by a group of experts drawn together by the Turkish-based Movement for Rights and Freedoms, that followed the Bogoev version in offered brevity and a focus on permissiveness rather than restriction.[138] In September the final version of the law prepared by the committee was submitted to parliament for approval. According to human rights activists and religious minorities this version represented only a marginal improvement on the earlier drafts, and still proposed giving extensive powers to a state agency with extensive rights to interfere in the affairs of religious communities and gave considerable discretion to local officials in interpreting the law in their territories.[139] This version was then approved by parliament on 12 October 2000, but since then its final approval has stalled and as of mid-2002 the outcome remained unclear. The new government elected in June 2001 has expressed little interest in the religious question, and much may depend upon political struggles between those keen to assert Bulgarian distinctiveness and those keen to meet the human rights requirements of European Union membership and integration into a democratic Europe.

Conclusion

Some of the differences emerging here between the Polish and Bulgarian cases mirror those in Southern Europe, notably in the way in which the focus in the Catholic countries has been more on constitutional 'recognition' rather than the advocacy of 'discrimination'. The Polish hierarchy followed the Spanish example in arguing for the acquisition of formal legal status in the context of the fundamental law, though it seems to have adopted a much more aggressive approach in pursuing this goal, a product perhaps of its misreading of the degree of societal authority it had gained through its defence of Polish liberty during the communist period. Equally, it is in the Orthodox country that more attempts have been made to protect the position of the majority church by restricting the rights of religious minorities. Yet as we shall see in chapter 5 the impetus for this has come as much from nationalist politicians as from a church weakened by decades of repression and division.

Notes

1. K. Daniel and J. Cole Durham, 'Religious identity as a component of national identity: implications for emerging church–state relations in the former socialist bloc', in A. Sajo and S. Avineri (eds.), *The Law of Religious Identity: Models for Post-Communism* (The Hague: Kluwer Law International, 1999), p. 126.
2. For a general overview of Polish history see Norman Davies, *God's Playground: A History of Poland* (Oxford: Clarendon Press, 2 volumes, 1981).
3. K. Dawisha, *Eastern Europe, Gorbachev and Reform* (Cambridge: Cambridge University Press, 1988), pp. 58–9.
4. Numerous books deal with these developments, but one useful essay written at the time is J. Rupnik, 'Dissent in Poland, 1968–78: the end of revisionism and the rebirth of civil society', in R. Tokes (ed.), *Opposition in Eastern Europe* (London: Macmillan 1979), pp. 60–112.
5. For a good overview see Timothy Garton Ash, *The Polish Revolution* (London: Granta and Penguin, 1983/1991).
6. 'New evolutionism', in Adam Michnik, *Letters from Prison and Other Essays* (London: University of California Press, 1985), pp. 135–48.
7. J. Linz and A. Stepan, *Problems of Democratic Transition and Consolidation* (Baltimore: Johns Hopkins University Press, 1996), p. 272.
8. S. Ramet, *Nihil Obstat: Religion, Politics and Social Change in East-Central Europe and Russia* (Durham and London: Duke University Press, 1998), pp. 93–9; Daniel and Cole Durham, 'Religious identity as a component of national identity', pp. 126–8.
9. See Adam Michnik's essay on 'The church and the left', which pointed out that in recent years the church has become a bastion in defence of human dignity, and stressed the need for cooperation between secular and religious critics of the regime. A. Michnik, *The Church and the Left* (Chicago: Chicago University Press, 1993).
10. 'Notes on church and state', *Journal of Church and State*, 18: 2, 1976, p. 398.
11. Cf. Rupnik, 'Dissent in Poland, 1968–78'; J. Casanova, *Public Religions in the Modern World* (Chicago: University of Chicago Press, 1994), pp. 94–101.
12. J. Jershschina, 'The Catholic Church, the communist state and the Polish people', in S. Gomulka and A. Polonsky (eds.), *Polish Paradoxes* (London: Routledge, 1990), p. 95.

13. Szjakowski, 'The Roman Catholic Church in Poland', paper given at PSA conference, Southampton University, April 1984, p. 20; a more triumphalist, if debatable, view is expressed by George Weigel who argues that the visit was even more significant, because at this time John Paul II started to dismantle what Lenin had started at the Finland Station in 1917. G.Weigel, *The Final Revolution: The Resistance Church and the Collapse of Communism* (New York, Oxford University Press, 1992).

14. *Religion in Communist Lands*, 8: 3, 1980, pp. 239–40.

15. For a good overview of the Solidarity period see Ash, *The Polish Revolution*.

16. Ibid., pp. 280–1; I. Korba, 'Five years underground: the opposition and the church in Poland since martial law', *Religion in Communist Lands*, 15: 2, 1987, pp. 179–81.

17. Casanova, *Public Religions in the Modern World*, p. 108.

18. On these talks see W. Osiatynski, *The Round-Table Negotiations in Poland*, Working Paper No.1, Centre for the Study of Constitutionalism in Eastern Europe, 1991.

19. *Keston News Service (KNS) 379*, 11 July 1991, p. 15.

20. *Open Media Research Institute* (OMRI), 168, 28 August 1995.

21. A dilemma pointed to by Weigel who, though sympathetic to the church's position, argues that it has not always learnt the arts of democratic persuasion. Weigel, *The Final Revolution*, pp. 156ff.

22. *KNS 364*, 6 December 1990; *Transition*, 3 November 1995, p. 45.

23. Quoted in T. Beeson, *Discretion and Valour: Religious Conditions in Russia and Eastern Europe* (London: Fount, 1982), p. 168. This chapter also provides a useful overview of the situation of religion in communist Poland up until 1980.

24. R. Taras, *Consolidating Democracy in Poland* (Boulder: Westview, 1995), p. 117.

25. Ramet, *Nihil Obstat*, p. 294.

26. A. Kwasniewski, leader of the reformed communists, quoted in Taras, *Consolidating Democracy in Poland*, pp. 200–1; Adam Michnik, 'Post-communist Poland: religious liberty for all?', *East–West Church Ministry Report*, 3: 3, 1995, pp. 1–3.

27. Casanova, *Public Religions in the Modern World*, pp. 110–11.

28. Cf. *KNS 354*, 12 July 1990, p. 14 and 25 October 1990, p. 11; and Radio Free Europe, 6 August 1990.

29. *KNS*, 27 June 1991.

30. Cf. 'Notes on church–state', *Journal of Church and State*, 34: 3, 1992; *BBC Summary of World Broadcasts (SWB)*, EE/1654, B/3, 3 April 1993; M. Ebeolz, 'The Roman Catholic Church and democracy in Poland', *Europe-Asia Studies*, 50: 5, 1998, p. 821.

31. See Anna Sabbat-Swidlicka, 'Polish ombudsman over-ruled on religious instruction', *RFE/RL Research Report*, 2: 28, 9 July 1993; Mark Brzezinski, *The Struggle for Constitutionalism in Poland* (London: Macmillan, 1998), pp. 178–82; S. Ramet, *Whose Democracy? Nationalism, Religion and the Doctrine of Collective Rights in Post-1989 Eastern Europe* (Oxford: Rowman & Littlefield, 1997), p. 101.

32. US State Department, *Annual Report on International Religious Freedom for 1999: Poland*, Section 1.

33. *SWB* EE/1576, B/11, 1 January 1993 and EE/1629, B/5, 5 March 1993; Anna Sabbat-Swidlicka, 'Church and state in Poland', *RFE/RL Research Report*, 2: 14, 2 April 1993.
34. *Religious Freedom for 1999: Poland*, Section 1.
35. US State Department, *Report on Human Rights Practices for 1996* (Washington DC, 1997).
36. *The Independent*, 17 and 18 May 1991, 27 November 1991.
37. Sabbat-Swidlicka, 'Church and state in Poland', pp. 47–8.
38. *OMRI*, 168, 29 August 1996; 170, 3 September 1996; 230, 27 November 1996; J. Karpinski, 'Poles divided over church's renewed role', *Transition*, 5 April 1996, pp. 11–13.
39. Brzezinksi, *The Struggle for Constitutionalism in Poland*, p. 1.
40. Ibid., p. 74; 'Notes on church and state', *Journal of Church and State*, 18: 2, 1976, p. 398.
41. Brzezinski, *The Struggle for Constitutionalism in Poland*, pp. 106–10.
42. In March 1994 its parliamentary deputies were mandated to vote against ratification. *SWB*, EE/1958, A/9, 29 March 1994.
43. Cf. *SWB*, EE/2439, C/6, 20 October 1995 and EE/2635, C/5, 4 May 1996; F. Millard, *Polish Politics and Society* (London: Routledge, 1999), pp. 136–8.
44. *SWB*, EE/2055, 23 July 1994; J. Karpinski, 'The constitutional mosaic', *Transition*, August 1995, p. 9.
45. *SWB*, EE/1684, B/5, 10 May 1993.
46. Quoted in Brzezinski, *The Struggle for Constitutionalism in Poland*, p. 122.
47. *SWB*, EE/2092, A/10, 5 September 1994 and EE/2135, A/4, 25 October 1994.
48. Ibid., EE/2258, A/6, 25 March 1995.
49. Ramet, *Whose Democracy?*, p. 105.
50. *SWB*, EE/2334, A/7–8, 20 June 1996.
51. *SWB*, EE/2970, C/4, 18 March 1997; *OMRI* 43, 3 March 1997.
52. *OMRI* 58, 24 March 1997.
53. Cf. *SWB*, EE/2902, C/5–6, 25 April 1997 and EE/2910, C/9–10, 5 May 1997; Millard, *Polish Politics and Society*, p. 120.
54. *The Warsaw Voice*, 2 June 1996.
55. *Catholic World News*, 9 January 1998; the text can be found at http//www.giurisprudenza.unimi.it/~oli . . . Oand%20th%20republic%20of%20Poland.htm.
56. Ebeolz, 'The Roman Catholic Church and democracy in Poland', p. 838.
57. Cf. K. Boyle and J. Sheen (eds.), *Freedom of Religion and Belief: A World Report* (London: Routledge, 1997), pp. 359–60; A. Zagorska, 'Sharing the power: the growth of non-traditional religions in Poland', *Religion in Eastern Europe*, 18: 2, 1998, pp. 1–16; M. Pietrzak, 'La situation juridique des communautes religieuses en Pologne contemporaine', *European Journal of Church and State*, 6, 1999, p. 245.
58. http://www.uni-wuerzburg.de/law/p100000_html.
59. *KNS*, 6 July 2000.
60. *SWB*, p. 238; Daniel and Cole Durham, 'Religious identity as a component of national identity', pp. 131–2.

61. *KNS 354*, 12 July 1990 and *KNS 356*, 9 August 1990.
62. B. Yoder, 'Religion in Poland in 1994', in *Religion in Eastern Europe*, 14: 6, 1994, pp. 43–5; A. Korbonksi, 'A concordat but not concord', *Transition*, June 1995, pp. 13–17; Ebeolz, 'Religion and democracy in Poland', p. 833.
63. B. Tranda, 'The situation of Protestants in today's Poland', *Religion in Communist Lands*, 19: 1–2, 1992, pp. 37–44.
64. Casanova, *Public Religions in the Modern World*, pp. 110–11.
65. *SWB*, EE/2496, C/6, 29 December 1995; J. Richardson, 'New religions and religious freedom in Eastern and Central Europe: a sociological analysis', in I. Borovik and G. Babinski (eds.), *New Religious Phenomenon in Central and Eastern Europe* (Kraków: Nomos, 1997), pp. 264–5.
66. *OMRI 224*, 19 November 1996.
67. Richardson, 'New religious movements and religious freedom in Eastern and Central Europe', p. 262.
68. Ibid.; see also J. Luxmoore, 'Eastern Europe in 1996', *Religion, State and Society*, 25: 1, 1997, p. 90.
69. *KNS*, 27 March 2000.
70. *KNS*, 6 July 2000.
71. *KNS*, 27 March 2000.
72. *KNS*, 30 November 2000.
73. *KNS*, 17 November 2000; for a background case study see Rosa Lehmann, 'State, church and local response: the fall and rise of a Greek Catholic parish in socialist Poland', in T. Inglis, Z. Mach and R. Mazanek (eds.), *Religion and Politics: East–West Contrasts from Contemporary Europe* (Dublin: University College of Dublin Press, 2000), pp. 93–112.
74. Though note some evidence suggesting that amongst the younger generation the level of anti-Semitism is declining. US State Department, *2000 Annual Report on International Religious Freedom: Poland*, found at http://www.state.gov/www/global/ human_rights/irf/irf_rpt/irf_poland.html.
75. For a general history see R. Crampton, *A Concise History of Bulgaria* (Cambridge: Cambridge University Press, 1997); R. McIntyre, *Bulgaria: Politics, Economics and Society* (London: Pinter, 1988), pp. 15–53.
76. Cf. P. Tsvetkov, 'The politics of transition in Bulgaria: back to the future', *Problems of Communism*, May–June 1992, pp. 34–42; Linz and Stepan, *Problems of Democratic Transition and Consolidation*, pp. 333–43.
77. Ibid., p. 343.
78. R. Daskalov, 'A democracy born in pain: Bulgarian politics, 1989–97', in J. Bell (ed.), *Bulgaria in Transition: Politics, Society and Culture after Communism* (Boulder: Westview, 1998), pp. 9–38.
79. Some useful essays on the history of the Bulgarian Church can be found in G. Bakalov (ed.), *Religiya i tsyrkva v Bylgariya* (Sofia: Gutenburg Publishing House, 1999).
80. This section relies heavily on Ramet, *Nihil Obstat*, pp. 277–9; Spas Raikin, 'Nationalism and the Bulgarian Orthodox Church', in P. Ramet (ed.), *Religion and Nationalism in Soviet and East European Politics* (Durham: Duke University Press, 1989), pp. 352–77.
81. Crampton, *A Concise History of Bulgaria*, pp. 73–4.

82. For more detail on the Catholic experience see M. Koinova, *Catholics of Bulgaria* (Centre for Documentation and Information on Minorities in Europe – Southeast Europe, CEDIME-SE, 1999).
83. M. Koinova, *Muslims of Bulgaria* (Centre for Documentation and Information on Minorities in Europe – Southeast Europe, CEDIME-SE, 1999).
84. Ibid.
85. R. Hoare, 'Bulgaria', *Religion in Communist Lands*, 18: 2, 1990, pp. 172–80.
86. On the schism see Ramet, *Nihil obstat*, pp. 282–5; S. Raikin, 'The schism in the Bulgarian Orthodox Church, 1992–92', in Bell, *Bulgaria in Transition*, pp. 207–31; various reports in *KNS*, especially on developments in the late 1990s: 3 December 1998 and 27 February 1999.
87. See K. Engelbrekt, 'Bulgaria's religious institutions under fire', *RFE/RL Research Report*, 25 September 1992, pp. 60–6; Koinova, *Muslims of Bulgaria*; K. Kanev, et al., *Report on Bulgaria* (English document from around late 1995 or early 1996 documenting state of religious liberty in Bulgaria); on all these events see Emil Cohen and Krassimir Kanev, 'Religious freedom in Bulgaria', *Journal of Ecumenical Studies*, 36: 1–2, 1999, pp. 250–3.
88. *KNS*, 7 November 2000.
89. A. Zhelyazkova, 'Bulgaria's Muslim communities', in Bell, *Bulgaria in Transition*, p. 166.
90. Kanev, *Report on Bulgaria*.
91. For a general survey of the constitutional debate see E. Tanchev, The constitution and the rule of law', in Bell, *Bulgaria in Transition*, pp. 65–90.
92. According to a review of constitutional and legal provisions relating to religion in Kanev, *Report on Bulgaria*.
93. *Obektiv*, February 1999 (an occasional publication produced by the Bulgarian Helsinki Group).
94. Kanev, *Report on Bulgaria*.
95. *Tolerance*, January 1998, p. 2.
96. *Radio Free Europe*, 58, 22 March 2000.
97. I am grateful to Krassimir Kanev of the Bulgarian Helsinki Committee for giving me a soon to be published report on religious minorities which contained this information, Interview, June 2000.
98. According to Dr N. Nedelchev, General Secretary of the Bulgarian Evangelical Alliance, June 2000.
99. J. Chin, Political attitudes in Bulgaria', in *RFE/RL Research Report*, 20 April 1993, p. 40.
100. *KNS*, 10 February 2000.
101. The text can be found in a press release of the Tolerance Foundation, Sofia, 17 December 1999.
102. See the text of the UDF draft produced by the Tolerance Foundation and Human Rights Without Frontiers, published in *Compass Direct*, 15 July 1999 and commentary on revised draft on 17 December 1999.
103. Cf. Engelbrekt, 'Bulgaria's religious institutions under fire', p. 61; Boyle and Sheen, *Freedom of Religion and Belief*, p. 280–1.
104. *BBC SWB*, EE/2250, B/4, 27 January 1996.
105. For a broad overview see Cohen and Kanev, 'Religious freedom in Bulgaria', pp. 243–64.

106. http://www.uni-wuerzburg.de/law/bu00000_.html.
107. Kanev, *Report on Bulgaria;* Koinova, *Catholics of Bulgaria,* p. 25.
108. Kanev, *Report on Bulgaria.*
109. There are numerous such cases, but see the report of Human Rights Without Frontiers, 6 November 1998, which details the harassment of Jehovah's Witnesses in Plovdiv whose members were subject to persistent harassment, and whose literature was publicly burnt at the instigation of district mayors.
110. *Obektiv,* June–September 1997, pp. 16–17; Tolerance Foundation, *Report on Religious Freedom in Bulgaria in 1997* (Sofia, 26 February 1998).
111. Boyle and Sheen, *Freedom of Religion and Belief,* p. 284.
112. Kanev, *Report on Bulgaria.*
113. *Tolerance,* January 1998, pp. 4–5.
114. Reuters, 15 August 1997.
115. International Helsinki Federation, *Annual Country Report on Human Rights,* 1 June 2000, p. 1.
116. *Tolerance,* June–September 1997, pp. 11–12; HRWF, 2 July 1998 and 18 October 1998.
117. *Obektiv,* September 1996–January 1997, p. 10; *Baptist Times,* 1 June 1995; interview with Latchezar Popov, Rule of Law Institute, Sofia, June 2000.
118. Kanev, *Report on Bulgaria;* Koinova, *Catholics of Bulgaria,* p. 22; Cohen and Kanev, 'Religious freedom in Bulgaria', p. 250.
119. US State Department, *Annual Report on International Religious Freedom for 1999: Bulgaria* (henceforth *Bulgaria, 99*) found at http://www.state.gov/www/global/human_rights/irf/irf_rpt/1999/ irf_bulgaria99.html, p. 2.
120. Numerous examples can be found in the reports of the Tolerance Foundation and the Bulgarian Helsinki Group cited earlier; such attacks were still being reported in 2001. See the press release of the Tolerance Foundation of 4 July 2001, at http://groups.yahoo.com/group/balkanhr/message/2451.
121. US State Department, *Annual Report on International Religious Freedom for 2000: Bulgaria* (henceforth, *Bulgaria, 2000*).
122. See various reports from the Tolerance Foundation.
123. *Bulgaria, 99,* p. 3.
124. Boyle and Sheen, *Freedom of Religion and Belief,* p. 286.
125. Tolerance Foundation, *Report on Religious Freedom in Bulgaria in 1997,* pp. 1–2.
126. HRWF, 22 December 1998.
127. For a general overview of the Muslim position see W. Hopken, 'From religious identity to ethnic mobilisation: the Turks of Bulgaria before, under and since communism', in H. Poulton and S. Taji-Farouki (eds.), *Muslim Identity and the Balkan State* (London: Hurst & Co., 1997), pp. 54–81.
128. International Helsinki Federation, *Annual Country Report on Human Rights,* 1 June 2000, pp. 1–2.
129. *European Baptist Press Service,* 17 November 1993; *Baptist Times,* 23 December 1993.
130. A more detailed report can be found in HRWF 2 July 1998.
131. *Tolerance,* January 1998, p. 7.
132. F. Corley, 'Bulgarian churches protest against new religion regulations in Sofia', in *Keston News Service,* 18 March 1999.

133. *Obektiv*, February 1999.
134. Press release of Tolerance Foundation, 6 July 1999.
135. For a detailed legal analysis see W. Cole Durham, 'Analysis of proposed Bulgarian legislation restricting religious freedom', *Obektiv*, January–April 2000, pp. 15–18.
136. See the press release of the Tolerance Foundation, 17 December 1999.
137. See their appeal to the president, prime minister and chairman of the National Assembly, attached to a Tolerance Foundation press release on 9 February 2000; and Bjelajac, 'Appeal from the minority churches'; see also the detailed legal commentary produced by World Advocates, USA, and 'The Rule of Law Institute' (undated document given to me by Latchezar Popov, chairman of the latter institution); further comments focused on the way in which all three of the drafts had the capacity to politicise registration decisions by assigning the final word to the Council of Ministers rather than the courts, offered occasionally vague terminology in describing what was permissible or not, vested excessive discretion in the hands of local officials, and appeared to discriminate against believers who were not citizens of Bulgaria. Cole Durham, 'Analysis of proposed Bulgarian legislation restricting religious freedom', pp. 15–18.
138. Ibid., p. 18.
139. Tolerance Foundation Press Release, 8 November 2000.

4 The former USSR: Russia and the successor states

Our study so far has concentrated on Southern and Central Europe, but it was developments in the field of religion–state relations in the former USSR that initially stimulated this attempt at comparative research. It was in the Soviet Union that there first emerged the communist political system that was to form the basis for the creation of polities of a similar type in various parts of the world. Policies pursued by Moscow often provided an exemplary model for other communist rulers to follow, though many of these states eventually modified them to suit local circumstance. In the field of religion this meant seeking to eliminate religious influences from public life, though different states varied in the extent to which they made this a priority. Even within the fifteen republics that made up the USSR during the post-Stalin years, anti-religious policies were pursued with varying degrees of enthusiasm and success. Under Mikhail Gorbachev the official commitment to the creation of an atheist society was dropped and by the early 1990s nearly all of the newly independent republics had adopted policies and laws that were more favourable to religion and which formally reduced or removed state intervention in religious life. In the case of Russia the legal situation prevailing in the early 1990s allowed for the emergence of a religious free market in which both indigenous religious minorities as well as the far less numerous 'new religious movements' could flourish and propagate their teachings. Though the latter groups had far fewer adherents than indigenous communities, a sensationalist media and a fearful Orthodox Church contributed to a rhetoric centred on an 'invasion of the sects' that was undermining Russian unity and destroying families at a time of great uncertainty. For that reason, in Russia and many of the other post-Soviet states there emerged calls for the passage of stricter legislation that would reinforce the position of 'traditional' religious communities and impose some limits on the activities of 'sects'. In a study of this size it is impossible to do justice to developments in all of the fifteen successor states, and here we simply offer an account of how Russia has dealt with the questions of 'recognition' and 'restriction', and present a series of very brief sketches illustrating how six post-Soviet states in different geographical regions and with different religious traditions have handled this issue.

The Russian Federation

The political context: imperial collapse

Following the Russian defeat of the Mongol horde at the battle of Kulikovo Field (1380) the geographical and political reach of the Russian state steadily extended, until by the end of the nineteenth century it included Central Asia and the Caucasus to the south, comprised parts of modern Central and Eastern Europe, as well as Finland, in the west, and reached the Pacific Ocean in the east. By that time the centre of political power had shifted to the city of St Petersburg where the Romanov tsars ruled with varying degrees of skill and with the support of a relatively small bureaucratic elite. The last of these rulers was Nicholas II, a man whose ambition to pass on his patrimony unchanged was constrained by his limited political skills, jealousy of talented ministers, and general inability to grasp the political realities of the day. All this came to the fore during the 1914–18 war, which heralded the collapse of the Russian imperial system and very rapidly culminated in the triumph of the Bolsheviks.

The new system that eventually matured under Stalin was very different from the inefficient and relatively benign authoritarianism of the old regime, and came to be characterised by many scholars as the supreme example of a 'totalitarian' polity. Such a regime was distinct from traditional authoritarian systems in being controlled by a mass party dominated by a single individual, in utilising terror and a pervasive secret police force to bring society into line, and in the state's domination of all aspects of economic life.[1] By the 1960s, however, many commentators were expressing unease at such characterisations, pointing to the way in which the 'classical' model ignored other defining features of these regimes – notably their commitment to rapid social change. Such scholars argued that the model failed to do justice to differences amongst communist systems, that it was too static and made no allowance for change, and that it was a product of Cold War thinking. Instead a veritable host of new conceptualisations appeared, though as these were appearing in the West dissenters within the Soviet bloc began to revert to the totalitarian characterisation albeit with a stress on 'totalist aspirations' rather than the actual ability of these types of state to control everything that went on in their realms. For all this, most seemed to agree that the Soviet-type regime was a qualitatively different form of political order from any that had existed hitherto.[2]

However one conceptualised these states, there could be little doubt that the USSR remained one of the most tightly controlled societies in the world and that it had proved relatively successful in neutralising dissenting views. With Stalin's death all this began to change. Under Khrushchev there were sporadic and uneven reform attempts, but under Brezhnev the element of political regularisation that developed in terms of procedures, and a willingness to involve experts in decision-making, disguised the reality of an economic and political system that was finding it increasingly hard to cope with the changes taking place both within the USSR and in the outside world. In an effort to increase their legitimacy Soviet leaders periodically flirted with Russian nationalism, especially during the Great Patriotic War but also under Brezhnev, though it was not always clear how that might strengthen Moscow's appeal in the non-Russian borderlands. Despite this, Russia remained the only one of the fifteen republics without its own communist party – except for the period 1956–66 when a Russian party bureau was established – and in consequence had no means of exerting influence on its own behalf outside the Soviet party apparatus, though of course many minority nationalities pointed out that this was generally dominated by Russians.[3]

Gorbachev came to power in 1985 committed to reforming the system, but in the event presided over its collapse. Having set the pace with the rhetoric of glasnost and perestroika, and having pushed through a series of institutional reforms, Gorbachev found himself left behind by the speed of change from late 1989 onwards. Power gradually ebbed away from the centre to the street, the labour unions, the national republics and newly elected legislatures at all levels of the system. Within the Russian Federation Gorbachev faced mounting political opposition, on the one hand from the newly created and highly conservative Russian Communist Party that emerged in 1990, and on the other from Russia's new democratic institutions under the leadership of Boris Yeltsin. When conservatives staged a coup attempt in August 1991 it was Yeltsin and the Russian parliament that led the resistance and eventually won out, and in consequence it was they who reaped the benefit of the Soviet collapse when it came at the end of that year.

In essence the transition in Russia stemmed from a failure of the Soviet political system and the collapse of central control over many of the ethnically defined republics. The regime that emerged from that transition is still in the process of change and remains hard to characterise, but what is clear is that Russia – unlike Spain, Greece and possibly Poland – is not yet a consolidated democracy. Many of the forms of democracy have been established: the legal guarantee of civil rights (albeit not always implemented), a quasi-free media, a partial if sometimes selective rule of law and the regular holding of elections. Yet elections have not led to governmental turnover, and the presidential election held in March 2000 was organised in such a way as to dramatically reduce the possibility of anyone defeating Vladimir Putin. The levels of criminality and violence remain high, as can be seen from the number of political assassinations, the forceful resolution of the presidential–parliamentary conflict in 1993, or the attempted military solution of the Chechen problem. In addition, the evolution of economic reform has led to the enrichment of a tiny minority, alongside the impoverishment of the majority who are thus marginalised and increasingly believe they have no impact upon the activities of their political rulers. As numerous commentators have pointed out, some of these problems stem from the sheer scale of the reform needed to transform Russia in comparison to some other 'third wave' states, for here we are dealing with a society that has a very limited democratic tradition, no experience of a modern market economy, and no clear definition of what Russia is in political, geographical and even metaphysical terms.

The religious context: the death and rebirth of 'holy Rus'

Prior to 1917 Orthodoxy had been the dominant religious tradition for the best part of 900 years, and had been strongly identified with the fate of the nation from the time of the partial defeat of the Mongol horde at Kulikovo. During subsequent decades the church worked closely with the state in promoting a sense of Russian unity, through language, literature and symbol, and for a brief period the two sides were united in a single family as the young Mikhail Romanov who became Tsar in 1613 ruled in tandem with his domineering father, the rather worldly Patriarch Filaret.[4] In the mid-seventeenth century Patriarch Nikon sought to raise the status of the spiritual power above that of the state, but having split the church on doctrinal matters he was later deposed by a secular authority keen to assert its supremacy. This move was reinforced by Peter the Great whose church reforms in the early eighteenth century institutionalised the subordination of the Orthodox hierarchy to the state, effectively turning the church into a branch of the civil service.[5] This was the pattern that prevailed until the end of the nineteenth century, and the occasional appearance of devout *startsy* (spiritual elders) or committed parish priests could not disguise the overwhelmingly submissive nature of the church as an organisation.

It was this church that virtually all Russian revolutionaries of the nineteenth century opposed and which they saw as a brake on economic, social and political progress. For some, hatred of Orthodoxy was accompanied by an idealisation of sectarian movements – akin to Engels' rather rosy-eyed view of the revolutionary potential of Thomas Munzer's movement in sixteenth-century Germany – and for a brief period the Bolsheviks published a magazine aimed explicitly at religious minorities. When they first came to power in late 1917 Lenin and his colleagues concentrated their attention on the Orthodox and generally left minorities alone. The first victims of regime violence included several bishops and many clergy, but from the late 1920s onwards, as Stalin consolidated his power, all religious groups came under attack. In part this campaign was motivated by anti-religious zeal, but it also reflected Stalin's efforts to impose control over all aspects of autonomous social life. By the end of the 1930s virtually all religious institutions had been closed and the vast majority of religious activists had been swallowed up by the purge machine, whether through physical elimination in the execution cellars or though internment in the gulag. Only Hitler's invasion of Russia in 1941 brought some respite and those who survived were brought out of prison or retirement to encourage resistance and bring comfort to the victims of war.

After the defeat of Germany this partial religious tolerance was maintained for a while as Russia embarked upon a process of rebuilding. The official commitment to the eventual elimination of religion remained, but the party accepted that this was likely to be a long-term process requiring a variety of means. If religious institutions, however limited their numbers, were to be allowed to exist the state would have to perfect the means of *control*, with state and security agencies monitoring very carefully the daily life of religious communities and watching out for any undue excesses of religious enthusiasm on the part of clergy or laity. *Repression* remained as an option, but it seemed as though the memory of the 1930s would be sufficient to keep most believers cautious in manifesting their beliefs. For those of a more enthusiastic nature the courts, camps and psychiatric hospitals remained available, and were widely used under Khrushchev – when a more militant anti-religious campaign was waged – and during certain periods of Brezhnev's tenure in office. Finally, *educational and propaganda* measures were taken to undermine religious values and promote an alternative world-view and vision of humanity. These might include formal propaganda measures in the workplace and educational institutions, media campaigns, and the promotion of non-religious rituals to mark the major events of an individual's lifetime.[6]

For all this, it was apparent that at least a residual religiosity remained amongst many Russians by the early 1980s and that the existing number of places of worship remained inadequate for those who wished to participate in religious life. As Gorbachev's reforms began to take hold from 1987 onwards it was clear that religion could not be excluded from public life any longer, and during 1988 the release of the majority of religious prisoners coincided with the very public if controlled celebrations of the millennium of Christianity in Russia. During the following year religious communities gained numerous de facto rights to open churches, engage in educational and charitable activities and participate in public life, and these rights were given legal backing in a new USSR law on religion approved in October 1990 and followed one month later by a Russian Federation law which effectively created a religious free market in that republic.

The dissolution of the USSR left each of the fifteen new states to develop their own models of church–state relations and, though most formally committed themselves to the separation of church and state, a variety of models emerged. In some a radical religious pluralism emerged, whilst in others the state in tandem with other actors sought to prevent minority entry into the religious market. Within the Russian Federation the initial position was that of absolute pluralism, and during this period many religious organisations, both domestic and international in origins, set up shop in Russia. Though the vast majority of these were probably indigenous in nature and many had deep historical roots within the country, it was the wealthy foreign-funded missionaries and the more exotic and seemingly dangerous 'sects' or 'cults' that increasingly attracted media attention. As we shall see, 'traditional' churches, nationalist politicians and the media increasingly spoke of the dangers posed to the national culture or the nation's physical and psychological health by these groups and called for legal restraints on their activities.

'Traditional religions' and the pursuit of recognition

The Russian Orthodox Church, like other traditionally dominant religious communities discussed in this study, has always denied that it seeks to become a state church or to acquire undue advantage in the new Russia. In the words of Metropolitan Kirill of Smolensk:

The era when Orthodoxy was the official state religion in the Russian Empire was far from being a 'golden' one for our Church. Accusations that the Russian Orthodox Church now wishes to regain state religion status are thus absurd. That would mean it is trying to deprive itself of freedom.[7]

Other Orthodox spokesmen stressed that even should the church wish to regain such a status, it lacked the resources and energy to develop a truly close relationship with a state that for its part was prepared to use religion but lacked any commitment to granting the church serious political influence. What the church did desire, however, was protection against unfair competition for an organisation weakened by seventy years of state atheism, and recognition that this was the religious community that had shaped Russian identity through the ages and enjoyed the support of the majority of the population.[8]

For all these disclaimers there could be little doubt that from the early 1990s onwards the Russian Orthodox Church, though lacking formal establishment, enjoyed a public status unavailable to other religious communities. Black-robed hierarchs and priests were present at most significant public occasions, with the Patriarch offering blessings at presidential inaugurations and local priests participating in the initiation of new institutions or economic ventures. For their part leading politicians of all types were keen to be seen attending religious services, to be shown on the television deep in conversation with bishops, and arguing for special protection to be granted to the Orthodox Church. Even the former party ideologist and leader of the Russian Communist Party Gennady Zyuganov constructed an ideological dish that included patriotic–Orthodox ingredients.[9] The Patriarch frequently denied any desire to get involved in political affairs and generally adopted a position supportive of the current officeholders, though he did offer the church's territory and services for mediation during the October 1993 stand-off between the president and his parliamentary opponents.[10]

The church's special position was also evident in other areas, including the military, finance, culture and education. In March 1994 Patriarch Aleksii welcomed Defence Minister Grachev to his official residence and following the meeting the two men signed an agreement beginning 'we...fully representing the Orthodox Church and the Russian Armed Forces'.[11] Not all were happy with this meeting and several Muslim spokesmen criticised the lack of religious equality in the armed forces.[12] Five years later the head of Russia's Council of Muftis Ravil Gainutdin raised this issue again, noting that the agreement with the Orthodox had led to the creation of over 100 chapels on military bases, but that the military had refused to sign any similar agreement with the Islamic community despite the fact that Muslims made up 20 per cent of conscripts.[13]

On the financial front the state continued throughout the 1990s to offer subsidies for the restoration of churches and monasteries, and granted the church several lucrative tax concessions, with that on the importation of cigarettes proving the most controversial. On the cultural front the Patriarch in 1994 signed an agreement with the Ministry of Culture on the use of religious buildings,[14] albeit one that did not prevent tensions between church leaders and cultural workers arising over the best ways of preserving important buildings and icons. Finally, the church acquired some new rights in the fields of education, though there was no serious attempt to create a network of religious-based schools along the lines found in some West European states. Instead this took the form of a rather piecemeal introduction of religious education into schools and the appearance of Orthodox symbols in prominent positions in educational establishments. Not all were happy at the intrusion of clerics into education, and one critic caustically observed:

In my time each school year opened with either a Leninist lesson or a lesson on courage. . . . The oldest pioneer leader reverently laid flowers before Lenin's bust. As God is my witness I can see no progress. Every school year must now begin with a prayer of thanksgiving for the children's happiness. Prayers are offered up for Russia. . . . The former pioneer leaders make obeisance before an icon.[15]

The 1997 law on religious associations required education to be secular in character, though it offered parents the opportunity to request additional classes in religious education. In practice, where such classes were offered they tended to have a predominantly Orthodox flavour and when it was proposed to introduce theology courses into higher education from September 2000, the guidelines laid down by the Ministry of Education envisaged that this be heavily Orthodox in orientation.[16]

In practice this growing prominence of the Orthodox Church emerged on an ad hoc rather than systematic basis. Each development added to the image of a socially and culturally dominant Orthodox Church but in terms of formal criteria for religious establishment represented a very weak movement towards the creation of a state church. Indeed, the legal settlement inherited from the last years of the Gorbachev era appeared to preclude any formal recognition of the position of the Russian Orthodox Church. The 1990 Russian law promised freedom of religion to all groups and made no special mention of the Orthodox or any other religious community. During mid-1993 the Russian parliament discussed what were described as amendments to the law, though in practice these would have changed the existing settlement beyond recognition. The prime aim of these amendments was to restrict the activities of foreign missionary organisations. The draft discussed in parliament during the early summer of 1993 was described by the Patriarch as satisfying 'the expectations of the Orthodox clergy and the people of the Church'.[17] More importantly for this section, Article 8 of the law as eventually approved required the state to 'render support' to 'the traditional confessions of the Russian Federation', these being described as 'those religious organisations whose activity preserves and develops the historical traditions and customs, national cultural originality, art and other cultural heritage of the peoples of the Russian Federation'.[18] Though these amendments fell with Yeltsin's forcible dissolution of parliament, they indicated that many within the Orthodox Church and amongst the political elite hoped to provide the dominant religious tradition with some formal recognition of its special place within the new political settlement.

Following the disbanding of parliament in October 1993, Yeltsin hastily pushed through a new constitutional draft that would reinforce his powers in relation to those of the legislative assembly. The new text offered little change in the religious sphere, promising religious equality to all, offering privileged status to none and maintaining the official commitment to a secular state and the separation of church from state. The Orthodox Church appears not to have made any serious efforts to influence the wording of these clauses, and only some of the more radical Orthodox brotherhoods offered public criticism of the existing draft. For example, at a meeting of the Christian brotherhoods shortly before the constitutional referendum in December 1993 there were calls for members to vote against the draft on the grounds that it recognised the equality of all religious believers, something that they argued made little sense in the Russian context. At the same time they recommended that in the forthcoming parliamentary elections believers should only vote for candidates committed to restoring the 1993 amendments to the law on religion.[19] In the event, the constitutional text was approved, with Article 14 proclaiming that:

The Russian Federation shall be a secular state. No religion shall be declared an official or compulsory religion. All religious associations shall be separate from the state and equal before the law.

This commitment was reinforced by Article 19, which prohibited any restriction of civil rights on the basis of religious affiliation.[20]

Over the next three and a half years various draft laws on religion were put forward, some of a restrictive nature and others more liberal in intent. One draft advanced in mid-1995 by a member of the ultra-right Liberal Democratic Party proposed defining Orthodoxy as the 'church of the majority'. A bill sponsored by the government maintained the stress on equality and singled out no religious group, but this was in turn opposed by the Orthodox who put forward their own version. From 1994 onwards around one-third of Russia's eighty-nine regions approved their own sets of laws or instructions which in many cases aimed at restricting the rights of 'non-traditional religions'. Many of these local laws imposed tight restrictions on religious activities and missionary work, though many excluded favoured groups from jumping the legal hurdles necessary to carry out such work. For example, in Murmansk exceptions were made for the Orthodox, Old Believers and Muslims, whilst in Kalmykia the governor issued a decree permitting only Buddhism, Islam and Orthodoxy to function in his province.[21]

Those arguing for a legal recognition of the 'traditional' religions did so largely in terms of protection from unfair competition or using the language of national self-preservation. In early 1997 Patriarch Aleksii could be found arguing that equality before the law did not mean that all religions were of equal significance in Russia, whilst a group of patriotic writers argued that Russian statehood had been formed in the 'bosom of Orthodoxy' and that defence of this church was essential to the effort to recreate a sense of national consciousness.[22] As originally passed in June of that year the law named four 'traditional' religions – Orthodoxy, Islam, Buddhism and Judaism – but singled out Orthodoxy as 'an inalienable part of Russia's historical, spiritual and cultural inheritance'. Islam was formally recognised as equal to Orthodoxy, and then came Judaism and Buddhism, which were respected but not inalienable parts of Russia's heritage, after which came the rest who appeared to have a more limited range of rights. Liberal deputy Valerii Borshchev suggested that as the constitution promised equality to all, the new law was in breach of the fundamental law in singling out specific religious communities, and asked why pagans and the Old Believers were not included amongst the category of traditional religions.[23]

Public opinion seemed equally unenthusiastic about the proposed changes, with one survey indicating that 49 per cent of Russians disagreed with the privileging of the Orthodox Church, though a substantial minority (27 per cent) felt that it should be given special treatment.[24] Boris Yeltsin also appeared sceptical, for initially he vetoed the law on the basis of its seeming breach of both the constitution and international agreements to which Russia had signed up. In particular he opposed the unconstitutional privileging of Orthodoxy. Yet in October 1997 he proved willing to sign a very slightly amended version of the law that still failed to answer many of his earlier criticisms. In its new redaction the preamble to the law affirmed the rights of all to freedom of conscience and described Russia as a secular state, but went on to refer to:

the special role of Orthodoxy in the history of Russia and in the establishment and development of its spirituality and culture; respecting Christianity, Islam, Buddhism, Judaism and other religions constituting an integral part of the historical heritage of the peoples of Russia.[25]

Broadly speaking this phrasing satisfied representatives of the 'traditional' religions, as well as some of the more conventional Christian groups who now had gained some form of constitutional approval, albeit in a preamble which offered nobody specific rights or obligations and had no formal legal implications. In the years after adoption of the 1997 law there were occasional attempts to strengthen the status of traditional religions further – as in 1999 when the LDPR returned to the fray with suggestions that legal recognition should be restricted to those groups which had functioned in Russia for over 100 years and that the 'traditional' status should only be granted to Orthodoxy and Islam.[26] But these were essentially proposals from the fringe of the political elite and, though President Putin has exhibited a more genuine understanding of Orthodoxy than his predecessor or other politicians and has been respectful of the church, he has been unwilling to permit it political influence or further legal privilege.[27]

During his first two years in office Putin made few detailed comments about religion. Where he did discuss it was in relation to 'religious extremism' associated with Chechen fighters or the events of 11 September 2001, or in the condemnation of foreign missionaries to be found in the National Security Concept adopted shortly after he became president. From the middle of 2001, several versions of a quasi-official state religious policy were produced by state bodies. In each the emphasis was very much on the maintenance of a secular state, in which 'traditional' religious communities were to enjoy greater respect but no formal privileging. More noteworthy, however, was the proposal for the re-creation of a state body responsible for monitoring religious affairs which some saw as harking back to Soviet-era religious controls, though a few suggested that such a body might help to prevent the dominance of any single religion.[28] Then in early 2002 a law amending the 1997 law was introduced into the Russian parliament that spoke of different categories of 'traditional' religious groups. 'Traditional religious organisations' were those which had possessed a centralised organisation on the territory of the Russian Federation for at least fifty years, with over one million members, and which were 'an inalienable part of the historical, spiritual and cultural heritage of the peoples of Russia'. Then came 'traditional religious organisations of individual peoples of the Russian Federation present for over fifty years and with over 100,000 members and which were part of the heritage of those peoples'. Thirdly came 'historical traditional religious organisations' which could be centralised or local organisations present for no fewer than fifty years and were thus also part of the heritage of the country. Finally were representatives of 'foreign traditional religious organisations' which were part of the heritage of the corresponding states. The authors of this law claimed that whilst this would allot state preferences it would not entail any encroachment on freedom of conscience or the rights of religious minorities.[29] At the time of writing, the status of this draft remains unclear, but in the form described here it does appear to reinforce distinctions and offer differential rights to religious groups and in language at least to continue the formal privileging of some groups over others. And how this will tie in or reinforce Putin's seeming commitment to a secular state in which Orthodoxy has primary respect but no privilege remains to be seen.

Handling 'otherness': regulating religious pluralism

The RSFSR law 'on freedom of worship' approved at the end of 1990 confirmed and deepened the legal guarantees of religious freedom contained in the USSR law on freedom of conscience approved in October of that year. The Russian law offered religious freedom to all and guaranteed the right of each individual to hold religious beliefs or none, and to change them as they wished. At the same time it promised equality to all religious groups, the separation of religion from the state, and stated that citizens and foreign residents would enjoy the same rights with regard to religious freedom. Some regulatory features of the old system were retained, with those religious organisations seeking juridical personality required to register with the appropriate central or local authorities, but the underlying assumption was that providing there was no breach of the law any groups of believers who so chose would be granted registration. At the same time it was made clear that Russian courts were to consider international agreements entered into by the state on matters relating to religion as legally superior should they clash with the Russian law.[30]

The de facto consequence of this law, and the rapidly changing political atmosphere in Russia, was the creation of a religious free market and the temporary reduction of the state's role in the religious sphere, though arguably this was as much a product of the generally chaotic nature of administrative life in the early 1990s as of principle. In this context existing religious communities experienced considerable growth in institutional terms and saw participation in their activities increase. For most of the major institutions this entailed a reopening of previously closed places of worship, and the legalisation of many minority communities that had previously functioned 'underground' or semi-legally. At the same time the hierarchical churches were faced with acute personnel shortages as a growing number of individuals sought a religious celebration of the major rites of passage. Alongside these developments came the emergence of 'new religious movements': some, such as the White Brotherhood or Mother of God Centre, indigenous to the country, and others coming from outside. Yet many of the Protestant and neo-Christian groups seen as 'new' had in fact deep historical roots in Russia. These included the Baptists, Adventists, Pentecostals and the Jehovah's Witnesses, and even the Hare Krishnas had been active since the late 1970s. Others such as the 'health and wealth' branches of Pentecostalism or Scientology had hardly begun to penetrate the country prior to 1990.

For many commentators, and indeed for the general public, the facts were less important than the wider perception that this relatively lightly regulated market situation was permitting an 'invasion of the sects' which was leading to the break-up of families and undermining the position of the 'traditional' religious communities. The reality was more complex, for whilst there were a few well-publicised and well-financed religious campaigns by outside religious activists, much of the missionary work being done within the Russian Federation was the work of individual enthusiasts, sometimes alone and sometimes in collaboration with indigenous believers. Whilst critics spoke of five million drawn into the poorly defined category of 'new religious movements', informed commentators gave much more conservative estimates. For example, Sergei Filatov suggested that at most 10,000 people had stayed with the indigenous White Brotherhood, Vissarionites and Mother of God Centre, whilst less than 5,000 had been attracted for any length of time to the Moonies. Moreover, some of these groups, including the Roman Catholics and the Hare Krishnas, had publicly stated their concern to avoid 'illegitimate' forms of proselytism. Orthodox concerns were understandable, insofar as in a few parts of the country non-Orthodox movements did outnumber the national church in terms of both institutions and personnel, but were clearly exaggerated.[31]

In the face of this perceived growth of religious organisations and movements it was perhaps not surprising to find the Orthodox leadership during the early 1990s beginning to ask whether the religious free market was getting out of control. We shall explore the arguments in a later chapter, but broadly speaking the church's critique focused on their own inability to cope with 'unfair competition' as a result of seven decades of institutionalised anti-religion, and the improper methods being utilised by some of the minority religious groups which they felt focused too heavily on the vulnerable elements within society and deliberately sought to 'poach' from the Orthodox flock.[32] These arguments were taken up elsewhere in the public arena, with the newly free media finding the activities of religious 'cults' irresistible, and politicians seeing the potential political advantage in associating with the cause of the Orthodox Church. In June 1993 the liberal nationalist politician Sergei Stankevich was writing about the destruction of families by 'exotic sects' and called for greater legal controls over their entry to Russia. Around this time the press published a series of articles on sectarian activity and carried pleas from anxious parents who had 'lost' their children to unfamiliar religious groups.[33] All of this provided the background to the first abortive attempt in the spring and summer of 1993 to change the regulatory framework within which religious organisations functioned.

The proposed amendments produced by the parliamentary committee on freedom of conscience in collaboration with a council of experts were made known to a restricted audience in late 1992, but almost at once met with a storm of protest from the major religious communities.[34] For the Orthodox the major problems stemmed from the failure of the drafters to involve the church and the perception that the changes would reintroduce a high degree of state control over religious life. At the same time Patriarch Aleksii, in a letter to committee chairman Fr Polosin, argued that the text as proposed would do little to combat the activities of rich foreign missionary organisations that were carrying out illegitimate proselytising activities within the country. Discussion continued over the following months and in June 1993 the bill, which effectively replaced rather than amended the 1990 law, was given a preliminary airing in the upper chamber of the Supreme Soviet. During this debate Fr Polosin argued that whilst the 1990 law had been a positive step forward, the legislators had not foreseen the entry to the country of a huge number of sects whose activities were disrupting families and causing social concern. For that reason the proposal aimed at limiting the possibilities open to foreign-based organisations, which could no longer function in Russia without an invitation from an officially recognised indigenous religious organisation.

Perhaps inevitably these provisions elicited a hostile response from Protestants and Catholics, the former concerned at the restriction of missionary activity and the latter concerned at how the clauses on foreign-based organisations would affect religious orders and the position of the majority of priests who were not Russian citizens. During the early summer debate continued and on 14 July the slightly amended bill had its first formal reading, resulting in its approval by an overwhelming majority. Human rights activists, religious activists and some legal experts continued to protest – with Yuri Rosenbaum, one of the drafters of the 1990 law, describing the draft as contravening international agreements and involving the state in heresy hunting[35] – but with the support of the Orthodox hierarchy and some parts of the Muslim leadership the bill was sent forward for presidential approval. After some delay he sent it back unsigned, arguing that in its present form the law contradicted the constitution and international agreements to which Russia had assented, and therefore Yeltsin asked for changes despite supporting the law's general intention to provide a more appropriate regulatory framework. In the subsequent second reading held on 27 August the parliamentary committee chairman noted Yeltsin's expressions of concern over the general state of spirituality in Russia, and therefore proposed introducing a new section in Article 8 as follows:

The state renders support to religious organisations whose activities preserve and develop the historical traditions and customs, the national–cultural distinctiveness, art and cultural heritage of the peoples of the Russian Federation.[36]

The presidential representative taking part in the debate expressed his unease about the formulation but it was immediately approved by parliament, as were the retention of the clauses banning foreign missionary activity. In practice the debate proved pointless because at the end of September Yeltsin dissolved parliament and the proposed law fell with the rump assembly, though the debate was far from finished.

Though the draft law fell, by the mid-1990s many regions within the Federation were beginning to develop their own regulatory framework for religious organisations and in most cases these tended to be restrictive in nature. According to Homer and Uzzell the first such documents appeared in Kazan during 1993 when the mayor issued an ordinance that spoke of the protests engendered by the activities of charismatic groups, whilst in September 1994 the Tatar republic proposed banning all 'totalitarian charismatic groups'.[37] In some areas there was little concern for legal regulation and much depended upon the whim of officials, as in the northern province of Arkhangelsk where the authorities who once granted a Baptist group land to build a church suddenly took it back, arguing that the Baptists were 'not our people'.[38] Perhaps best known off all were the regulations produced in the Tula region at the end of 1994, rules that were to became a model for other regions in subsequent years. Such regional laws, affecting around one-third of Russia's eighty-nine regions by 1996, varied from region to region. According to Homer and Uzzell, they generally included a tightening of procedures for the legal recognition of religious communities, intrusive monitoring of religious life, discrimination against 'foreign' groups, limits on the use of public space and free speech, and violations of the rule of law by local officials who often enjoyed considerable discretion in deciding which particular groups to harass.[39] At the same time, members of religious minority communities in some areas reported that the Tula draft was being promoted by local Orthodox hierarchs as a model to follow, and that in individual cases the local clergy were behind efforts to restrict the activities of religious groups. There were also suggestions that the new situation was permitting the de facto revival of the careers of former officials of the Soviet-era Council for Religious Affairs, many of whom were reappearing as expert advisers to local administrations.[40]

At the centre the Russian Orthodox Church, in alliance with several politicians and newspaper outlets, maintained its campaign for a more restrictive approach throughout the mid-1990s, with Patriarch Aleksii arguing for a much greater selectivity by local officials and media outlets in deciding which religious groups could take up airtime or make use of public facilities.[41] Towards the end of 1995 the government sponsored a new bill stressing the equality of all religious groups and opposing the privileging of any single denomination, but this was strongly opposed by parliamentary supporters of the church.[42] During 1996 there took place a series of debates and a process of constant redrafting which eventually produced a new draft law similar to the proposed amendments of 1993. That favoured by the Patriarchate would have banned the activities of foreign religious organisations unless their activities were carried out under the auspices of the recognised Russian communities who invited them. At the same time, it required a re-registration process for all religious communities that would enable the authorities to check up on their activities and ensure that they were not responsible for 'violating public morality' or 'stirring up religious tension'.[43] The draft law 'on freedom of religion and religious associations' which eventually emerged towards the end of 1996 went a long way to meet the demands of the Russian Orthodox Church. Even then not all were satisfied, and in a letter to the press in January 1997 a group of 'patriotic' writers argued that only the traditional religions should be permitted to have access to the media or undertake charitable and educational activity. One month later a meeting of the Orthodox bishops' council proposed a reference to the Russian Orthodox Church as the 'church of the majority'.[44]

The details of the parliamentary debate have been adequately described elsewhere and need not concern us here. As noted earlier the law approved in late July 1997 was initially vetoed by Yeltsin on the grounds that it breached the constitution and international agreements entered into by Russia, that it contradicted itself by describing the state as secular and then permitted the state to make religious judgements, and gave one religious community an inappropriately privileged position. Over the next eight weeks the president was subject to extensive, and possibly counterproductive, lobbying from outside of Russia and sustained pressure from the country's Orthodox hierarchy and parts of the parliamentary establishment. In consequence, in late September Yeltsin approved virtually the same law he had objected to in July. And whilst it might be argued that the drafters of the law were responding to some legitimate concerns, there can be little doubt that from a legal and human rights perspective the text of the law as eventually approved was problematic. In particular, Russian legal scholars pointed out that in several respects the final version contradicted constitutional provisions for religious equality and freedom of association, and for the equal treatment of foreigners. It also breached the constitutional ban on the imposition of retroactive legislation insofar as it worsened the situation for already registered religious associations if they could not prove they had been around for fifteen years (see below).[45]

Various features of the law as finally approved met with a critical response from domestic and international human rights experts.[46] Above all many pointed to the element of inequality implicit in the distinction between traditional and non-traditional groups, though other parts of the law as well as the constitution promised religious equality to all. Further distinctions were also made between centralised and local religious communities, and between religious organisations and religious groups. Registered organisations duly registered with the Ministry of Justice enjoyed not just juridical personality, but a wide range of rights to carry out worship, purchase property, employ people, produce literature, carry out charitable work and conduct services in prisons, hospitals and other public organisations, and develop contacts and joint projects with foreign religious communities. Members of religious groups not registered with the state simply had the right to meet in premises belonging to members and propagate the faith amongst their own members. The situation was further complicated by registration requirements that required those seeking legal recognition to provide documentary evidence that they had legally existed on the territory in question for at least fifteen years. As this meant that they had to have existed during the early 1980s it seemed possible that interventionist local officials could use this clause to deny recognition to many groups that had functioned for decades but had been denied recognition during the Soviet period. Amongst such groups were many Baptist and Pentecostal communities, and the Roman Catholics who had only a handful of places of worship in 1982 but by the mid-1990s had nearly 200 functioning parishes. Even should 'new' groups acquire registration, if they could not meet the fifteen-year requirement they had to undertake the onerous and bureaucratic registration process on an annual basis until they had existed for the necessary length of time. For those groups struggling to achieve registration one option would be to unite in a centralised religious organisation, defined by possession of three local communities, for once created all parishes belonging to that organisation would receive registration automatically. At the same time only those centralised organisations that could prove a *legal* existence of fifty years or more could utilise the word 'Russian' in their title, effectively limiting its usage to the Russian Orthodox Church. Finally, all existing religious communities were obliged to re-register by the end of 1999 or face liquidation.

Almost immediately it became apparent that the fifteen-year rule would create problems, especially given the law's general tendency to allow discretion to local officials in interpreting which groups had existed legally prior to 1982. On a strict interpretation over half of the religious congregations functioning by the mid-1990s had no formal legal recognition prior to that date, though many could get around this by joining up with a centralised religious union – a tactic adopted by many Pentecostal and charismatic groups. Others utilised their Soviet prison records or court judgements showing that they had been sentenced for the act of creating a congregation under the old regime, and suggested this provided evidence of a de facto functioning religious community. This approach appears to have been accepted by the Ministry of Justice, which several months after the passage of the law issued an instruction explaining to local officials that religious communities were only required to provide proof of existence not formal legal recognition.[47]

Such interpretations did not prevent local officials from using the new law to justify restrictive actions against those religious communities they disliked. For example, in the Khakassian Republic the local official responsible for religious affairs, Nikolai Volkov, took a very strict line in his dealings with the revived Lutheran community and the charismatic Glorification Church, both of whom he saw as non-traditional churches. In each case he sought to close them down on the grounds that they had not existed for the requisite fifteen years, and seemed particularly perturbed by the fact that the activist Lutheran deacon did not confine himself to work amongst the German population of the region. During the autumn of 1998 the church was briefly closed down, though the community produced documents showing Lutheran activity in the region since 1972, and in practice the local court's decision was quickly overturned by a Supreme Court judge.[48] On occasions the fate of religious communities could depend upon the vagaries of electoral politics, as in the southern city of Taganrog where some 7,000 Muslims had been seeking to rebuild a mosque demolished in the Soviet period. Having been granted a plot towards the end of 2000 the community found its site under attack by Cossacks, who joined with local Orthodox priests on a television programme in which it was claimed that the mosque was being funded by Chechen field commanders and would become a centre of fanaticism. Fearful of losing his position to the Communist Party candidate in forthcoming mayoral elections, it appears that the incumbent chose to block construction of the new mosque despite earlier agreements.[49]

During the late 1990s the law continued to be used in some areas as a justification for the harassment of minority religious groups, but the situation varied considerably across the territory of the Russian Federation, with some areas witnessing the emergence of genuine religious pluralism and others seeing attempts to close down or severely limit minority religious activity. Even within regions differences emerged, as in Rostov-on-Don where the city authorities adopted a restrictive approach to Protestant communities whilst the regional authorities let them worship without any hindrance.[50] Restrictive practice varied considerably, but in many areas local officials used the law to prevent 'non-traditional' religious groups from making use of public property – as in Tula where the Baptists and Adventists lost the right to make use of a local cinema, despite the appeals of the institution's manager who needed the rent – or carrying out preaching and evangelistic activities in public squares.[51]

A further consequence of the law related to the activities of foreign believers, whether those living and working in Russia generally or those seeking to carry out religious work within the Federation. According to Jeremy Gunn the law in its original form could be interpreted so as to prevent a group of Indian Hindu engineers currently working in Moscow from holding meetings to discuss Krishna or Vishnu.[52] More importantly perhaps, the law left unclear the position of foreign religious activists working within Russia, though its intention to reduce the number of missionaries was made clear during parliamentary debates. For institutional churches such as the Roman Catholic Church the problem was exacerbated by an instruction from the Ministry of Justice stating that only Russian residents could serve religious communities, a provision that if interpreted in a rigid fashion would deprive the majority of Catholic parishes of pastoral care.[53] In consequence of this stance priests in various parts of the country had to make repeated trips to Poland or elsewhere to gain the necessary visas, often given for short periods, to work in Russia.[54] For the Protestant communities the major problems affected the independent Pentecostal, charismatic and evangelical communities who invited foreign missionaries to preach or pastor their flocks, or which in some cases were created as a result of foreign initiatives. In the latter cases political considerations occasionally played a role, as in the Kirov region where one Orthodox priest argued that whilst the Americans were bombing Yugoslavia it would be impossible to find any common ground with the Baptists. More radical still were comments emanating in mid-2000 from officials and clergy in the Russian far east who suggested that the emergence of missionary groups in that region were part of a wider US plan to annex the territory to America.[55] Of course such arguments were extreme, but the fact that they were brought into use to justify constraints on missionary activity is symptomatic of a wider concern to limit the actions of 'non-traditional' religious groups.

What became apparent in the year or so following the introduction of the new law was the degree of licence it gave to local officials to develop their own religious policies, with some choosing benign neutrality and others adopting an extremely hostile attitude towards minority religions in general or picking out particular communities for harassment. According to Larry Uzzell there was initially no systematic worsening of the situation of 'non-traditional' groups but a general reinforcement of the attitude of those determined to bring to an end their activities.[56] This affected not only state officials but also extreme nationalist groups in some communities who saw the law as providing justification for physical attacks on 'alien' religious elements. For example, in early 1998 at an evangelical rally in Yoshkar-Ola members of the Russian National Unity Party sought to disrupt the meeting by giving Nazi salutes and handing out anti-Semitic literature.[57] Such attacks were often encouraged by the reporting of the local press, which in some areas singled out specific religious communities for denigration and sensationalist reporting. In the Krasnodar region several media outlets devoted many column inches to the local charismatic groups who were carrying out street evangelism, whilst papers throughout the country devoted considerable attention to the Jehovah's Witnesses, described in one central newspaper as amongst the most 'odious' sects in Russia.[58]

The framers of the law had argued that its aim was to combat the activities of 'destructive sects' and 'totalitarian cults', and not to curb the legitimate activities of religious minorities, but the text of the document made no reference at all to brainwashing, kidnapping of children, abusive proselytism or any of the other activities ascribed to such groups in the debate leading up to the law's adoption. An early survey of its impact suggested that the law as such was rarely applied to the more 'obvious' groups but largely to indigenous religious communities. Thus, of sixty-nine incidents recorded by Elliott and Corrado, some fifty-two affected Protestants (thirty-seven of them indigenous communities), eight Roman Catholics, and only five groups described by them as 'cults'. In addition, one Old Believer community and six Orthodox groups had been affected by the law: the former could not be more 'Russian' and the latter were groups engaged in 'reformist' activity or refusing to accept the authority of the Moscow Patriarchate.[59]

Though many of the problems affecting religious minorities arise from the 1997 law, other issues have also aroused controversy. Non-traditional communities have expressed unease about the negative and often sensationalist reporting of their activities in the media. Police harassment and detention of those involved in missionary work is frequent, with complaints coming from Catholics, Pentecostals, Mormons and others about document checks of those attending quite legal church meetings. More importantly, some sources suggests that less than 80 per cent of these cases are reported because people outside of the metropolitan centres still fear reprisals if they protest official or quasi-official actions.[60] The other persistent problem that has nothing to do with the 1997 law arises from the failure of Russia to adopt legislation on conscientious objection, despite the recognition of this as a basic right in the 1993 constitution (Article 59). Russia in 1919 became one of the first states to make provision for alternative service, but this came to an end in 1939 and conscription became the norm. During the mid-1990s several Jehovah's Witnesses were jailed for refusing to serve or forcibly transferred to army units, and the problem of conscientious objection was exacerbated further by the war in Chechnya which led increasing numbers of draftees to claim religious or moral objections to this specific conflict.[61]

Perhaps inevitably, the vagueness of sections of the law and the manner in which it was implemented in the years following 1997 led to legal challenges being mounted both to specific aspects of implementation and the law as a whole. Simultaneously there were some individuals within the state apparatus, particularly within the Ministry of Justice responsible for supervising the law's application, who appeared keen to soften some of its more controversial features. Conversely, other official agencies brought cases before the courts in an effort to use its terms to restrict the activities of religious minorities. During the autumn of 1998, for example, the Moscow procuracy sought to close down the local community of Jehovah's Witnesses under Article 14 of the 1997 law, which listed the reasons for depriving religious communities of registration. When the judge dismissed some of the sloppy argumentation used by the procurator – for example, attempting to denigrate the Witnesses by pointing to their failure to celebrate Christmas – the Moscow Directorate of Justice intervened to cite three more specific grounds for their dissolution: the refusal to undertake military service, the destruction of families and the infringement of the rights of the person arising from their doorstep evangelism. Though the case was protracted, the procuracy's case was rather undermined in May 1999 when the Ministry of Justice somewhat reluctantly agreed to register the central organisations of the Jehovah's Witnesses – though this has not prevented their communities from facing an uphill struggle to register in many places.[62]

In late 1998 two challenges to the law were mounted in the constitutional court, one brought by the charismatic Glorification Church in the Khakassian Republic and one by the Jehovah's Witnesses in Yaroslavl. Both of these communities had been refused registration under Article 27, which required that they provide evidence of a fifteen-year existence, though by the time the case reached the court in October 1999 both had been registered as members of a centralised religious organisation. At the preliminary hearing Constitutional Court Judge Valeri Zorkin received a letter from the administration's human rights ombudsman Oleg Mironov arguing that the law encouraged discrimination against some faith communities, and from Andrei Sebentsov, adviser to the prime minister on church–state relations, which suggested that as nearly two-thirds of existing religious communities had not been registered in 1990 the letter of the law would lead to the curtailment of the activities of many groups. Against this Duma deputy Valeri Lazarev argued that the fifteen-year rule gave the authorities time to check out the teachings and activities of unknown groups and ensure that they did represent a genuine religious trend. Judge Zorkin responded by asking whether it would then be appropriate to apply a similar rule to political parties. One month later the constitutional court ruled that the Article was constitutional. Simultaneously it argued that this should not be taken to mean that those organisations existing prior to the adoption of the law or belonging to centralised organisations would have to meet the fifteen-year requirement or be subject to annual re-registration. This would only apply to groups created after adoption of the law. More controversially, in explaining its judgement the court made rather loose use of terms such as 'sects' – which the ruling allowed the government to ban – 'recruitment' and 'psychological pressure', phrasing calculated to give administrative officials considerable leeway in denigrating or harassing minority groups. The judgement did not, however, do away with the distinction made between religious groups and religious organisations, and maintained the discretion available to local authorities in interpreting what was to count as evidence for fifteen years of existence for those communities who did not belong to centralised religious organisations.[63] For all this, during 1999–2000 a number of religious congregations were able to gain recognition by going to the courts, which frequently criticised the inadequacy of the evidence provided by local officials and administrators.[64]

Under the terms of the 1997 law all religious organisations were required to register by the end of 1999 or face closure, yet by the end of that year only about half had managed to do so, and eventually parliament approved and President-elect Putin signed a decree extending the period until the end of 2000, albeit with the proviso that those not registered by then would automatically lose their legal recognition.[65] Yet this extension proved too late in some areas, notably in the Voronezh region where in early 2000 the authorities not only proposed that parliament adopt a harsher law but also instituted court proceedings against twelve Christian and one Jewish organisations that had not acquired registration by the end of the previous year – though these actions were later dropped after central intervention.[66] When the revised deadline was reached at the end of 2000 it appeared that around 40 per cent of those desiring registration had still failed to achieve it. In some cases this was because they had not turned in sufficient information, in others because the local administration had failed to handle their applications in time, and in yet others because officials simply refused to recognise specific religious groups.[67] Despite appeals from the parliamentary commissioner for human rights President Putin refused to support an extension of the registration period. In consequence, officials in some regions have been able to use delaying tactics in order to deny registration to groups they dislike, occasionally in collusion with Orthodox bishops, as in the Kolomna region where Metropolitan Yuvenali sought to hinder construction of a mosque in mid-2001.[68] Despite this, most sources suggest that where federal decision-making bodies have become involved the process of registration has proceeded smoothly in most cases.

Under Putin efforts to recentralise power in general may have helped minority religious groups insofar as there is an effort to bring local practices into conformity with those favoured by Moscow. Nonetheless, some regional authorities have persisted in efforts to create their own legislative regulation of religious bodies. For example, in 2001 the Belgorod regional parliament adopted an anti-missionary law that went beyond previous laws that attempted to ban foreign missionary activity in seeking to prevent any dissemination of religious beliefs outside the walls of recognised religious institutions. Yet the federal security and justice ministries have repeatedly expressed unease about such laws and have attempted to minimise their importance.[69] Certain religious communities – notably the Jehovah's Witnesses, Mormons and some Pentecostal-charismatic groups – have also faced persistent problems as officials, Orthodox clerics, the media and 'anti-cult' specialists seek to restrict their activities. In Moscow the ongoing attempt to ban the Moscow branch of the Jehovah's Witnesses was reopened in mid-2002 despite the Justice Ministry's formal recognition of the movement.[70] And in late 2001 the banning of the Moscow branch of the Salvation Army as a militaristic organisation attracted international attention, though a February 2002 Constitutional Court ruling appeared to override this decision based on a contested understanding of the 1997 law.[71] Moreover, it is clear that some elements within the political elite remain hostile towards genuine religious pluralism, as is evident in the various draft laws on 'extremism' circulating in the first half of 2002. After much discussion a hybrid presidential bill was passed in the lower house of the Duma at the end of June, though this remains to be approved by the president and Federation Council. This defined 'religious extremism' in terms of activities aimed at subverting the constitutional order, encouraging terrorism, inciting religious or other forms of hatred, and propaganda of religious superiority.[72]

At the time of writing it is impossible to evaluate the possible implications of this law for religious minorities, but in general their position within Russia remains fluid and interpretation of the 1997 law still varies from region to region. Some areas have become notable for their tolerance towards religious minorities, whilst the authorities in others such as Cheboksary or Lipetsk continue to harass those groups seen as non-traditional.[73] Equally, it remains the case that the choice of which group to harass depends very much upon the attitude and enthusiasm of local officials, thus confirming the view of critics that one of the more unsatisfactory aspects of the law was the degree of discretion it gave to local authorities. Though in some regions there is little restriction of the rights of religious minorities, it is probably the case that of the five countries we have surveyed so far it is the Russian Federation that has found it hardest to come to terms with religious pluralism.

Sketches from the successor states

With the achievement of independent status at the end of 1991 each of the fifteen successor states began to develop their own policies towards religious institutions and to think afresh about the place of religion in public life. Formally, all committed themselves to the establishment of full religious liberty after decades of state-directed anti-religious activity, but in practice the extent to which some religions were favoured and others discriminated against varied from country to country. In this section we offer six sketches, illustrating development in three regions of the former USSR: the Baltic, the Caucasus and Central Asia. Each of the countries discussed is relatively small, and historically they are rooted in different religious traditions: Catholic, Protestant, Orthodox, Armenian-Catholic and Muslim. Though all of them are associated with a dominant tradition, Latvia's Catholic and Protestant communities are in reality fairly evenly matched, whilst in Kyrgyzstan a sizeable Slavic-European population has created a significant Christian minority. Whilst these sketches focus on the issues of 'recognition' and discrimination dealt with in the other case studies, they are inevitably less detailed. Their purpose is to give a flavour of the trends emerging in the 1990s and into the new century and thus enrich our later discussion of the factors that may serve to shape the politics of religious liberty in transitional societies.

Lithuania

The southern Baltic republic of Lithuania has a proud history of state-hood dating back to the mid-thirteenth century, but around 1386–7 formed an alliance with Poland that led to the acceptance of Christianity by Lithuania's rulers. This alliance lasted into the eighteenth century, until successive partitions of Poland led to the country becoming a part of the Russian Empire, albeit with the maintenance of strong Polish in-fluences. As a result of the First World War Lithuania regained its inde-pendence and, after a brief period of democracy, was ruled by author-itarian regimes from 1926 until the Molotov–Ribbentrop Pact of 1939 led to military occupation by the Red Army. After a period of terror the Soviets were thrown out by the advancing Nazi forces in 1941 and during their dominance around 200,000 of the country's Jews were mur-dered, before the Red Army returned bringing further terror and im-posing a new political system in which all key decisions were taken in Moscow.[74]

The imposition of Soviet rule met some resistance in Lithuania and not until the early 1950s were the anti-Moscow partisans effectively de-feated. In the meantime some 40,000 had lost their lives as a direct result of civil war, whilst tens of thousands of people described as 'represen-tatives of the bourgeoisie' had been imprisoned or deported to Siberia and the Russian far east. For the dominant Catholic Church these early years were especially harsh, with the execution of one leading hierarch and the deportation of many others. Here as elsewhere in the Soviet Union church property was confiscated, religious education prohibited and priests closely monitored by state agencies. After Khrushchev's fall in 1964 there was some moderation of anti-religious policies, but no let-up in the state's efforts to appoint compliant church leaders and limit the number of those entering religious life. Despite this, during the 1960s and 1970s the Catholic Church was to play a major role in promoting the defence of religious, national and civil rights. From 1972–89 the samizdat *Chronicle of the Lithuanian Catholic Church* published eighty-one volumes focused mainly but not exclusively on the abuse of religious rights, and activist priests joined with secular intellectuals in a wider campaign for liberalisation.[75]

The accession of Mikhail Gorbachev to power in Moscow was to prove a turning point in Soviet history and the Baltic states were to be amongst the first to take advantage of the new freedoms that emerged from 1987 onwards. Though the church supported democratisation in general it was wary of getting too deeply involved in the Sajudis movement created in mid-1988, an organisation that quickly moved from an advocacy of greater autonomy to the campaign for independence. Nonetheless, as a result of political change the church acquired greater freedoms as the 'national church' was given increasing prominence in public life. For all this the public role of the Catholic Church since the achievement of independence has been far more subdued than some had hoped and others feared. Despite the existence of a Christian Democratic Party few politicians looked to clerics for advice on policy-making, whilst the church itself has turned inward to some extent as it faces a reality where the initial religious enthusiasm of the early 1990s has ebbed.[76] Though over 70 per cent of Lithuanians still consider themselves to be Catholic most reports suggest that only 10–15 per cent of the population regularly attend church. Other religious communities active in the republic include the Orthodox and Old Believers – mainly drawing in the Russian population; a variety of Protestant organisations – including Lutherans, Reformed, Baptists, Pentecostals and Adventists, as well as newer charismatic groups; Muslims, Jews and various 'new religious movements'. Though there is some public discussion of the 'sect' issue, those involved in new religious movements probably number less than 3,000.

With regard to the issue of formal 'recognition' there is no legal privileging of the Roman Catholic Church as such, and Article 43 of the constitution adopted in 1992 explicitly rules out the creation of a state religion. This same article does, however, speak of the state recognising 'traditional Lithuanian churches and religious organisations, as well as other churches and religious organisations, provided that they have a basis in society and their teaching and rituals do not contradict morality or the law'. Those groups categorised as traditional were defined in the 1995 Law on Religious Communities as the Latin and Greek rite Catholics, Lutherans, Reformed, Orthodox and Old Believers, Jews, Sunni Muslims and Karaites. These groups are differentiated from other groups primarily by having the right to receive financial assistance from the state, to buy land and to teach their religious beliefs in state schools where parents request this. In May 1999 parliament amended the law on religious communities to provide state funding for the educational institutions of traditional religious organisations.[77] Officials have defined 'traditional' as those organisations that have been active in Lithuania for more than 300–400 years, so most other groups have little hope of achieving this status. At the same time it has not been ruled out that other groups might come to join the category of 'state recognised' if they can prove their positive contribution to Lithuanian society over a period of twenty-five years. The original law appeared to envisage such groups having the same rights as 'traditional' ones, but subsequent legislation appeared to strengthen the status of the latter.[78] In 1998 the Baptists, who had been present in Lithuania for 150 years, applied for traditional status but had their application turned down by parliament. In 2000 they applied for 'recognised' status and this was eventually granted on 12 July 2001, though it only gave them the right for certain tax privileges and their clergy exemption from military service. Still lacking, however, was the possibility of owning land, or teaching religion in school.[79]

Where the Catholic Church does enjoy some informal 'recognition' is in the presence of religious dignitaries at public functions, and through special agreements between the state and the Vatican signed in August 2000. Amongst other things these provide for cooperation in the sphere of education, recognition of military chaplains, and the addition of Assumption Day to the list of other religious holidays recognised by the state.[80] More ambiguously, because of the religious demography of the country it also likely that the flavour of religious education in school for those whose parents choose it will be predominantly Catholic. In practice, none of these developments has served to constrain the activities of religious minorities and most religious groups that wish to register with the state have been permitted to do so. Whilst traditional groups do not have to register their statutes to achieve legal status, other groups have to do so and two have seen their applications turned down – a meditation centre and the Lithuanian pagan community. Another exception was the Chabad Lubavich community, which the Ministry of Justice originally argued was not 'traditional' to the country, but in mid-1999 the Ministry eventually recognised it as such.[81] Though minorities occasionally complain that officials favour the Catholic Church, by and large those seeking to establish churches, carry out youth or missionary work, and organise charitable activities have been able to do so.[82]

As suggested earlier the 'sect problem' has not loomed as large here as in some of the successor states. Nonetheless, in April 2000 the government responded to parliamentary pressures and created an intergovernmental commission to investigate whether the activities of religious or spiritual groups complied with the law. Subsequently it has been reported that the security services maintain some degree of surveillance over the activities of groups deemed to be 'cults', including the Unification Church, the Jehovah's Witnesses and the Russian-based 'Vissarionites'.[83] Despite this, it is probably true that of all the countries discussed in this study Lithuania's national church is amongst the least formally privileged 'national' church, whilst its minorities have experienced very little in the way of legal and institutional constraints.

Latvia

In many respects Latvia's political history parallels that of Lithuania, with dominance by external forces the norm for much of its existence.

Russian influence began to grow under Peter the Great who attached the northern parts of the country, including the capital Riga, to the Empire in 1721 whilst the rest was gradually incorporated over the next eighty years. During the nineteenth century ordinary Latvians experienced what some saw as a double occupation, as the fact of Russian rule was largely disguised by the dominance on the ground of German-speaking nobility. One feature of this Germanic influence was the promotion of the Lutheran Church as the church of the nation, albeit one closely controlled by secular powers for long periods of its existence and also having to compete with a substantial Catholic community. The outbreak of war in 1914 led to chaos followed by the creation of independent statehood, but as in Lithuania this experiment was brought to an end by the Molotov–Ribbentrop Pact and the subsequent fifty years of Soviet dominance, interrupted only briefly by the Nazi occupation.

Soviet rule in Latvia was much more overtly Russian-dominated than in Lithuania and despite occasional protests the republic witnessed little of the national and religious dissent characteristic of its Catholic neighbour. Only under Gorbachev did social activism develop and only then did religious activists seeking to revitalise the Lutheran Church also begin to participate in the activities of an emerging civil society.[84] Though prominent for a brief period religious organisations and religious issues featured only marginally in the transition process and during the initial years of the democratisation of Latvia. For most such groups the primary focus in the 1990s was on internal reform, coming to terms with the new order and trying to find ways of retaining and gaining members in a largely secular society. Unlike the Lithuanian Catholics, the Lutherans in Latvia generally lacked strong ties to the wider society and only around 15 per cent of the population belonged to the church in any formal sense, though some surveys suggested that nearly 40 per cent of the population considered themselves to be Lutheran.[85] There was also a far greater degree of religious variety here, in part a product of the much larger Russian population much of which claimed to be Orthodox. Baptists, Pentecostals and other evangelicals competed with the Lutherans for the Protestant 'share of the market', and had a stronger presence and tradition here than in Lithuania, whilst the Roman Catholic share of the population was around 500,000. In addition there were about 10,000 Jews who had survived the Holocaust, and a handful of new religious movements which some sources suggested were more active in Latvia than in Lithuania.[86] Finally, one should note attempts to revive a national religion known as Dievturiba, started at the beginning of the twentieth century but effectively wiped out within the country during the Soviet period. Re-emerging during the last decade of the Soviet period, by the late 1990s there were reportedly twelve congregations that met on an occasional basis to offer 'holy speeches' praising work, beauty and the homeland.[87]

The place of religion in the new Latvia is defined briefly by the constitution and its legal regulation is carried out under the terms of a 1995 Law on Religious Organisations. Article 99 of the constitution simply states that everyone has the right to freedom of thought, conscience and religion, and maintains the commitment to a separation of church and state. Here there is no formal 'recognition' of the Lutheran or other churches as in any way special from the perspective of the state and, in practice, when religious leaders are involved in public events they usually come from all of the 'mainstream' churches. As in Lithuania, however, there is a general tendency to make an unofficial distinction between traditional and non-traditional religious communities, as is evident in the inclusion of Catholics, Lutherans, Latvian Orthodox, Old Believers, Baptists and Jews on the Advisory Committee on Religious Affairs attached to the Ministry of Justice. Under a law approved in September 1998 the five Christian churches mentioned here also have the right to teach religion in schools to those whose parents approve, and the training of their teachers is funded by the state.[88]

The activity of religious groups is regulated by the Law on Religious Organisations, approved in September 1995 and amended in 1996. Under the terms of this law religious communities seeking legal status must register with the Ministry of Justice, though it is still possible to meet without such registration. For those seeking legal recognition all that is formally required is that ten Latvian citizens express the desire to form an organisation and provide the necessary documentation. These documents are analysed by a Ministry Department, which may also seek the views of the Advisory Council on which representatives of the six traditions noted above are represented. This in turn would appear to give them some scope for blocking the development of non-traditional religious groups, though there is little evidence that they have acted in this way. Religious groups without registration may function freely, but they have no right to own property or receive tax exemptions, and have more limited rights to carry out religious activities in public places. For new groups that do not belong to existing church associations there is a requirement to re-register every year for ten years. There is also a ban on the registration of more than one religious union of a particular confession which effectively means that splinter or dissident groups, such as the Latvian Free Orthodox Church and a few Lutheran and Baptist offshoots, cannot acquire legal recognition. The law permits foreign missionary activity but only by those with invitations from Latvian religious organisations.[89]

Generally legislation on religion appears to have been interpreted in a liberal fashion, and by mid-1999 the Ministry of Justice had registered over 1,000 congregations, including: 301 Lutheran, 241 Catholic, 110 Orthodox, 81 Baptists, 65 Old Believers, 53 Pentecostals, 52 new religious movements, 44 Adventists and a handful of communities representing both traditional religions and independent Protestant churches.[90] During the mid-1990s a few communities faced difficulties in gaining registration. These included the Jehovah's Witnesses who were not given legal recognition until 1998, several charismatic groups and new religious movements whose activities were the subject of some sensationalist press reporting and public concern, and the Christian Scientists who for a while were refused registration after opposition from the Doctors' Association.[91] There were also reports that representatives of the traditional churches were playing a role in supporting anti-cult activity that tended to blur the boundaries between genuinely dangerous activities and the simple propagation of teachings that the historic churches found unacceptable.[92] The other problem that faced the Jehovah's Witnesses in particular related to the question of conscientious objection, as there was no legal provision for alternatives to military service. A law approved in late 1999 granted a limited right to other forms of public service for people who would not bear arms, but only to those who had been certified as preparing to become pastors or ministers in religious communities.[93] By and large, however, it is possible to conclude that Latvia has managed to develop a relatively liberal regime for the regulation of religious matters. This does not single out a single religious community for favour, though it does make a distinction between 'traditional' religious communities that have greater access to the state and non-traditional groups that in practice, at least in some cases, are seen as less legitimate in, if not dangerous to, the new nation-state.

Georgia

More than a thousand miles to the south of the Baltic, the Caucasian states of Georgia and Armenia have faced many of the same pressures in coming to terms with pluralistic politics, though here political and religious debates have taken a harsher form and have occasionally been accompanied by more violent actions. According to legend, Georgia was the land of Colchis, where Jason found the Golden Fleece and, more importantly for our purposes, in 331 it was one of the first countries to accept Christianity. Its subsequent history is too complex to trace here, but much of Georgia's history has revolved around a struggle to preserve some degree of independence whilst trapped between rival empires. At the beginning of the nineteenth century the country was incorporated into the Russian Empire and then, after a brief period of social democratic-dominated independence in 1917–21, it was occupied by the Red Army. With the imposition of Soviet rule came the repression of independent political forces and in the 1930s the liquidation of part of the Georgian elite. Inevitably the Georgian Orthodox Church, which had provided Stalin with some of his education, suffered from the general attack on religion and reportedly some 1,500 churches, mosques and synagogues were closed down during this period.[94] As elsewhere in the USSR the Nazi invasion brought a degree of respite for the mainstream churches and after the war the Georgian Orthodox Church was encouraged to join the World Council of Churches. Under Brezhnev the republic was dominated by the figure of Eduard Shevardnadze, a man who clamped down on more overt manifestations of nationalism but simultaneously encouraged a degree of economic reform and a controlled defence of Georgian interests.

Under Gorbachev, Shevardnadze was brought to Moscow as foreign minister and until 1989 his successors resisted growing nationalist challenges. This changed after the massacre of over twenty demonstrators in Tbilisi in April 1989. In 1990 nationalist forces triumphed in parliamentary elections, and in May 1991 the radical Zviad Gamsakhurdia was elected president of the republic. His inability to accept political opposition and intolerant attitude towards ethnic minorities quickly bred civil war and ethnic strife and, after Gamsakhurdia had been removed from office in early 1992, Georgia turned back to the experienced hand of Shevardnadze to guide them through the troubled 1990s.[95] Whilst these events were unfolding the position of religious communities changed little, though inevitably Gorbachev's reforms dramatically reduced the degree of state intervention in community life and allowed all religious organisations to open new places of worship to meet the needs of their adherents. In consequence, the 70 per cent or more of the population identifying themselves as Orthodox acquired more institutional opportunities to meet their religious needs, though the church itself experienced some traumatic debates over their past relationship with the Soviet state and was forced by more 'fundamentalist' clergy to withdraw from the World Council of Churches in 1997.[96]

Commitment to Georgian Orthodoxy was very much a feature of nationalist movements developing in the 1970s and 1980s, though in Gamsakhurdia's case this was accompanied by a deep suspicion of a hierarchy seen as tainted by its past associations with the Soviet regime. Even the canny Shevardnadze saw the potential role of Orthodoxy in providing some form of social solidarity during uncertain times and early in the 1990s he was baptised into the church. From around 1989 Orthodox church leaders and priests were, as in Russia, increasingly visible in public life and the historic role of the church was recognised in Article 9 of the 1995 constitution where it was declared that 'the state recognises the special importance of the Georgian Orthodox Church in Georgian history'. Though it went on to speak of the independence of the church from the state, in practice church institutions were given a tax-exempt status and some subsidies for the restoration of church property.[97] Following the Russian parliament's adoption of a more restrictive law on religion, elements within the Georgian Orthodox Church backed various legal drafts that would have 'protected' it and the people from the activities of 'non-traditional' religions. In consequence, the Ministry of Justice presented a bill to parliament that would have rendered traditional religions eligible for state support whilst requiring other groups to exist for at least twenty-five years before they could achieve the same status. Despite this pressure and periodic calls for some such legal changes, by mid-2000 a sufficient parliamentary majority had yet to be found for any further 'recognition' of 'traditional' religious groups.[98]

Alongside the Orthodox were to be found representatives of the Armenian Apostolic Church, a few Roman Catholics, a long-flourishing Baptist community, Pentecostals, Seventh Day Adventists, Jehovah's Witnesses, Jews and Muslims (about 5 per cent of the population). From the 1980s there also appeared groups of Baha'is, Hare Krishnas and a variety of Pentecostal and charismatic religious communities often stimulated by the efforts of foreign missionaries. Leaving aside the Muslims, the various religious minority groups drew in around 100–120,000 people from a population of around 5.5 million.[99] Constitutionally religious minorities have complete religious freedom (Articles 9 and 19), and at the time of writing there is no special legislation on religion or any requirement that religious groups register as such, though those wishing to carry out philanthropic work are required to seek formal recognition as charities and religious organisations may register as social organisations under the civil code. Despite this legislative liberalism, the period from the mid-1990s has, as in other former Soviet republics, witnessed occasional outbursts of 'anti-sectarianism' in the media and political arena. Moreover, in certain parts of the country religious minority groups have experienced petty harassment at the hands of local officials. In some cases the problems revolve around property, with the Jewish, Roman Catholic and Armenian Apostolic communities finding it difficult to regain properties taken during the Soviet period or transferred to the Orthodox Church.

More fundamental challenges have been posed to the activities of groups such as the Jehovah's Witnesses or charismatic groups seen as isolating themselves from society or who conduct their worship in a style that many officials find alien. Since around 1995 the Witnesses have faced persistent problems, with the impounding of their literature by customs officials, interference in their meetings and a one-man campaign against them waged by nationalist deputy Guram Sharadze. With the support of defrocked priest Basil Mkalavishvil, and for a while seemingly backed by a declaration from the church leadership attacking 'totalitarian forces', Sharadze has sought through the courts to ban the Witnesses and revoke the registration under civil law that they acquired in 1998. In early 2000 one court refused to ban the community, arguing that they found 'no aggression of any kind in their religious literature', and the judge urged religious tolerance on Georgia. Sharadze returned to the fray following the well-publicised death of a Witness who refused a blood transfusion and in mid-2000 a Tbilisi court upheld his appeal that their registration should be removed.[100]

The other major groups to experience harassment have been the charismatic and neo-Pentecostal congregations emerging during the 1990s. As many of these do not own buildings, their meetings have to be held in private property or in the open air, and this has led in several cases to police raids. Typical of such cases was the treatment of the Grace Church in Tbilisi whose rental agreements with local halls were torn up by officials, and which on several occasions experienced heavy-handed police action that included the beating up of several members of the community. Relatively high levels of religious violence continued into 2001 and 2002 with frequent reporting of physical attacks on Witnesses, Pentecostals and even Catholics, often resulting in the hospitalisation of those affected.[101] Subsequent attempts to take legal action against the police were rejected by the courts,[102] and consequently in 2001 the Jehovah's Witnesses filed a case at the European Court of Human Rights calling on the Georgian government to punish those responsible.

None of these cases appears to have been initiated by the central state, and officials within the government apparatus have expressed distaste for the activities of conservative churchmen and nationalist politicians who attack religious minorities. Thus when an ageing bishop called for the execution of all sectarians in early 2002 the Georgian Patriarchate disassociated itself from the remarks, whilst President Shevardnadze has held several meetings with religious leaders aimed at promoting inter-religious harmony. Moreover, in mid-2002 the government circulated a draft law on religion that aimed to provide some legal guarantees for religious groups, though early comments from non-Orthodox groups focused on the way it followed other post-Soviet legislation in favouring 'traditional' groups.[103] It is too early to discuss what the impact of such legislation might be but it is hard to see how a legal text in itself can curb persistent religious violence directed against minorities. Moreover, the failure of the courts to provide adequate protection for minorities suggests that the rule of law is not fully established, and that de facto 'recognition' of the Orthodox community in Georgia does go hand in hand with some restriction of religious rights for those belonging to other groups.

Armenia

Like its Georgian neighbour Armenia dates its acceptance of Christianity to the beginning of the fourth century.[104]After the Council of Ephesus (431 AD) the Armenian Church was one of five oriental Orthodox churches that became separated from the Western Church and subsequently they only accepted the decisions of the first three ecumenical councils. During later centuries the country experienced the rule of the Byzantines and Persians, followed from the end of the fifteenth century by the Ottomans. Throughout this period the church played a key role as defender of the nation and in effect the Patriarch served as national leader. During the nineteenth century various Armenian nationalist movements began to emerge in both the Ottoman Empire and in Russia where many Armenian intellectuals took refuge. The events of 1915, which most Armenians view as genocide, put a temporary break on national aspirations but at the same time created a potent symbol of identity and fed into national consciousness in ways that would continue to shape Armenian thinking throughout the century. For this reason it was not surprising that many Armenians saw Russia as a lesser enemy and proved rather apathetic when the Bolsheviks took power from a nationalist government in 1920.

During the 1930s Moscow increasingly imposed its harsh style of rule on the republic, brutally collectivising agriculture and attacking the influence of the church. Numerous churches were closed and destroyed, hundreds of priest exiled or shot, and in 1938 Catholicos Khoren I was murdered by the secret police. A partial revival after the war saw the opening of around fifty churches (compared with 491 in 1914), whilst the church leadership embarked upon a policy of close collaboration with the state. Though individual priests and believers spoke out against repression, by and large the church did not play an active role in the development of nationalist politics until the late 1980s when some activists appealed to its leadership for support or adopted religious imagery in promoting their cause. In 1988 a campaign emerged to reclaim the ancient Armenian territory of Nagorno-Karabakh, now situated in Soviet

Azerbaijan, a campaign that proved capable of mobilising hundreds of thousands and served as a focus for a growing nationalist movement. In consequence of this and developments in Moscow, Armenia achieved independence at the end of 1991, though by then conflict over the disputed territory had cost hundreds of Armenian and Azeri lives.

In religious terms the vast majority of Armenians consider themselves members of the national church, even though most have little idea of its doctrines and participate in its rituals on an irregular basis. A few, however, belonged to other faith communities, with a small Roman Catholic community active from the twelfth century onwards, and various American-based Protestant missions involved in the country from the mid-nineteenth century. At the time of independence there were also small communities of Russian Orthodox, Baptists, Pentecostals, Hare Krishnas and Jehovah's Witnesses, who have now been joined by Mormons and Western-backed neo-Pentecostal and charismatic groups.

Though the constitution promises freedom of religion to all, the 1991 Law on Freedom of Conscience and Religious Organisations clearly singles out the national church as distinctive. The preamble to the text describes the Armenian Apostolic Church as 'the national Church of the Armenian people and as an important bulwark for the edification of its spiritual life and national preservation'. The law goes on to reserve for the church the exclusive right to preach and disseminate the faith and to carry out educational work, whilst proselytism is strictly prohibited (Sections 8 and 17). A subsequent decree issued by President Levon Ter-Petrossian in 1993 spoke of the need for closer control over minority religions so as to enable the national church better to 'build and strengthen the religious consciousness of the Armenian people'.[105] One consequence of these definitions was that the Armenian Apostolic Church was recognised as a church, whilst other religious entities were registered as local communities.[106] Indeed, it soon became apparent that the state's Council for Religious Affairs viewed its primary task as defending the interests of that church, if necessary at the expense of minority groups.[107]

Under the terms of the 1991 law minority groups may only obtain official recognition if they are based on 'historically recognised holy scriptures' and if their doctrines 'form part of international contemporary religious-ecclesiastical communities'. Having gained recognition from the Council for Religious Affairs (later abolished) such groups may own property, hold services on their premises and, with special permission, in hospitals, prisons and army units, have access to the media, and engage in charitable work. They may not, however, get involved in politics or receive funding from abroad. The presidential decree of 1993 went on to impose further restrictions on the activities of foreign preachers, whilst some newer religious movements were subsequently required to re-register after including bans on proselytism in their statutes.[108] During the mid-1990s an 'anti-sect' campaign developed, with media attacks on new religious movements in the press and during 1995 a series of violent attacks on minority communities. Amongst those affected were the Hare Krishnas, whose members were beaten up and whose temple was burnt down, and several Protestant churches, with a grenade reportedly thrown into the house of one Pentecostal pastor. Though such actions were probably the work of vigilante groups, the authorities made little effort to track down the perpetrators.[109]

This campaign against non-traditional groups was reinforced by parliamentary amendments to the law on religion approved in 1997. These tightened the registration requirements by raising the number of people needed to seek legal recognition from 50 to 200, a change that essentially froze out the Hare Krishnas who lacked sufficient adherents, but appears not to have prevented the re-registration of other previously recognised groups. Only the Jehovah's Witnessses (who some reports claim to number as many as 18,000) have consistently been refused registration throughout the 1990s, with officials initially suggesting that this was because they refused military service but more recently focusing on the fact that proselytism is integral to their beliefs. Nonetheless, the issue of service in the armed forces remains important in a country that is on a permanent state of military alert. During the course of the decade a handful of Witnesses served prison terms for draft evasion and many young men were reported to be hiding so as to avoid the call up.[110] In early 2000 there were some reports that the authorities might register the community prior to the hearing on the country's application to join the Council of Europe, but a nationalist campaign in the media during the spring appears to have halted any progress on this issue.[111] Over the next two years there have been persistent pressures on the Jehovah's Witnesses, with several court cases brought against members, but though in most cases the higher courts have found for the community they still face an uphill struggle to gain legal registration. Overall, the situation in Armenia is not that dissimilar to Georgia insofar as petty restrictions and occasional violence have seriously affected the work of minorities, though in Armenia the formal privileging of the national church is far more extensive.

Kyrgyzstan

Prior to late 1991 the territory comprising the modern republic of Kyrgyzstan had no tradition of independent statehood. The Kyrgyz nomads had been divided into tribal structures over which dominant khans periodically sought to impose control, but by the end of the century this mountainous territory had become a part of the Russian Empire. During the 1930s a sizeable proportion of the cultural and political elite was wiped out by Stalin and from then until the late 1980s Kyrgyzstan was formally to prove one of the most loyal of the fifteen republics. Only in 1989–90 did social activism and ethnic conflict develop and only under Askar Akaev, the executive president selected by parliament at the end of 1990, did the country embark upon a programme of reform. Though a reluctant convert to independence, Akaev rapidly embraced the slogans of marketisation and democratisation, and made frequent use of the rhetoric of pluralism and civil society. During the early 1990s the atmosphere in Kyrgyzstan was very different from that of neighbouring states where stiff repression was meted out to both secular and religious oppositionists. Here there emerged a wide range of social organisations championing the cause of religious and ethnic minorities, social groups, the homeless and pensioners, as well as an array of political parties, though few of the latter had any serious organisational basis or mass social support. By the mid-1990s, however, there were signs that the political elite was losing its enthusiasm for pluralism, and electoral manipulation and the arrest of several opposition figures during 2000–2 suggested that Kyrgystan's experiment with pluralism was coming to an end.[112]

Though Kyrgyzstan is commonly thought of as an Islamic country, the religion of the prophet came relatively late to this mountainous corner of Central Asia.[113] Despite periodic efforts at Islamicisation, traditional belief structures remained strong, rooted in the close ties of the nomadic herders to the natural world and evident in both a cult of ancestors and a totemistic veneration of certain animals – notably the wolf, the horse and other creatures central to daily life. Only under the Russian rulers of the late nineteenth century did Islam begin to penetrate the consciousness of the people, as St Petersburg sought to create religious and administrative structures that they could control to some degree. During the Soviet period religious organisations in Kyrgyzstan faced many of the same pressures as they did throughout Central Asia. Initially there were some attempts to placate religious feeling, with religious courts and schools allowed to function during the early 1920s, but by the end of the decade Islamic and other religious groups within the republic began to face severe pressures from the state authorities.[114] Following the Great Patriotic War some mosques were allowed to reopen and Kyrgyz Muslims were subordinated to a Central Asian Muslim administration based in Tashkent. At the same time there was something of a revival of 'folk Islam' with 'unofficial' religious activists seeking to preserve elements of the faith despite the relative paucity of institutional structures. When Khrushchev launched a renewed anti-religious campaign in the late 1950s there were just over eighty registered religious associations functioning in the republic, and, compared with some Soviet republics, Kyrgyzstan came off lightly during the Khrushchev period, seeing just under a quarter of religious communities closed down. Yet in the following decades there were repeated and vicious press campaigns against some religious minorities, though these often masked a distinct lack of anti-religious enthusiasm on the part of the ethnic Kyrgyz running day-to-day affairs.

Gorbachev's reforms initially brought little change to Kyrgyzstan, and concessions were late in affecting the Soviet Muslim community. Nonetheless, by the end of 1990 mosques were beginning to reopen and Muslim prayer leaders to enjoy a greater public visibility. In late 1991 the republic adopted a new law on freedom of conscience, modelled on the Soviet law passed the previous year, and under its provisions there rapidly emerged a genuine religious free market which benefited both traditional and new religious communities. Though older churches such as the Lutherans and Orthodox looked set to gain institutionally, this was offset by the emigration of sizeable proportions of their potential flock – around 80 per cent of ethnic Germans and 30 per cent of Russians during the 1990s. At the same time they faced competition from other groups which proved more attractive to the young and which were more able to recruit on a multi-ethnic basis. Some, like the Baptists, had been active in the republic for many decades but had primarily worked within Slavic and European population groups. In the mid-1990s, however, some of them began to conduct services and make converts amongst the Kyrgyz, a development that was to contribute to growing inter-religious tensions in the middle of the decade. Alongside these were a number of evangelical and charismatic missionary organisations, and new religious groups including Baha'is, the Hare Krishnas, and the Unification Church whose impact was often exaggerated because they tended to recruit amongst the children of the better educated or from the social and cultural elites.

For the Muslim community this was also a time of institutional expansion, as hundreds of mosques were opened, religious leaders were able to gain a proper religious education, and ordinary Muslims able to make the haj for the first time. At the same time there appeared activists keen to purify Kyrgyz Islam of the accretions gathered during years of foreign occupation, and to do away with practices such as elaborate funeral ceremonies. This trend was reportedly encouraged by Sadyqan Kamalov, Kyrgyzstan's first independent mufti, and in 1993 he was replaced for his alleged close ties to Islamicists. Until 1995, however, government intervention in religious affairs was minimal and only in 1996 was a special State Commission on Religious Affairs created whose aim was to bring more order into the religious sphere.[115] And since that time there have been signs that the government has sought a greater degree of religious control, both in order to limit the possibility of Islamic 'fundamentalism' affecting the republic and to prevent inter-religious conflict.

The two major 'traditional' religions operating in Kyrgyzstan during the 1990s were the Muslim and Orthodox communities, though Baptists, Lutherans and Mennonites had been present since the beginning of the century, whilst others such as Adventists, Pentecostal and Jehovah's Witnesses had been active in the republic for many decades. From the late 1980s onwards Muslim and Orthodox functionaries were to be found at major state gatherings, the key religious festivals were turned into public holidays, and the institutions of the two dominant traditions were to receive some very limited state subsidy. This was particularly the case where ancient mosques were repaired as part of a programme of national-cultural reconstruction or where the state sought to make good the damage caused by years of Soviet neglect.[116] In practice, however, the poverty of the state made it difficult to provide any substantial support for religious institutions.

At the legal-constitutional level, religious communities entered the period of political independence on an equal footing. The 1991 law on freedom of conscience and religious associations signed into law by Akaev at the end of 1991 promised religious freedom and equality to all, expressly forbade giving advantages to any religious group, and maintained the Soviet commitment to the separation of church and state.[117] Between late 1992 and early 1993 the media and public figures gave considerable attention to the approval of a new constitution and, addressing parliament, in December 1992 the president proposed that the constitutional preamble might include a clause referring to the importance of the moral values of Islam and other religions.[118] In letters to the press this phrase attracted limited attention, though some felt it better to talk of religious values in general rather than single out one set in particular, and others wanted the preamble to stress the secular nature of the state.[119] In the end, however, it was decided to omit any reference to religious values and the constitution eventually adopted on 5 May 1993 made no reference to any particular religious group.[120]

Not until the mid-1990s did the issue of 'recognition' surface again, albeit in the context of debates over how to control potential threats posed by 'religious extremism' and deal with the social tensions said to result from religious diversity. Various groups argued for restriction on the rights of minorities, and a few intellectuals and parliamentary deputies called for some form of legal definition that set apart those religious communities with deep roots in the Kyrgyz republic. During the course of 1997 a draft law on religion was circulated that in certain respects followed the Russian model, though the head of the state Commission on Religious Affairs, Emilbek Kaptagaev, and the chairman of the Legislative Assembly's parliamentary Commission on Education, Science and Culture, Jolborsu Jorolbekov, expressed a desire to avoid the mistakes of their Russian counterparts.[121] The draft that appeared at the end of 1997 did in fact promise equality for all religious confessions, but in several places referred to an undefined category of 'traditional religious organisations' and appeared to give them greater rights than 'non-traditional religions'. For example, only the former category had the right to preach in public places or through the mass media (Article 9).[122] Further discussions took place in parliament in March 1999 when deputies introduced various amendments, but by mid-2000 the law had still not been approved and there had been no formal assignment of a *primus inter pares* status to Islam or Orthodoxy.

Though the 1991 law on freedom of conscience had created a religious free market in Kyrgyzstan, there were occasional reports of religious tensions, especially when ethnic Kyrgyz and Uzbeks converted to Christianity.[123] In general, however, the government remained willing to tolerate foreign missionaries during the early 1990s and was oriented towards an American model of religion–state relations. This began to change in the middle of the decade when the media published a series of articles and letters attacking certain minority groups and calling for legal constraints on their activities. Such articles often focused on letters from the families of 'cult' members complaining that their loved ones had been seduced by new religious movements, or quoted intellectuals who argued that the activities of such groups undermined efforts to create a new sense of social solidarity and national identity.[124] Occasionally Muslim and Orthodox leaders joined together in calling on the government to take legal action against religious movements that took advantage of vulnerable young people and broke up families.[125] This call for a more interventionist approach to religious questions was also directed at Islamic groups promoting a more purist or 'fundamentalist' vision of the faith. During 1995 the security forces had started to warn of the increased influence of 'fundamentalism' in the southern regions of the country, with many of the thousand or more mosques there being used to spread more purist approaches to religion. In response the government banned the teaching of religion in secular schools, and set up the state commission on religious affairs whose chairman presided over the removal of the sitting mufti at the end of 1996.[126]

In November 1996 President Akaev issued a decree 'on measures for realising the rights of the citizens of the Kyrgyz Republic to freedom of conscience and religious practice'. Under this decree all religious organisations and foreign missionary groups were required to re-register with the Ministry of Justice, after an initial checking of their documents by the state commission. According to deputy justice minister Cholponkul Arabaev this was merely an accounting device to enable the government to discover what religious groups were active in the republic, and did not represent an attempt to return to Soviet models of control over religious life.[127] Two months later a further government resolution attacked some religious groups who attracted recruits under false pretences and made converts amongst those who traditionally adhered to Orthodoxy or Islam. At the same time it attacked those who sought to spread more radical Muslim teachings, and noted that in some cases children were being kept out of schools and forced to attend unregulated religious schools.[128] Finally, at the end of 1997 the state security service set up a special sub-committee to monitor the activities of religious organisations and sects.[129] It was in this context that parliament started to discuss a new law on religion in 1997, one that would have imposed some restriction on the rights of religious minorities, and denied non-registered groups the right to carry out religious activity in any form.

In practice this new interventionism brought little change in the daily life of most religious minorities, though perhaps it did help to create an atmosphere where petty harassment became possible or more acceptable. Most religious communities that had been registered in the early 1990s were re-registered again in 1997–9, though one or two had some difficulties. For example, the Korean-based Presbyterian Church had temporary problems in gaining legal recognition for its educational institute, but primarily as a result of bureaucratic wrangles over whether this was the responsibility of the Ministries of Education or Justice.[130] There were also complaints about state favouritism after the State Commission intervened in a conflict between the Russian Orthodox Church and a priest who defected to the jurisdiction of the Russian Orthodox Church Abroad.[131] The Christian group that appeared to face the most problems was the charismatic Church of Christ whose adherents were expected to make wholehearted commitments and whose exuberant worship attracted the attention of politicians and journalists alike. In a succession of articles they were attacked for breaking up families and holding services that were said to resemble the gatherings of the Russian hypnotist Kashpirovsky, though on other occasions they were given the opportunity to defend themselves and one leading member spoke of how the church had taken her away from a life of crime.[132] Baptists also began to experience problems in the south of the republic during 1999, with their meetings periodically disrupted in the Kyzyl Kiya district and press attacks on the activities of their preachers.[133]

Most seriously affected, however, were minorities within the dominant Islamic traditions, for here the activities of a more militant group of activists often led to the establishment of close and restrictive state control over the daily life of mosques and religious leaders. After the 11 September 2001 attacks on the World Trade Center and Kyrgyzstan's decision to host forces of the anti-terror coalition, there emerged signs that the government was increasingly keen to control and contain its own religious radicals. New police campaigns led to the arrest of people suspected of belonging to the banned Hizb-ut Tahrir organisation, and a decree on publishing activity issued in February 2002 included a provision for auditing existing religious congregations so as to elicit the number of illegally functioning groups. In addition, during the spring of that year it emerged that a new draft law on religion was being prepared in parliament that would effectively increase state control of religious organisations and make registration with the Ministry of Justice compulsory for any group that wanted to organise collective religious activity. For all this, within the context of Central Asia, Kyrgystan's treatment of religious believers in the 1990s was relatively liberal. 'Traditional' religious groups did enjoy a pre-eminence in public life but this was not accompanied by substantial legal privilege or political influence. Most religious believers were able to practise their faith freely and register such places of worship as they chose, providing they did not involve themselves in public affairs. Here the pressure on minorities was still primarily social rather than state-directed, though post-11 September the general concern with 'religious extremism' may push the government into adopting a more restrictive approach to religious liberty issues.

Turkmenistan

Prior to the Russian conquest in the last third of the nineteenth century the territory of modern Turkmenistan was populated by various Turkmen tribes with little sense of nationhood and no common political structure. Nominally subordinate to the khans of Khiva and Khokand, they by and large governed themselves, though an often syncretic attachment to Islam provided some form of an overarching set of norms and values. The Russian occupation brought little change to the nomadic life of most of the population, and only after the Bolshevik revolution, and the eventual breaking of local resistance that lasted into the late 1920s, did the Turkmen begin to experience fundamental changes in their way of life.

Under Stalin the benefits of education and literacy campaigns were accompanied by collectivisation, limited industrialisation, and the physical elimination of a substantial section of their political and cultural elites. Inevitably religious institutions and personnel suffered considerably, until the war moderated the excesses and permitted a limited and controlled revival of Islamic institutions under the leadership of a new Muslim leadership based in Uzbekistan. To some extent this was accompanied by a revival of folk Islam, evident in pilgrimages to 'holy places' and elaborate celebrations of rites of passage. The new religious policy developing under Gorbachev during the late 1980s led to a revival of institutional Islam, as the number of legally recognised mosques in the republic grew from four in 1985 to over seventy by the beginning of the 1990s.

From late 1985 Turkmenistan was ruled by Saparmurad Niyazov, who was appointed first secretary of the republican communist party by Gorbachev to clean up corruption but who was to prove an unenthusiastic reformer. After the collapse of the USSR Niyazov moved quickly to assert his own control and since then has created his own peculiar style of personal dictatorship. Accompanied by a personality cult of Stalinist proportions, in which towns, currency and buildings are named after the leader (*Turkmenbashi*), he has stamped harshly on any manifestations of dissent, utilising the 'fundamentalist threat' to justify the continuation of authoritarian rule.[134] In the religious sphere the ethnic predominance of Muslim peoples ensured that Islam remained the dominant tradition during the 1990s, but other communities were also active. There were a small number of Russian Orthodox churches which attracted many of those Russians who chose to stay in the republic after 1991. More problematic was the position of other religious groups that had enjoyed a tenuous status under the Soviet system and continued to do so in the new order. Amongst these were to be found members of the Armenian Apostolic Church (whose community dates to the nineteenth century), Baptists, Pentecostals, Adventists, Jehovah's Witnesses and Baha'is.

Constitutionally Turkmenistan remains a secular state and guarantees the equality of all before the law regardless of their religious beliefs. In practice, however, Islam enjoys a dominant status and Niyazov has been keen to utilise Islamic symbols in his attempts to build a new Turkmen identity. To that end he has sought to maintain tight control over Islamic institutions, whose leaders (paid by the state) actively promote the image of the president as father of the people and defender of the faith. Morning broadcasts on state radio start with a prayer, and the history of Islam is taught in all state schools.[135] Yet this represents a somewhat ambiguous privileging for the Muslim community, entailing as it does a high degree of subservience to the state and government interference in the selection of Muslim (and Orthodox) clergy. More importantly, the government's fear of 'fundamentalism' has meant close supervision of Islamic activities of all sorts and the repression of any religious leader encouraging undue enthusiasm on the part of his local community. For example, during early 2000 the mullah Hoja Ahmed Orazgylych was deported from Ashgabat with his family to a district on the Iranian border, whilst the mosque he built was demolished and his 1995 translation of the Koran into Turkmen denounced by President Niyazov as 'evil' and all copies ordered to be burnt. This in turn formed part of a wider campaign in recent years which has seen the closure of all but one Islamic educational institutions and the failure to re-register many existing mosques.[136]

Whilst the constitution provides for no formal 'recognition', the Law on Freedom of Conscience and Religious Organisations as amended in 1995 and 1996 effectively permits the registration of only Islamic and Russian Orthodox congregations. Under this law only those who can find 500 citizens of the same faith in one locality can gain registration, and all those who meet without registration are deemed to be meeting illegally (though the law does not state this to be so). In practice this removes the possibility of registration from all minority groups, for whilst many of them can meet the requirement nationally, none has any significant concentration of members.

The amendments to the law fundamentally changed the religious situation in Turkmenistan. During the early 1990s minority groups often faced petty harassment and there were social pressures on those who sought to make converts amongst ethnic Turkmen or Uzbeks. From the mid-1990s, however, the state has actively intervened to limit the activities of 'non-traditional' groups and by the end of the decade was employing repressive methods reminiscent of the Khrushchev years in its battle against the 'sects'. According to the amended law all religious groups had to re-register and consequently all the minorities, as well as perhaps half of all Muslim communities, lost their registration: for example, the Bahais who had only gained recognition in 1994 lost it in 1997 and since then have been permitted to open their centre just once a year to celebrate *Novruz*, the New Year.[137] In consequence, all of these groups started to meet illegally, a development that from 1998 onwards brought increasing pressure from the state authorities. Particularly harshly treated were the Baptists, who had begun to work more actively amongst ethnic Turkmen. During 1999 the police conducted a series of raids on Baptist meetings, threatening those involved and occasionally beating up people who protested about their actions. Since the summer of 1999 one ethnic Turkmen Baptist has been sentenced to four years' imprisonment under fabricated criminal charges, others have been subject to internal exile, and those with Russian citizenship deported.[138] Other groups facing official pressure include the Jehovah's Witnesses for their proselytising activities,[139] the Hare Krishnas, two of whose temples were demolished and their leader deported in mid-1999, and the Adventists whose Ashgabat church was demolished at the end of the same year.[140] Finally, one might note the case of the Armenian Apostolic Church whose members have been present in Turkmenistan since the nineteenth century when Armenian traders became active in the region. At the time of the Bolshevik revolution there were half a dozen churches, but these were forcibly closed down during the 1920s and 1930s. In January 1999 the local Armenian community appealed to the authorities for permission to use a church taken from them under Soviet rule and applied for registration, but by mid-2002 this application backed by the Armenian ambassador to Turkmenistan had met with no response.[141] All of this suggests that whilst there is little formal privileging of Islam in Turkmenistan, there is overt discrimination against members of minority churches that is comparable to that experienced in the post-Stalinist period in the Soviet Union. Despite occasional Turkmen promises of improvement to international bodies, the position of religious minorities in Tukmenistan remains precarious whilst the formal 'recognition' granted to Islam remains of very doubtful benefit to its adherents.

Conclusion

This study of the Russian experience and brief round-up from some of the successor states has elaborated the variety of ways in which post-Soviet transitional polities have handled the question of religious 'recognition'. Only in two have the constitutions singled out the national religion, whilst in several others legal texts make distinctions between traditional and non-traditional religions. In Russia, Georgia and Armenia representatives of the 'national' religion have been more prominent in public life; in Turkmenistan Islam has enjoyed state favour, but only at the expense of complete subservience. In five of the seven cases the initial period of transition was marked by the emergence of a religious free market. From the mid-1990s onwards, however, 'anti-sect' campaigns developed in number as attempts were made by politicians and representatives of the dominant religious tradition to tighten up legislation on religion. In particular, there were attempts to make it harder for 'non-traditional' groups to flourish, efforts that in parts of Russia and Armenia, and in more extreme fashion in Turkmenistan and neighbouring Uzbekistan, sometimes moved from administrative restriction to overt repression. Such changes were justified with reference to the need to build national solidarity, protect national religions from unfair competition, or with reference to the need to combat the threat of religious extremism, and it is to some of these arguments that we shall turn in the next chapter.

Notes

1. A classic statement of the totalitarian thesis can be found in C. Friedrich and Z. Brzezinski, *Totalitarian Dictatorship and Autocracy* (New York: Praeger, 1956).
2. On this debate see M. Crouch, *Revolution and Evolution: Gorbachev and Soviet Politics* (London: Philip Allan, 1989), pp. 204–13.
3. On Russian nationalism under Brezhnev see J. Dunlop, *The New Russian Nationalism* (New York: Praeger, 1985); D. Hammer, *Russian Nationalism and Soviet Politics* (Boulder: Westview, 1989); S. Carter, *Russian Nationalism: Yesterday, Today, Tomorrow* (London: Pinter, 1990).
4. For a useful overview see F. Kazemzadeh, 'Reflections on church and state in Russian history', in J. Witte and M. Bourdeaux (eds.), *Proselytism and Orthodoxy in Russia: The New War for Souls* (New York: Orbis, 1999), pp. 227–38.
5. J. Cracraft, *The Church Reform of Peter the Great* (London: Macmillan, 1971).
6. For a fuller study see J. Anderson, *Religion, State and Politics in the Soviet Union and the Successor States* (Cambridge: Cambridge University Press, 1994).
7. Quoted in V. Fedorov, 'Barriers to ecumenism: an Orthodox view from Russia', *Religion, State and Society*, 26: 2, 1998, p. 143.
8. See the comments quoted in Jane Ellis, *The Russian Orthodox Church: Triumphalism and Defensiveness* (London: Macmillan, 1996), pp. 148–52.
9. J. B. Urban and V. Solovei, *Russia's Communists at the Crossroads* (Boulder: Westview, 1997), pp. 87–120.
10. *Nezavisimaya gazeta*, 9 October 1993; *Moskovskie novosti*, 17 April 1994; Ellis, *The Russian Orthodox Church*, pp. 152–4.
11. *Moskovskie novosti*, 13 March 1994.
12. Ibid., 29 April 1994.
13. *Radio Liberty/Radio Free Europe (RL/RFE)*, 5 May 1999.
14. *Russkaya mysl'*, 8 May 1994.
15. *Ogonyok*, 6, 1992, pp. 8–9.
16. *Keston News Service (KNS)*, 14 March 2000.
17. Quoted in Ellis, *The Russian Orthodox Church*, pp. 183–4.
18. Cf. *Moskovskie novosti*, 19 September 1993; H. Berman, 'Freedom of religion in Russia', in Witte and Bourdeaux, *Proselytism and Orthodoxy in Russia*, p. 276.
19. *Russkaya mysl'*, 23 December 1993.
20. Quoted in T. Sinuraya, 'Religious freedom in Russia', *European Journal of Church and State*, 6, 1999, p. 250.
21. On these developments see Berman, 'Freedom of religion', pp. 277–8; L. Homer and L. Uzzell, 'Federal and provincial religious freedom laws

in Russia', in Witte and Bourdeaux, *Proselytism and Orthodoxy in Russia*, pp. 284–320.

22. Cf. *Rossiiskie vesti*, 6 January 1997 and *Rus pravoslavnaya*, 23 January 1997; for more on the arguments see chapter 5.
23. *Nezavisimaya gazeta*, 24 July 1997.
24. *Izvestiya*, 8 September 1997.
25. English translation taken from http://www.stetson.edu/~psteeves/relnews/freedomofconscienceeng.html.
26. *KNS*, 6 October 1999.
27. See the comments of Alexander Morozov in *Nezavisimaya gazeta – religii*, 9 August 2000.
28. *KNS*, 13 June 2001.
29. *KNS*, 5 February 2002.
30. On the 1990 law see Ellis, *The Russian Orthodox Church*, pp. 160–3.
31. For a general overview see the chapters by Shchipkov, Filatov and Vorontsova, Filatov, and Elliott and Deyneka, in Witte and Bourdeaux, *Proselytism and Orthodoxy in Russia*, pp. 77–108, 163–84 and 197–223.
32. See Patriarch Aleksii's comments on abuse of freedom of religion inherent in the activities of groups which take advantage of 'the peoples' material difficulties' or who make converts though 'flagrant pressure on the individual that deprives him of his God-given freedom', *Nezavisimaya gazeta*, 15 July 1993; in private conversations more cynical observers saw this campaign in terms of creating an issue that would distract public attention from the media discussion of the hierarchy's compromises with the old regime.
33. Cf. *Nezavimaya gazeta*, 16 June 1993 and *Argumenty i fakty*, No. 28, July 1993.
34. This next section relies heavily on Ellis, *The Russian Orthodox Church*, pp. 170–90 and Berman, 'Freedom of religion', pp. 275–6.
35. *Nezavisimaya gazeta*, 23 July 1993.
36. *Moskovskie novosti*, 19 September 1993.
37. Probably the best overview of these developments can be found in Homer and Uzzell, 'Federal and provincial religious freedom laws in Russia', pp. 284–320.
38. Quoted in S. Filatov, 'Russkaya pravoslavnaya tserkov' i politicheskaya elita', in S. Filatov et al., *Religiya i politika v postkommunisticheskoi rossii* (Moscow, 1994), p. 111.
39. Homer and Uzzell, 'Federal and provincial religious freedom laws in Russia', pp. 288–91.
40. This also happened in other former Soviet republics, and during a visit to the Kyrgyz state commission on religion in 1997 I found the former CRA commissioner occupying an advisory position and an office across the corridor from the chairman; on Russia see Ellis, *The Russian Orthodox Church*, p. 169.
41. *Kommersant Daily*, 9 June 1995.
42. Berman, 'Freedom of religion', p. 277.
43. *KNS*, 4, 1996, May.
44. *Rus pravoslavnaya*, 23 January 1997; *Nezavisimaya gazeta*, 27 February 1997.

45. See the various analyses contained in *Nezavimaya gazeta*, 24 July 1997 and 25 September 1997; Sinuraya, 'Religious freedom in Russia', pp. 260–2.

46. J. Gunn, 'The law of the Russian Federation on Freedom of Conscience and Religious Associations from a human rights perspective', in Witte and Bourdeaux, *Proselytism and Orthodoxy in Russia*, pp. 239–64.

47. *KNS*, 21 January 1998.

48. On this cases see *KNS*, 4 February 1998, 3 April 1998, 7 October 1998 and 28 November 1998.

49. *KNS*, 8 December 2000.

50. Ibid., 28 November 1998.

51. Ibid., 17 April 1998.

52. Gunn, 'The law of the Russian Federation', p. 247.

53. *KNS*, 21 and 22 January 1998.

54. The Jesuits also had problems in registering as a 'Russian' organisation, though they pointed to a charter signed by Tsar Paul I in 1800 granting them legal recognition. *KNS*, 21 April 1999.

55. Cf. *KNS*, 23 June 1999 and 5 July 2000.

56. Ibid., 23 April 1998; by far the best single source of information of local developments is provided by *Keston News Service* whose correspondents travel widely in the Russian Federation; and most of these cases are confirmed by reports in the Russian media, or that portion of it which reports on minority religious communities.

57. Ibid., 4 February 1998.

58. Ibid., 21 September 1999; *Rossiiskaya gazeta*, 13 October 1999.

59. M. Elliott and S. Corrado, 'The 1997 Russian law on religion: the impact on Protestants', *Religion, State and Society*, 27: 1, 1999, pp. 109–34.

60. US State Department, *2000 Annual Report on International Religious Freedom: Russia* (found at http://www.state.gov/www/global/ human_rights/irf/irf_rpt/ irf_russia.html).

61. Amnesty International, *Russian Federation: The Right to Conscientious Objection to Military Service* (AI Report, April 1997).

62. Cf. *Nezavisimaya gazeta*, 21 October 1998; *KNS*, 22 October 1998, 17 February 1999, 3 March 1999 and 11 May 1999.

63. *KNS*, 15 October 1999, 21 and 26 November 1999, 17 December 1999.

64. US State Department, *2000 Annual Report on International Religious Freedom: Russia*.

65. *Nezavisimaya gazeta*, 12 April 2000.

66. *KNS*, 6 March 2000.

67. ITAR-TASS News Agency report posted on Paul Steeve's website.

68. *KNS*, 4 May 2001.

69. *KNS*, 31 May 2001.

70. *Moskovskie novosti*, 23 July 2002.

71. http://www.newsmax.com/archives/articles/2001/7/10/214306.shtml; *KNS*, 5 October 2001, 6 December 2001, 4 March 2002.

72. *KNS*, 3 July 2002.

73. See the numerous reports on regional variations contained in virtually every issue of *Keston News Service* over the period 1998–2000.

74. A useful introduction to Lithuanian history can be found in V. Stanley Vardys and J. Sedaitis, *Lithuania: The Rebel Nation* (Boulder: Westview, 1997), chapters 1–2.

75. V. Stanley Vardys, *The Catholic Church, Dissent and Nationality in Lithuania* (Boulder: Westview, 1978); M. Bourdeaux, *Land of Crosses: The Struggle for Religious Freedom in Lithuania, 1939–78* (Chulmleigh: Augustine Publishing Company, 1979).

76. For a good general survey of developments in the Baltic see F. Hoppenbrouwers, 'Romancing freedom: church and society in the Baltic states since the end of communism', in *Religion, State and Society*, 27: 2, 1999, pp. 161–73.

77. US State Department, *2000 Annual Report on International Religious Freedom: Lithuania*.

78. US State Department, *Annual Report on International Religious Freedom for 1999: Lithuania*; Vardys and Sedaitis, *Lithuania*, pp. 206–7.

79. *KNS*, 13 July 2001.

80. US State Department, *2001 Annual Report on International Religious Freedom: Lithuania*.

81. US State Department, *2000 Annual Report on International Religious Freedom: Lithuania*.

82. *East-West Church and Ministry Report*, 8: 1, 2000, pp. 7–10.

83. US State Department, *2000 Annual Report on International Religious Freedom: Lithuania* (see also the 2001 report).

84. J. Dreifelds, *Latvia in Transition* (Cambridge: Cambridge University Press, 1996), p. 168; M. Sapiets, 'The Baltic churches and the national revival', *Religion in Communist Lands*, 18: 2, 1990, pp. 155–68.

85. J. Rubenis, 'Rebirth and renewal in the Latvian Evangelical Lutheran Church', *East-West Church and Ministry Report*, 5: 4, 1997.

86. For statistics see Hoppenbrouwers, 'Romancing freedom', p. 162.

87. Solveiga Krumina-Konkova, 'Development of new religious movements in the social and cultural context of contemporary Latvia', paper presented at a conference on 'Religious and spiritual minorities in the twentieth century: globalisation and localisation', Bryn Athyn, Pennsylvania, June 1999.

88. Hoppenbrouwers, 'Romancing freedom', pp. 168–70.

89. The basic features of the law are set out in R. Balodis, 'Religious organisations in the Latvian state: their rights and obligations', *Religion, State and Society*, 27: 2, 1999, pp. 233–8.

90. US State Department, *Annual Report on International Religious Freedom for 1999: Latvia*.

91. US State Department, *2000 Annual Report on International Religious Freedom: Latvia*.

92. See Krumina-Konkova, 'Development of new religious movements in the social and cultural context of contemporary Latvia'.

93. A. Nils, 'Amendment to the law on compulsory service adopted in Latvia: effects on Jehovah's Witnesses', *Human Rights Without Frontiers*, 7 March 2000.

94. R. Gachelidze, *The New Georgia*, (London: University College of London Press, 1995), p. 34.

95. S. Jones, 'Georgia: the trauma of statehood', in I. Bremmer and R. Taras (eds.), *New States, New Politics: Building the Post-Soviet Nations* (Cambridge: Cambridge University Press, 1997), pp. 505–43.

96. Interview with Fr Vassily Kobahidze in *Bulletin of the Moscow Patriarchate's Department for External Church Relations*, 1 August 1997.

97. An English translation of the Georgian constitution can be found at http://www.politicalresources.net/georgia.htm.

98. US State Department, *Annual Report on International Religious Freedom for 1999: Georgia.*

99. Ibid.

100. On this case and other issues surrounding the Jehovah's Witnesses see *KNS*, 11 June 1999, 7 July 2000; *Segodnya*, 7 July 1999; *Human Rights Without Frontiers*, 1 March 2000; *The Georgian Times*, 26 April 2000; statement of Georgian Orthodox Church condemning sectarianism on Paul Steeve's 'Religion in Russia' website, 2 May 2000.

101. *KNS*, 11 January and 8 July 2002.

102. *KNS*, 11 June 1999 and 20 August 1999: *Human Rights Without Frontiers*, 22 October 1999.

103. *KNS*, 9 July 2002.

104. For a general overview see N. Dudwick, 'Armenia: paradise regained or lost', in Bremmer and Taras, *New States, New Politics*, pp. 471–504; Felix Corley, *Armenia and Karabakh: Ancient Faith, Modern War* (London: Catholic Truth Society, 1992).

105. The 1991 law and 1993 presidential decree can be found at http://www.sain.org/Armenian.Church/law.txt.

106. Interview with L. Khachadrian, Chairman of the State's Council of Religious Affairs, taken from *Window Quarterly*, 2: 3, 1991.

107. K. Boyle and J. Sheen (eds.), *Freedom of Religion and Belief: A World Report* (London: Routledge, 1997), pp. 265–71.

108. Ibid., pp. 268–70.

109. *News Network International*, 19 May 1995.

110. US State Department, *Annual Report on International Religious Freedom for 1999: Armenia.*

111. *KNS*, 27 June 2000.

112. For more detail see John Anderson, *Kyrgyzstan: Central Asia's Island of Democracy?* (Reading: Harwood, 1999).

113. For a broader overview see John Anderson, 'Religion, state and society in the new Kyrgyzstan', *Journal of Church and State*, 41: 1, 1999, pp. 99–116.

114. Useful material on some pre-revolutionary developments can be found in A. Tabyshalieva, *Vera v Turkestane* (Bishkek, 1993).

115. A phrase used by its first chairman Emilbek Kaptagaev in an interview with the author, September 1997.

116. For example, in 1992–3 Orthodox believers petitioned Akaev for support in restoring the Resurrection Cathedral in Bishkek, and in January 1993 the president did visit the cathedral and hand over one million roubles. *Slovo Kyrgyzstana*, 12 January 1993; *BBC Summary of World Broadcasts (SWB)*, SU/1593, B/1, 22 January 1993.

117. The text can be found in *Sovetskaya Kirgiziya* (soon to be renamed *Slovo Kyrgyzstana*), 13 February 1992.

118. Reported in the Moscow paper *Nezavisimaya gazeta*, 9 December 1992.

119. Cf. *Slovo Kyrgyzstana*, 2 February 1993 and 23 February 1993.

120. The final text can be found in *Slovo Kyrgyzstana*, 21 May 1993.

121. The former in an interview with the author, September 1997, and the latter in an interview with *Vechernii Bishkek*, 27 November 1997.

122. *Proekt. Zakon Kyrgyzskoi Respubliki. O religii i religioznykh organizatiyakh* (undated text approved by the president in author's possession).

123. *Izvestiya*, 10 January 1992.

124. Cf. *Slovo Kyrgyzstana*, 23 August 1996; *Vechernii Bishkek*, 17 June 1997.

125. *Slovo Kyrgyzstana*, 4 June 1996.

126. On these developments see Anderson, 'Religion, state and society in the new Kyrgyzstan', pp. 107–12.

127. Interview with the author, September 1997.

128. *Nasha gazeta*, 4 February 1997.

129. *Vechernii Bishkek*, 23 December 1997.

130. Interview with church official, September 1997.

131. *Vechernii Bishkek*, 23 October 1998 and 2 November 1998.

132. *Vechernii Bishkek*, 21 May 1997, 3 December 1997, 4 June 1999 and 24 September 1999.

133. *KNS*, 29 May 1999; *Vechernii Bishkek*, 10 June 1999.

134. D. Nissman, 'Turkmenistan: just like old times', in Bremmer and Taras, *New States, New Politics*, pp. 634–49; John Anderson, 'Authoritarian political development in Central Asia: the case of Turkmenistan', *Central Asian Survey*, 14: 4, 1995, pp. 509–27.

135. *Turkmenskaya iskra*, 8 June 1992 and 27 October 1992; *Segodnya*, 5 February 1992.

136. *KNS*, 3 August 2000.

137. US State Department, *Annual Report on International Religious Freedom for 1999: Turkmenistan*.

138. See the reports, mostly by Felix Corley, in *KNS*, 13 August 1999, 22 January 2000, 8 February 2000 and 13 March 2000.

139. Six were reportedly in prison in early 2002. *KNS*, 22 March 2002.

140. *KNS*, 8 September 1999, 22 January 2000.

141. US State Department, *Annual Report on International Religious Freedom for 1999: Turkmenistan*; *KNS*, 23 January 2000.

5   Justifying religious 'recognition' and/or discrimination

In all of the transitional societies we have examined so far there have been wide-ranging debates over the place of religion, though in some countries the issue has enjoyed a greater political salience than others. In these discussions different actors have put forward a variety of arguments to justify granting some churches formal 'recognition' in the new polities, or to defend legal discrimination against religious minorities. The emphasis of the individuals and institutions involved in this discussion vary according to their ideological and institutional needs, but a number of broad types or families of argument are evident from a reading of the available sources. These include suggestions that the dominant church:

- is the religious community of the people, of the majority, or of the nation, and thus deserves some formal 'recognition';
- has the right to exercise some form of 'moral guardianship', and requires the state to provide some form of protection from unfair competition;
- all this is reinforced by a general need in transitional societies for order and stability in the face of uncertainty, and this requires regulation of inappropriate or divisive religious activity;
- and in any case, why should our country slavishly follow models of church–state relations developed elsewhere that reflect different cultural and religious contexts, and that have the potential to undermine the process of national rebuilding currently being undertaken?

Not all of these arguments play with the same force in every country and, as we shall note in the next section, it is by no means always the case that the justification of 'recognition' and/or discrimination comes primarily from the traditionally dominant religious institutions.

The actors

In most of the societies we are dealing with the pressure for legal privilege, control or restriction has come from a variety of sources, most obviously from the *traditionally dominant religious community*. Prominent religious

166

institutions may point to their role as the national church or the church of the majority whose 'first amongst equals' status is simply a 'sociological fact'. They may, as in Poland, point to their role in making democratisation possible. In the post-communist states they might suggest that the assaults of anti-religious communists so weakened their position that some form of state protection is necessary. And some, whether Catholic or not, have a hankering for the pre-Vatican II teaching that 'error has no rights'. For this reason church leaders utilise their access to political elites and the media to press their case, often alone, but sometimes in tandem with other major but non-threatening religious groups – as in Russia where sections of the Muslim leadership supported the passing of the 1997 law – or with secular allies.

These latter groups may include some unlikely bedfellows. At the fore-front are often to be found *conservative nationalists* who view the church as an institution that played a key role in forging national identity, as a use-ful support for their own policy preferences, and a bulwark against 'alien' implants whether religious or cultural. In Bulgaria and Russia such ar-guments have also been made by *reformed, or old-style, communists* – both often keen to appropriate nationalist arguments and eager to find new sources of legitimacy in the emerging political order. On occasions this unholy alliance might be joined by *liberal intellectuals*, using arguments based on the need to protect the cultural inheritance of the country but also using elitist or 'good taste' arguments about the vulnerability of the masses to the activities of religious 'sects'.

At the institutional level pressure may come from *state agencies*, espe-cially in the post-communist countries where the bureaucratic disposition to control remains strong, and in both Bulgaria and Russia some of the officials responsible for religion under the old regimes remain in office to-day. In many countries *security agencies*, seeking to justify their continued existence or to find a role, may play a part in calling for restrictions on groups with the real or imaginary capacity to threaten the fragile social and political stability of the new political orders. Away from the centre *local politicians and administrations* are often at the forefront of attacks on religious 'cults', as in Greece where local officials continued to obstruct church building by Jehovah's Witnesses even after the central state had, under international pressure, given them some legal recognition.

These attacks and campaigns are frequently taken up by the local or even central *media*, which exaggerate the number of 'sect' members or run sensationalist 'anti-cult' stories that frequently bear little resemblance to what actually goes on in the community concerned – witness the attempts to attribute child sacrifice to the Jehovah's Witnesses in some Varna pa-pers in the mid-1990s.[1] During transitional periods throughout the world the media rapidly throws of the shackles of the past and occasionally sinks to levels that would make the British tabloids seem a model of responsibility! All of this has an effect on *public opinion*. Though a small section of the population may have genuine fears and anxieties when it sees friends and family members 'lost' to unfamiliar religious groups, this is an issue that can be easily manipulated by the media and by politicians. It is easy to play on the concern that an 'invasion of the sects' is taking place, and that this represents just part of a wider social malaise that has seen 'order' overturned by democratic chaos. For that reason members of the public may agitate for the restriction of minority rights or form campaigning anti-cult groups, though such surveys as are available suggest that this is rarely matched by any public enthusiasm for the formal privileging of specific religious groups.[2]

Finally, one might point to the more indirect role of *international* actors and the domino effect. Shterin and Richardson have noted the ways in which Western anti-cult movements and literature influenced pressure groups and policy-makers within Russia, leading groups that usually reject external models as inappropriate to make a selective use of Western experience to achieve particular ends.[3] There also seem to be cross-currents within the former Soviet space, with many of the draft laws appearing in Bulgaria, Romania and some of the former Soviet republics appearing to be modelled to a lesser or greater extent on the Russian model, and even relatively liberal Poland witnessed calls in the late 1990s for some tightening of the requirements to be fulfilled by religious groups before they can operate.

The arguments

(a)   Majoritarianism and the national church

During the run-up to the constitutional debate in Spain the Catholic church was not happy to find that an early draft excluded any reference to the place of the national church. Addressing a religious gathering in November 1997 Cardinal Enrique y Tarancón pointed out that:

the Church is a social reality... and politics has to bear in mind and respect the real life of the people; it cannot ignore the fact that a large majority of the Spanish people belong to the Catholic Church.

For this reason the Cardinal argued that there had to be some recognition of the church's position in the political reorganisation of the country, and that the church could not simply be treated as one religion amongst many.[4] Similar arguments surfaced during the Polish constitutional debates of the mid-1990s, with Cardinal Glemp and other bishops frequently referring to the need to take proper account of the wishes of the people. In 1994 the Secretary of the Bishops' Conference, Tadeusz Pieronek, argued that given the country's history and the role of Catholicism in recent events, there was a need for some formal recognition of the 'public and social role of the Church'. Two years later, commenting on the failure of the constitutional draft to meet Catholic demands, he argued that 'this constitution does not meet the basic expectations of Polish believers who are in a majority'.[5] In similar vein Russian Orthodox spokesmen Fr Andrei Kuraev could argue that 'the equality of religions before the law does not mean their equality before the culture and history of Russia', and that some formal 'recognition' of this fact should not be seen as diminishing the rights of others.[6]

The use of simple majoritarian arguments was not, however, without its problems and as a general rule was used selectively and perhaps thus undermined as a line of argument. In particular, the Polish church was vehement in its rejection of majoritarianism when it came to issues of personal morality, with the hierarchy strongly opposed to holding a referendum on the abortion issue.[7] The same bishop Pieronek who utilised majoritarianism during the constitutional debate could argue elsewhere that:

for the Church an unquestionable shortcoming of democracy is its inseparable feature – the principle of the majority. . . . This principle cannot be applied to essential issues, that is, to those which relate to the principles of faith or morality, within the Church as well as outside it.[8]

Equally problematic was the notion of a religious majority in states where the overwhelming mass of the population were at best irregular church attenders. Whilst the problems of evaluating religious adherence cannot be explored here, in only one of our countries was there any evidence to suggest majority participation in religious ritual on a regular basis, i.e. Poland, where some sources claimed regular church attendance figures of over 50 per cent of the population.[9] In Spain and Greece less than a third of the population participated in religious activities once a month or more,[10] whilst in Bulgaria and Russia most surveys reported that around 2–6 per cent of the population were 'regular' attenders.[11] Russian surveys in turn also suggested that perhaps a half of those involved in religious practice were attending non-Orthodox places of worship, and that of those calling themselves Orthodox many held a strange amalgam of beliefs that had little to do with the historic doctrines of Orthodoxy. The limits of religious influence were also suggested by a Bulgarian study which stated that whilst 78.5 per cent considered themselves Orthodox, in times of trouble only 3 per cent turned to God and only 0.7 per cent turned to a priest.[12] In such circumstances, whilst it is true to say that there is a strong cultural identification with the traditional religious communities, it is not always clear that sociologically – at least in the 'Protestant' sense of active membership – they represent a majority of the population or even, in the Russian and Bulgarian cases, of those who actively practise a religious faith.

Overlapping with the majoritarian approach, and often utilised by political nationalists and secular politicians as well as by the churches themselves, is the argument that justifies privilege and/or discrimination with reference to the deep historical connections between a particular religious group and the nation. Throughout history, it is suggested, this particular religious community helped to shape national consciousness through its promotion of language and culture. It defended the national interest during times of trouble or foreign occupation and, in the communist context, served as a major pillar of national defence against an atheistic and denationalising regime. Here the argument is less for discrimination against others than a plea for a formal recognition of what are described as cultural and historical realities, though, as we shall see later, nationalism can also be used to justify differential if not discriminatory treatment of religious groups.

Such arguments appear in all the countries under consideration, though they seem to have lost much of their force in Spain. In Greece the connection of religion and nation remained much stronger, for here, despite the weak personal religious commitments of many nationalist politicians, Orthodoxy and Hellenism remained identified in the public consciousness. For Greek President Constantine Karamanlis the nation and Orthodoxy 'had become in the Greek consciousness virtually synonymous concepts which together constitute our Hellenic-Christian civilisation', and in 1989 Prime Minister Mitsokis could describe Orthodoxy as 'the support of the nation'.[13] Such an approach was also evident in Poland where the first post-communist prime minister argued that the church could not simply be relegated to the private sphere. Not a chauvinist nationalist, but a liberal-minded Catholic, Tadeusz Mazowiecki noted that:

In Poland, where the Church historically has played . . . and continues to play, an important role, there should be a profound discussion in which we resist . . . denial of the most important historical role of the Church in the public life of this country.[14]

Such appeals to the national contribution of the dominant church were even more frequent in Russia where in early 1997 a group of 'patriotic' writers used this approach to call for restrictions on religious minorities. Speaking of 'the historical past and national distinctiveness of Russia', they went on to talk of the historic relationship between Orthodoxy and the state 'in the bosom of which was formed Russian statehood and Russian culture'. Without these ties being reinforced in legislation they saw little hope of rebuilding a sense of Russian national identity.[15]

Arguments of this type were especially prevalent in those countries where Orthodox and Oriental churches predominated, and could be found in countries outside our study such as Romania where Patriarch Teoctist, supported by some nationalist politicians, called for formal 'recognition' of the Orthodox Church. In the context of a debate over a new law on religion in 1999, he argued that the Church was:

born at the same time as the Romanian nation and took part alongside it in all major historical events; most of the Romanians are Orthodox and the Orthodox Church has constantly enjoyed the public's greatest trust.[16]

Occasionally justifications of this type appeared in legal texts, as in the preamble to the 1991 Armenian Law on Freedom of Conscience and Religion where the Armenian Apostolic Church was described as the 'national church of the Armenian people' and as 'an important bulwark for the edification of its spiritual life and national preservation'.[17] The chairman of the Armenian Council for Religious Affairs used a parental analogy – albeit referring to the church in the paternal rather than the more usual maternal terms – to justify privileging the national church and inhibiting the activities of minorities:

The Armenian Church is the father of the Armenian people. The father was imprisoned and stripped of his children for seventy years. Now that father is free, others have come to adopt his orphaned children. What we need is to give the father a chance to reclaim his children. Some of the children would want to go to other homes and some would return to their father's home. It is up to the children. But, it is only fair to give the father a chance to embrace his children. . . . All we are saying is give the father, the Armenian Church, a chance.[18]

Though such arguments were generally phrased in terms of a need to recognise the special place of the national church, in some cases they spilt over into calls for a restriction of the rights of minorities. In more radical versions they could be taken to suggest that in some sense members of other religious communities were not really members of the nation or that their presence threatened the security of the nation. During the early 1960s several Spanish bishops opposed the extension of religious freedom on the grounds that it would contribute to the destruction of national unity.[19] Referring to Greece, Pollis has noted the way in which the notion of 'an ethno-national Greek ethnos as embodied in the state' could be taken to imply that only those who belonged to the religious ethnos were entitled to rights.[20] Yet few would have taken the argument so far as Solidarity Senator Kaczynski during the abortion debate in Poland, when he suggested that 'all good Poles are against abortion. Those in favour are an evil part of the nation.'[21] Of course, the latter statement is an extreme one, but this and some of the other ones quoted above do reflect a type of argument that justifies religious privilege and/or discrimination with reference to the fact that the dominant church is somehow representative of the majority and has special historical ties to that nation's fate. And as we shall see a little later, the argument from national tradition can be extended to develop more overtly nationalist reasoning that sometimes spills over into xenophobia.

(b)   *Moral guardianship, unfair competitition and the*
       'invasion of the sects'

These are overlapping lines of argument that emphasise the role that the traditional churches might be able to play in the transmission of moral values and in the protection of the population from some of the more dangerous consequences of pluralism. To do this more effectively, it is suggested, the national church – in the post-communist cases, weakened by decades of anti-religious assaults – needs some form of 'protection' and, possibly, some limitation on the rights of competitors. The moral guardianship argument comes up more often in relation to matters of education and morality than constitutional–legal issues, but is often implicit in these. Responding to the perception that political liberalisation has opened up the country to a wave of alternative values, permissiveness, individualism and consumerism, the traditional churches have pointed to themselves as fixed points of reference in an uncertain world. For that reason, and in the Catholic case reinforcing their argument with an appeal to 'natural law', they argue that their voice should be given special attention on some policy issues. Addressing the congregation at the coronation of King Juan Carlos, Cardinal Tarancón stressed that whilst the church supported legitimate democratic authority, this was only to the extent that it pursued the common good, the definition of which, he seemed to imply, would be decided by the religious institution.[22] Up to a point church activism in defence of its moral values represents a legitimate participation in the lobbying process characteristic of democratic orders, but the problem is how to make such arguments in ways that do not appear as special pleading for 'reserved domains' in public policy. At the same time, it is often hard for the church to find justifications that are acceptable to other groups or individuals within the society who will not accept a 'we must do this because God, tradition or the Bible says so'.

Arguments for 'recognition' or 'limitation' may be voiced in terms of the needs of the church – for protection against 'unfair competition' – or the needs of society – for protection against the 'excesses' of the sects. In the first case, particularly evident in the Orthodox countries, the argument is that during the transition period the national churches are weak, thanks to past atheistic policies (in the post-communist cases) or the impact of 'modernisation' (Greece). At the same time, the population is disoriented and vulnerable, inclined to fall prey to the blandishments of well-funded and organised religious groups from the outside world. Some of these debates came together in Greece, a country that is still not fully comfortable with its membership of the European Union and the implications this may have for its own distinctive cultural traditions. In the words of a 1990 encyclical issued by the archbishop of Athens:

> It is not at all an exaggeration to say that from the time of the establishment of the Greek state in 1839 at no time has our nation faced a more serious crisis than today. Our problem is not located only in our weak economy... our problem is spiritual, ethical and cultural. Our entry to the new world of a United Europe is connected with the agony and struggle for the safeguarding of our national, cultural and especially our spiritual and religious continuity.... Various propagandas from East and West flood our country and create tragic victims amongst those who have no foundation in the faith and tradition of our fathers.[23]

In such conditions the new religious movements are seen to be taking advantage of a population that is highly susceptible to new ideologies because of the rapid social changes taking place in the wider society.

In Bulgaria, Romania and many of the former Soviet countries frequent contrasts are made between the situations of the national churches and that of religious organisations supported by or coming from the outside world. The former have reduced institutional structures, a poorly educated clergy and a shortage of material resources, and their primary task in the short term appears to be one of rebuilding. To that end much of their activity in the 1990s has centred on the opening of churches, regaining of property, increasing the numbers of clergy and improving their educational level, and dealing with internal divisions within the church. Feeling themselves the victims of past excesses, these churches often attempt to develop close relations with the new political orders and acquire some form of legal 'recognition' of their 'special' status. Against them, so it seems,[24] are pitted wealthy foreign missionary organisations that can mount huge evangelistic campaigns, afford large amounts of publicity and media time, and offer 'inducements' of various sorts to those who join their communities. It is also the case that for citizens of many of these countries membership of religious communities may be encouraged by the offer of literature, food, English lessons or trips abroad. Though the intent may not be corrupt, it is not entirely surprising that some local commentators speak of such things as 'bribes' or 'illegitimate inducements'.[25] In part, this represents a reaction to the crass behaviour of some Western organisations, particularly those who construct ostentatious churches with modern equipment, often in suburbs that are otherwise poorly equipped.[26] Yet it is worth noting that such activities are often viewed negatively by indigenous religious minorities, and that many foreign missionaries do not operate on the grand scale. Nonetheless, the presence of so many foreign religious activists in Russia and Bulgaria, especially in the early 1990s, reinforced the feeling that in some sense outsiders were taking advantage of a vulnerable and disoriented population to poach believers from weakened traditional churches.

Alongside this there were the claims made by the largest religious communities that others were encroaching upon their canonical territory. This problem is especially acute in relation to Catholic communities active in Orthodox-dominated lands, as witnessed by the resistance of Russian and Greek Orthodox leaders to proposals that Pope John Paul II visit their countries – though he was eventually permitted to visit Greece in May 2001. On frequent occasions Russian Orthodox hierarchs, and less often Bulgarian and Romanian church leaders, have complained about attempts to create Catholic dioceses on 'their' patch, and Patriarch Aleksii reportedly once suggested that the Catholic expansion eastward was more dangerous than that of NATO.[27] In general the Orthodox position in Russia was well expressed by the Patriarch in an address to the Council of Bishops in 1997 where he stated:

the mission of the Catholic Church on our territory has taken on a proselytising character. . . . The Orthodox position on this question is clear: the Roman Catholic Church should direct its attentions only to those whose national-cultural roots belong to the traditional Catholic flock, and not to those who have Orthodox roots or are baptised in the Orthodox Church.[28]

In other words, whilst the Catholics should be able to organise amongst 'their own' nationalities – Poles, Lithuanians, Germans and other foreigners – they should not be active in ethnically Russian communities. From Moscow's perspective, the opening of dozens of Catholic parishes throughout Russia since 1991 represents a lack of fraternal spirit. Yet most sources suggest that the Vatican has discouraged proselytism, and Catholic leaders in Russia point out that nearly 300 churches existed in 1917, that Soviet oppression had reduced the number to six in 1991 and that today there are less than 200 functioning. In other words, even today the pre-Soviet status quo has not been achieved, so it is hard to speak about aggressive activity by the Roman Catholic Church, though individual Polish priests have been known to make use of anti-Orthodox rhetoric.[29] During early 2002 there were suggestions of tensions emerging between the Russian Orthodox Church and the Putin administration over the Catholic issue. The president himself spoke of Russian pride that a Slav had been elected to the papal throne and expressed the hope that John Paul II would be able to visit Russia. At the same time, he recognised that this would depend upon the establishment of better relations between the two churches. For their part Orthodox leaders continued to attack alleged Catholic proselytism in Russia, with Archbishop Yevsevi of Pskov and Velikie Luki appealing to Putin 'not to allow the destroyers of our homeland and nation – the Roman Catholic Church – to triumph on Holy Pskov soil'.[30]

Whilst many of these arguments were primarily of interest to those involved in religious movements, the question of the harm, real and imagined, caused to church and society alike by the activities of religious 'sects' or 'cults' was one that allowed churchmen to appeal more readily to popular opinion and policy-makers. Here the stress was on the objective dangers posed by such groups, but equally such arguments might be used in defending the advantaging of mainstream religious groups that do not encourage 'anti-social behaviour' such as conscientious objection or isolation from non-believers. Throughout much of Europe in recent years concern has been expressed about the activities of 'totalitarian' or 'destructive' cults,[31] and such concerns have been magnified in former communist countries where many of the religious movements concerned were poorly known prior to 1989. Leaving aside political manipulation of the issue, there are also genuine fears and anxieties expressed by friends and families when their members join religious groups about which they know little. Yet it remains the case that the terms 'destructive', 'totalitarian', 'cult' and 'sect' are used very loosely in this debate and often selectively. Thus whilst many Orthodox might be happy to dismiss Baptists as a 'sect', the latter in turn will use the same terminology when referring to Jehovah's Witnesses or Mormons. More disturbing, if theological debates are not our main concern, is the way in which reference to 'brainwashing' or 'moral corruption' makes it difficult to defend such groups against attempts to restrict their rights and often gives officialdom considerable leeway in deciding what are 'destructive' groups and how to deal with them.

In the countries we are considering much of the argument as developed by politicians and the media is carried on in an emotive and sensationalist manner that generally exaggerates the problem and utilises it to justify attacks on almost any religious minority. Analysing some 230 articles on 'sects' from the Latvian press, Nikander Gills pointed to various ways in which they were said to 'threaten our country': by undermining national identity and questioning the values taught by the traditional churches; by abducting children; by tearing up families; by destroying individuality; by controlling human behaviour; by making their members beg or commit fraud; by giving their members arms; by slandering the state; by physical and sexual abuse of members; by endangering human life (for example through the refusal of blood transfusions); and by creating an anti-social environment which cut members off from the wider society. Gills also noted the frequency with which sects and cults were compared to cancerous cells eating away at society's well-being.[32] The language used in such articles is often highly emotive, speaking of 'waves' of non-traditional religions 'flooding' the country and 'acting vigorously and cleverly so as to bewilder naïve youth'.[33]

For Patriarch Aleksii II of Russia, 'pseudo-Christian and pseudo-religious sects' were one of the major spiritual problems facing Russia in the 1990s, though he failed to define who were to be included in these categories.[34] This failure to define what groups were included and to provide evidence to back up claims about 'sectarian' activity was typical in many of the countries discussed here. All too frequently the rhetoric stepped into fantasyland, as in the case of the Bulgarian parliamentary deputy who stated that:

sects ruin the character, they brainwash, destroy the mind, and break up the values of the Bulgarians. . . . The awful calamity is that along with many of the sects and behind the cover of faith come drugs, organised crime, terrorist groups and money laundering.

Not one of the latter charges was accompanied by serious evidence and the words might be dismissed as the ravings of a fanatic had they not come from the mouth of the chairman of the parliamentary commission on religion and human rights.[35] In equally extravagant vein Bulgarian press articles spoke of politicians 'detained' by the sects and forced to defend them, or described charismatic preachers as 'soul bastards . . . turning our children into Janissaries'[36] – an image that might strike both anti-sectarian and anti-Islamic chords amongst the population.

In many of these countries parents, politicians and churchmen have joined forces to create anti-cult movements and organisations devoted to 'rehabilitating' those who join non-traditional organisations, whilst the special services of several countries have devoted resources to combating groups which use 'sophisticated and deeply immoral methods and techniques for the purposes of gaining new converts'.[37] In Russia anti-cult groups have been created with the support of the Orthodox hierarchy, and there have emerged cult specialists, such as the Moscow Patriarchate's Aleksander Dvorkin, who seek to expose the sins of the 'sects'. In general, such people and organisations claim to be concerned only with 'destructive cults', and justify their advocacy of harsher laws with reference to such organisations. At the same time, they tend to use rhetoric that creates an image of thousands if not millions of sectarians 'invading' the country and undermining the physical and mental health of the younger generation.[38] Perhaps Russia is atypical, but here numerous anti-sect sources speak of five million people having joined new religious movements during the 1990s,[39] though most sources suggest that even together indigenous Russian sects and foreign implants cannot have attracted more then 300,000 people during that period.[40] In consequence, it appears that the real target of many of these groups in Russia is virtually every group outside the fold of the dominant religions (Orthodoxy and Islam). Equally unclear is the extent to which restrictive laws approved in Russia, and under discussion in Bulgaria and elsewhere, will deal with genuinely destructive groups in ways that cannot be handled by the criminal law. Nonetheless, at the heart of the discussion is the assumption that it is healthier for church, state and society if the dominant or mainstream religion is given support and encouragement, and 'sects' or 'cults' are actively discouraged or constrained in their ability to organise. For Patriarch Aleksii this was not about denying people the right to choose their religious faith, a right he fully supported, but about preventing 'this choice from being imposed from without, especially by taking advantage of the peoples' material difficulties or through flagrant pressure on the individual'.[41]

(c)   Stability and the need for order

When calls for 'recognition' are accompanied by demands for restriction on some types of religious activity, it is sometimes suggested that these are necessary because of the peculiar circumstances of the transition period.[42] In particular, it is suggested that during times of great uncertainty and in a situation where society is under considerable pressure from the process of social and political change, there is a greater need than ever for a proper legal regulation of religious life. In part this is a reaction to the perceived chaos attendant upon democratisation, and a longing for some aspects of the old authoritarian or communist system that was at least characterised by a high degree of order. Alongside this there is sometimes heard the view that the lack of regulation in the religious sphere would not be accepted in other policy areas. Thus, Patriarch Aleksii could argue that if religious life were not properly regulated then any group, however dangerous, could come to Russia and preach whatever they liked.[43] And in a 1997 interview with the author, Emilbek Kaptagaev, then chairman of the Kyrgyz State Commission on Religious Affairs, drew an analogy with a market economy in arguing that the religious sector needed a proper regulatory framework if it was to function efficiently.[44]

In some circumstances the justification for curbs on religious freedom have been framed with reference to the need for social and political stability in fragile new political orders. Such claims have both social and political/security aspects. In Kyrgyzstan, officials have pointed to the problems that arise when Protestants and others try to evangelise the indigenous peoples, and funerals have often provided flashpoints as the Christian peers and Muslim families of the deceased convert struggle over the destiny of the body – in Central Asia there are separate burial grounds for the two communities. There have also been charges that much of the literature distributed in the region stirs up religious antagonism by denigrating traditional customs.[45] In Russia, there have been several cases where officials have hindered the activities of minorities on the grounds that these might stir up conflict, though one consequence of this approach can be to encourage groups who dislike minorities to organise protests so as to give the impression of religious tension. Thus, on various occasions, Russian nationalist groups have picketed religious meetings in an effort to get them banned. In the Tula province the authorities denied a group of Adventists access to public buildings on the grounds that their presence might stir up inter-religious conflict, as their preachers had attacked both Baptists and Orthodox during sermons.[46]

Alongside claims that an excess of religious diversity might threaten religious peace and social stability are suggestions that on occasions religious 'sects' pose a challenge to national unity, political stability or state security. Responding to Vatican II's commitment to religious liberty and moves to give this legal backing in Spain during the 1960s, Archbishop Alonso Munoyerro argued that such a move would destroy Catholic unity, whilst Franco's confidante Admiral Carrero Blanco predicted that the Council's teaching would 'lead us into religious and consequently political disintegration'.[47] All too often such arguments were self-serving, as in the utilisation of the grossly exaggerated 'fundamentalist threat' by the leaders of Central Asia to justify their maintenance of authoritarian rule. It is also an argument that appeals to security officials keen to justify their existence, and not just in transitional societies.

There have also been claims that religious movements provide a cover for espionage and other activities directed against state interests. A Russian Interior Ministry decree of late 1996 mentioned the Jehovah's

Witnesses, Unification Church, Mormons, various charismatic groups and the True Orthodox Church (an indigenous movement) as threatening because:

Using religion as a cover, the foreign representatives of the above mentioned organisations are creating networks, which enable them to gather socio-political, economic, military and other forms of information about the processes that define Russia's strategic position.[48]

During the mid-1990s Nina Krivel'skaya, a parliamentary deputy from the nationalist Liberal Democratic Party, carved out a niche for herself as a 'cult' specialist, and frequently made reference to the foreign origins of new religious movements whose activities she saw as part of a wider plan to penetrate Russia and the CIS. Such groups, she claimed, had plenty of money and often served as a means by which could be carried out 'open intelligence activities against the Russian state'.[49]

In both Russia and Bulgaria, the Mormons have been singled out by security agencies as groups particularly likely to be utilised by foreign intelligence agencies, a response perhaps to the fact that of all the foreign missionary groups they are most assiduous in providing their representatives with proper language training.[50] In the middle of 2000 there also emerged claims that the US government was using missionaries in an effort to break up Far Eastern regions and transfer them to American sovereignty. Magadan regional governor Valentin Tsvetkov argued that the main goal of missions in his region, which were spending 'enormous amounts of money', was 'not at all religious education, but control over the region and its natural wealth'.[51] During 2001 such arguments were given more authoritative backing in a book by Nikolai Trofimchuk entitled *Expansiya* (Expansion). Here the head of the religious studies faculty at the Russian Academy of State Service argued for placing 'spiritual security' on the same plane as national security. He also suggested that whatever their personal intentions, the vast majority of foreign religious activists in Russia served the political interests of the countries from the which the missionaries came.[52] Few of these claims are backed up with any evidence or have any grounding in reality but, leaving aside their political manipulation, they also reflect genuine concerns about the potentially divisive effects of religious diversity in states that in several cases are struggling to build effective new political orders.

(d)   Nationalism and 'doing it our way'

In Greece, Armenia and Russia, and to a lesser extent in Bulgaria, Poland and the Caucasus, many of the arguments revolve around issues of national identity, and form part of a wider discourse about the nation-building process. At its most extreme this takes the form of a xenophobia that treats all non-traditional expressions of religious faith as alien and a threat to the well-being of the nation, and rejects the experience of the outside world in dealing with religion–state issues as simply irrelevant to transitional societies. In its most extreme form this was perhaps best articulated by the Russian regional official who, when asked where the new religious movements came from, responded:

America – a sewage ditch. When it was created all sorts of rabble thronged there, and Protestantism and all sorts of non-traditional religions arose there. These things come from there.[53]

Such feelings were sometimes vehemently expressed at demonstrations staged by nationalist movements in Russia and Bulgaria, as during a Pentecostal conference in Sofia in the mid-1990s when Orthodox theological students denounced the 'arrogant aliens' who had nothing in common with Bulgarian traditions but still presumed to bring their message across the Atlantic.[54]

More typical, however, was a deep-seated resentment at the influx of foreign missionaries that followed the collapse of communism and the attitude adopted by many foreigners who saw themselves bringing faith and civilisation to countries about which in most cases they know very little. Metropolitan Kirill of Smolensk, effectively deputy leader of the Russian Orthodox Church, noted that after 1991:

hordes of missionaries dashed in, believing the Soviet Union to be a huge missionary territory. They behaved as though no local churches existed, no Gospel was being proclaimed. They began preaching without even making any effort to learn the Russian language. . . . Missionaries came from abroad with dollars, buying people with so-called humanitarian aid and promises to send them abroad for study or rest. They have bought time on radio and television and have used their financial resources to the utmost in order to buy people.[55]

Particularly disliked was the assumption of many foreign missionaries that those baptised in the Orthodox, or in Poland the Catholic, tradition were legitimate targets for conversion. In the view of Metropolitan Kirill and others this was a nothing more than 'spiritual colonialism'. There were also claims that those encouraging the growth of a religious free market had some distinctly non-spiritual objectives. Andrei Kuraev, for example, suggested that for some in Russia and outside, the coming of Protestantism was welcome because it would help to promote an individualistic mentality or ethic that would support the building of democracy and a market economy.[56]

Similar arguments, albeit with a broader cultural emphasis, were sometimes voiced by nationalists who argue that their countries have identities that have been shaped over centuries, in part by their religious traditions, and that they need no lessons from outside in how to manage their affairs. The Macedonian Internal Revolutionary Organisation, part of the Bulgarian governing coalition in the late 1990s, attacking the activities of a Pentecostal evangelist in Sofia, stated that:

We wanted to demonstrate that we belong to an ages old civilisation and culture with its own history of struggle and suffering in establishing its identity. . . . We wanted to remind people across the Atlantic that they must conform to certain phenomenon of the Bulgarian historical and political reality.[57]

Such argument also surfaced in discussions of the most appropriate model of church–state relations for the new states, with Poland's Cardinal Glemp early on expressing his concern that his country might uncritically opt for a European or American model that was not necessarily appropriate to the Polish context.[58] In Russia there was a particularly strong reaction to the US 'wall of separation' approach which one group of 'patriotic' writers described as running counter to 'the historical past and distinctiveness of Russia, and the mentality of its people', and as rooted in the 'individualistic amoralism' typical of American society.[59] In similar vein Fr Vsevolod Chaplin attacked the hypocrisy of Western critics and Russian liberals who cried foul when Russian bishops made comments on public life but saw no breach of separation when Bill Clinton attended church or permitted military chaplains to be active in the armed forces. Instead there was a need to 'build a model of church–state relations that takes into account the real position in the country . . . not take a utopian view which seeks to maximise or minimise the role of religion in society'.[60]

This rejection of Western models is in part a reaction to the West's perceived dominant liberal ethos and the promotion of concepts of church–state relations that effectively relegate religion to the private sphere. As early as 1991, the Polish Catholic bishops warned of a new threat facing the country:

Yesterday it was the East, but today the West will insist that Poland fully accept social, political and also whole-hearted religious liberalism. So we are confronted with a new form of totalitarianism, that is intolerant of good, of God's laws, so that with impunity we may propagate evil and in effect once again wrong the weakest.[61]

In similar vein Stefan Niesolowski, leader of the Christian National Union, reacted to the relativism of liberalism and the false assumption that a separation of church and state would lead to genuine state neutrality on religious matters. In terms reminiscent of US critics of the radical 'wall of separation' interpretation of the First Amendment, he demanded:

respect for Christian values in public life because otherwise the state will become possessed by other ideologies. There are no moral alternatives to Christianity. Of the other ideologies I have in mind in particular liberal ideology, aiming to build a morally relativist state, a completely secular humanist state, where clericalism is treated as an enemy.[62]

This concern with liberalism was also apparent in Russia and Greece. Constantine Scouteris, professor of church history at Athens University, argued that the West European experience since the Renaissance had been characterised by a loss of awareness of the proper human relationship to the world around, tending to create a situation in which humanity viewed the cosmos as a possession, At the same time, the impact of the last 500 years in Western Europe had destroyed any sense of community and created an undue emphasis on the individual pursuing his or her own rights regardless of context and consequences.[63] Greek and Russian Orthodox commentators frequently spoke of the threat to traditional consciousness posed by 'extreme liberalism'.[64] In several addresses during the late 1990s Metropolitan Kirill of Smolensk spoke of the dangerous consequences that might follow an overhasty integration of Russia into the Western civilisational sphere. Criticising both radical liberals and nationalists, he nonetheless argued that there was a new manner of reality:

that had arisen outside of all traditions and has been created under influence of post-industrial reality. At the foundation of this manner of life lie liberal ideas which have united within themselves pagan anthropocentrism, which entered European culture at the time of the renaissance, protestant theology, and Jewish philosophical thought. These ideas came to a head in the era of enlightenment in a certain complex of liberal principles. The French revolution was the culminating act of this spiritual and philosophical revolution.... It was absolutely no accident that this revolution began with the reformation, for it was the reformation that rejected the normative significance of tradition in the sphere of Christian doctrine.

It was this liberal ethos that dominated the West and Russia and her church should think very carefully before uncritically accepting ways of doing things that had evolved over time and in a very different context, and whose benefits for the spiritual development of humanity were far from obvious.[65]

In Greece, and to a lesser extent in Poland, the debate over liberalism was tied into controversies over their countries' future role in the European Union. Whilst opinion polls in Greece during the 1990s showed a high degree of support for European integration, many suspected that the roots of this were largely instrumental rather than affective in nature. At the same time, many conservative forces in Greek society remained suspicious of the possible consequences of such processes for national identity and the Greek way of life. From 1998 onwards this concern was articulately expressed through the speeches and addresses of the newly appointed Archbishop of Athens, Christodoulos. Even before his selection Christodoulos had pointed to the danger of 'subservient rulers sacrificing to the Moloch of Europeanisation our native heritage, who lead us perilously into European channels and rabidly strike at the two remained fortresses left standing; church and family'.[66] In May 2000 these arguments hit the political mainstream when the government announced its intention to implement a 1997 law that would have removed the question about religious identity from identity cards. Playing on the fact that the church had not been consulted, the media-savvy archbishop launched an offensive and pointed to surveys which showed that over half the population supported the retention of the religious question. Though some tried to calm the debate, hostile exchanges between church and government spokesmen pointed to major differences of understanding over the question of Greek identity. For Christodoulos this issue represented the thin end of the wedge, a first step in the campaign to marginalise the church in public life. Whilst he claimed to have no problems with involvement in Europe, the archbishop warned of the potential dangers ahead, for though

Europe may eventually fill our pockets, it may also empty our souls. We must struggle for this not to happen because, if it does, it will lead our country into decline and deterioration. We are at the heart of Europe. . . . We are first Orthodox Christians and then Europeans. First comes the national identity, then come all the others.

Addressing a rally of 100,000 in mid-June 2000 he stressed that Europeanisation was part of a wider process of globalisation, which though having positive effects might also lead to the levelling of cultures.[67] Similar anxieties, if less forcefully expressed, were also voiced in Polish and Bulgarian debates about the possibility of joining the European Union, though by 2002 Poland's Cardinal Glemp was somewhat reluctantly referring to membership as a 'historical necessity'.[68]

In the Greek context both churchmen and politicians tended to see the role of the Orthodox Church as more than simply meeting people's religious needs, and therefore protection of that church as in some sense central to the well-being of the nation. This has led secular critics to suggest that the revival of religion in the country during recent years had nothing to do with spirituality and everything to do with nationalism and what George Mavrogordatas calls a 'nation in danger mentality'.[69] The emphasis of church spokesmen was increasingly on the fact that threats to Orthodoxy represented threats to the nation, with the Holy Synod arguing in one document on the sects that they were dangerous because their activities aimed 'at the fading away of the national consciousness of their victims. This is why the matter is mainly a concern of the State, and not of the Church.'[70] This defensive or protective nationalism was also strongly apparent in Greek, and indeed Bulgarian, attitudes towards Turkic or Muslim minorities whose demographic patterns were seen as threatening the integrity of the Orthodox nation.

What Edwin Bacon calls 'cultural preservation' arguments were also prevalent in Russian debates, where it was implied that Orthodoxy embodied Russian culture and the church owned the spiritual rights to the Russian population.[71] The group of nationalist writers quoted earlier argued very strongly that unlimited religious pluralism was simply inappropriate in Russia and would have the potential to 'destroy traditional spiritual-moral values', and that a more restrictive law was required to protect 'the spiritual-cultural distinctiveness and national state interests of Russia'.[72] As in Greece the implication was that defence of the faith was an essential part of the process of nation-building and the reinforcement of national identity. This was made clear in many comments on the 1997 law, with Deacon Andrei Kuraev commenting that 'the main thing here is the future of Russia', and Sergei Dunaev, writing on the first anniversary of the law's approval, arguing that 'one year ago Russia declared her sovereignty in matters of religious distinctiveness'.[73]

Conclusion

What emerges from this chapter is the centrality of arguments about identity and belonging in the discussion of religious issues. In few of these countries has religion been a central political issue – except for brief periods, as during the Polish abortion and constitutional debates, or in Greece following the removal of the religious question from identity cards – but in a number of them it has acquired greater significance because of its role in discourses about national identity and models of future development. Certainly in Greece, Russia and to some extent in Georgia and Armenia, attempts to 'protect' the traditional religion or restrict the rights of minorities have been justified using a 'cultural preservation' or 'nation in danger' rhetoric. Moreover, in all the countries where this debate has taken place the dominant tradition has been Orthodox or 'Oriental' (Armenia). Alongside this goes a rejection of externally imposed models of church–state relations shaped by Western, individualistic liberalism, a rejection shared by at least some sections of the Polish Catholic Church. At one level this represents an affirmation of 'doing it our way', but as we saw in the arguments revolving around the 'invasion of the sects' it also has negative connotations stemming from a suspicion of 'otherness'. Thus, it is hardly surprising to find that the countries where intolerance is more prominent are also countries where identity questions remain to the fore. At the same time, the perception of 'threat' does not always correlate with the actual level of religious competition in a country, which may be high – as in Russia and to some extent in Bulgaria – but is relatively low in other 'threatened' countries – such as Armenia and Greece.

Notes

1. Cited in *Obektiv* (a periodical publication of the Bulgarian Helsinki Group), June–August 1998.
2. One survey carried out in 1997 showed that 27 per cent believed the Orthodox Church should be privileged and 40 per cent thought it should not; *Nezavisimaya gazeta*, 25 December 1997; but see also a survey of Russian ninth and eleventh grade school children which showed 35.9 per cent wanting to ban 'sects'. RIA Novosti, posted on Johnson's Russian List, 15 May 2000.
3. M. Shterin and J. Richardson, 'Effects of the Western anti-cult movement on development of laws concerning religion in post-communist Russia', *Journal of Church and State*, 42: 2, 2000, pp. 247–71.
4. Quoted in A. Brassloff, *Religion and Politics in Spain: The Spanish Church in Transition, 1962–96* (London: Macmillan, 1998), p. 95.
5. *BBC Summary of World Broadcasts (SWB)*, EE/2092, A/10, 5 September 1994, EE/2135, A/4, 25 October 1994, & EE/2063, C/6, 4 May 1996.
6. A. Kuraev, 'Ot strany pobedishvshego o ateizma k obshchestvu torzhestvuyushchego yazychestvo', in S. Filatov et al., *Religiya i politika v postkommunisticheskoi Rossii* (Moscow, 1994), p. 210; a more recent discussion of this argument can be found in *Nezavisimaya gazeta*, 17 July 2002.
7. A. Sabbata-Swidlicka, 'Church and state in Poland', in *Radio Liberty/Radio Free Europe Research Report (RFE)*, 2: 14, 2 April 1993, pp. 45–53.
8. Z. Mack, 'The Roman Catholic Church and the transformation of social identity in Eastern and Central Europe', in I. Borowik and G. Babinski (eds.), *New Religious Phenomena in Central and Eastern Europe* (Krakow: Nomos, 1997), pp. 75–6.
9. This seemingly rather high figure is quoted in US State Department, *2000 Annual Report on International Religious Freedom: Poland*.
10. During the mid-1980s surveys showed 86 per cent of Spaniards describing themselves as Catholic but only 31 per cent as practising, whilst in the early 1990s, 5 per cent described themselves as devout and 25 per cent as practising. V. Perez-Diaz, *The Rebirth of Civil Society* (London: Harvard University Press, 1993), pp. 173–4 and T. Lawlor and M. Rigby, *Contemporary Spain* (London: Longman, 1998), p. 326; reportedly a Greek Orthodox internal

report has suggested that only 3 per cent attended regularly on Sundays, but I have been unable to track down the evidence for this.

11. Surveys carried out in 1997–8 reported 55 per cent of Bulgarians and 48 per cent of Russians describing themselves as Orthodox, but only 8 per cent and 7 per cent respectively attending church more than once a month. S. White et al., 'Religion and political action in post-communist Europe', *Political Studies*, 48: 4, September 2000, pp. 688–9; E. Bacon, 'Religion and politics in Russia', in M. Bowker and C. Ross (eds.), *Russia after the Cold War* (Harlow: Longman, 2000), pp. 186–7.

12. I. Katsarski, 'Bulgarskoto pravoslavie i imperativite na modernizatsiyata', in G. Bakalov (ed.), *Religiya i tsyrkva v Bylgariya* (Sofia: Gutenburg Publishing House, 1999), p. 25.

13. Karamanlis quoted in K. Ware, *The Orthodox Church* (London: Penguin), p. 208; Mitsokis quoted in N. Kokosolakis, 'Greek Orthodoxy and modern socio-economic change', in R. Roberts (ed.), *Religion and the Transformation of Capitalism* (London: Routledge, 1996), p. 260.

14. Quoted in M. Brzezinski, *The Struggle for Constitutionalism in Poland* (London: Macmillan, 1998), p. 122.

15. *Rus pravoslavnaya*, 23 January 1997 (this is a regular religious supplement to the conservative nationalist paper *Sovetskaya rossiya*).

16. *Nine O'Clock News* (Bucharest), 10–12 September 1999; see also the comments of another Romanian Orthodox theologian who noted the way in which the Orthodox defended their claims 'both historically, as the original church of the Romanian people going back to the Roman empire, and culturally as the source of spiritual power which has consolidated the unity and integrity of Romania'. Quoted in I. Bria, *Romania: Orthodox Identity at a Crossroads of Europe* (Geneva: WCC Publications, 1995), p. 54.

17. http://www.sain.org/Armenian.Church/law.txt.

18. Interview in *Window Quarterly*, 2: 3, 1991.

19. J. Hughey, *Protestants in Modern Spain* (South Pasadena: William Carey Library, 1973), pp. 41–2.

20. A. Pollis, 'Greek national identity: religious minorities, rights and European norms', *Journal of Modern Greek Studies*, 10: 2, 1992, p. 179.

21. P. Michel, 'Religious renewal or religious deficiency: religion and democracy in Central Europe', *Religion, State and Society*, 20: 3–4, 1992, pp. 340–1.

22. Brassloff, *Religion and Politics in Spain*, pp. 86–7.

23. Quoted in Kokosolakis, 'Greek Orthodoxy and modern socio-economic change', p. 261.

24. Whilst some of these groups are wealthy, it is not always the case, and in Russia it may well be that income from various speculations in oil products, tobacco, alcohol and mineral water render the Russian Orthodox richer than many of the foreign missions, though there is some controversy as to the amounts involved and on what they are spent.

25. See the discussion of this in L. Uzzell, 'Guidelines for American missionaries in Russia', in J. Witte and M. Bourdeaux (eds.), *Proselytism and Orthodoxy in Russia: The New War for Souls* (New York: Orbis Books, 1999), pp. 323–30.

26. Several of the Korean-based Presbyterian churches I have visited in Central Asia in recent years have substantial properties encompassing a wide range

of facilities, from food kitchens to hi-tech audio equipment, that sits uneasily with their immediate surroundings.

27. *Kommersant Daily*, 24 July 1997.
28. *Rus Pravoslavnaya*, 6 March 1997.
29. S. Filatov and L. Vorontsova, 'Russian Catholicism: relic or reality', in Witte and Bourdeaux, *Proselytism and Orthodoxy in Russia*, pp. 93–107.
30. *KNS*, 12 February and 22 April 2002.
31. For example, in the summer of 2000 the French parliament adopted tough anti-sect legislation that created a new crime of 'mental manipulation' punishable by up to five year's imprisonment. For a discussion of this see the links at http://www.cesnur.org/testi/fr2K_index.htm.
32. N. Gills, 'New religious movements in Latvia in the mirror of the press', paper presented at the CESNUR Conference on 'Religious and Spiritual Minorities in the 20th Century: Globalisation and Localisation', Philadelphia, June 1999.
33. *Krasnaya zvezda*, 13 September 2000, translation taken from Paul Steeve's website.
34. *Rossiiskie vesti*, 6 January 1997.
35. Quoted in *European Baptist Press Service*, 17 November 1993.
36. Quoted in *Hate Speech in the Balkans* (Vienna: International Helsinki Federation for Human Rights, 1998).
37. According to a report of the Polish National Security Office quoted in J. Richardson, 'Minority religions in former communist countries: a sociological analysis', in Borovik and Babinski, *New Religious Phenomena in Central and Eastern Europe*, pp. 257–82.
38. I am grateful to Eileen Barker for drawing my attention to a wonderful document produced by the Russian Ministry of Health setting out some of the dangers of getting involved in such groups.
39. Cf. *Rus Pravoslavnaya*, 14 June 1997; *Izvestiya*, 4 July 1998.
40. Shterin and Richardson, 'Effects of the Western anti-cult movement on development of laws concerning religion in post-communist Russia', p. 257.
41. *Nezavisimaya gazeta*, 15 July 1993.
42. See the comments of Patriarch Aleksii interviewed in *Rossiiskaya gazeta*, 6 January 1997.
43. *Nezavisimaya gazeta*, 13 April 1996.
44. Interview in Bishkek, September 1997.
45. *Nasha gazeta*, 10 December 1997; for more detail see J. Anderson, 'Religion, state and society in the new Kyrgyzstan', *Journal of Church and State*, 41: 1, 1999, pp. 99–116.
46. *KNS*, 17 April 1998.
47. Brassloff, *Religion and Politics in Spain*, p. 15.
48. Quoted in *Frontier*, No. 3, 1997, pp. 4–5.
49. *Rus Pravoslavnaya*, 14 June 1997.
50. *Moskovskie novosti*, 26 July 1998; the Scientologists were also linked with foreign intelligence agencies in an article appearing in *Krasnaya zvezda*, 13 September 2000 (translated on Steeve's Russian Religious News website).
51. *KNS*, 5 July 2000.

52. *KNS*, 4 September 2001.

53. *KNS*, 19 March 1998.

54. *Obektiv*, February–May 1997, p. 24.

55. Metropolitan Kirill, 'Gospel and Culture', in Witte and Bourdeaux, *Proselytsim and Orthodoxy in Russia*, p. 73.

56. Kuraev, 'Ot strany pobedishvshego o ateizma k obshchestvu torzhestvuyushchego yazychestvo', p. 216.

57. Quoted in *Obektiv*, February–May 1997.

58. *The Independent*, 27 November 1991; Sabbata-Swidlicka, 'Church and state in Poland'.

59. *Rus Pravoslavnaya*, 23 January 1997.

60. *Nezavisimaya gazeta*, 26 June 1997.

61. Pastoral letter quoted in J. Szacki, *Liberalism after Communism* (Budapest: Central European Press, 1995), p. 177.

62. Quoted in Brzezinski, *The Struggle for Constitutionalism in Poland*, p. 122.

63. Interview with author, Athens, May 2000.

64. A phrase used by Patriarch Aleksii, quoted in J. Witte, 'Introduction', in Witte and Bourdeaux, *Proselytism and Orthodoxy in Russia*, p. 9.

65. *Nezavisimaya gazeta*, 26 May 1999.

66. *Athens News*, 30 April 1998.

67. Ibid., 30 and 31 May 2000, 1, 6, 9 and 15 June 2000; the author was in Greece during the early stages of this debate and witnessed a much smaller demonstration organised by an extremist para-church group where the identity card issue was linked to a variety of ills allegedly perpetrated by masons, Satanists and Protestants.

68. See the comments of the mayor of Plovdiv, Bulgaria's second city, who argued that 'yes, we want to join Europe, but we should protect our Christian faith, our Orthodox Church'. *European Baptist Press Service*, 17 November 1993; after a visit to Brussels in 1997 a group of Polish bishops professed themselves more amenable to the idea of European integration so long as ethics and moral values were not forgotten. *The Warsaw Voice*, 16 November 1997; *The Economist*, 16 March 2002.

69. G. Mavrogordatas, 'Church–state relations in the Greek Orthodox Case', paper presented to the ECPR Joint Sessions on 'Church and State in Europe', Copenhagen, 14–19 April 2000.

70. *Hate Speech in the Balkans*.

71. E. Bacon, 'Church and state in contemporary Russia: conflicting discourses', *Journal of Communist Studies and Transition Politics*, 18: 1, 2002, pp. 112–15.

72. *Rus Pravoslavnaya*, 23 January 1997.

73. *Trud*, 13 August 1997; *Nezavisimaya gazeta*, 15 July 1998.

6 Conclusion: modernisation, conflict, culture and religious liberty

Our study so far has focused on the place of religion in the life of transitional societies. To that end we have explored two issues: the extent to which 'traditional' or 'national' religious communities are granted a formal status in the new constitutional and legal order, and how these states handle the issue of religious pluralism. Clearly the issue of constitutional recognition has been more important in some of our cases than in others, and in the Greek case the very overt legal privileging of the Orthodox Church was something that had nothing to do with transition and was inherited from an earlier period. Though some politicians questioned the appropriateness of such definitions during the constitutional debates of the mid-1970s and there have been occasional attempts to raise the question of separation since that time, at present the close formal ties of church and state look set to remain well into the twenty-first century. For the other Orthodox or 'Oriental' churches, and indeed for the Muslim countries discussed briefly here, the issue of constitutional status as such has generally proved unimportant. Instead, the issue of 'recognition' has come to the fore in discussion of separate laws on religion emerging, with the exception of the Armenian case, in the late 1990s. In Russia, Bulgaria, Kyrgyzstan and Turkmenistan, laws or legal drafts have attempted to carve out a special role for 'traditional' religious groups and, to varying degrees, grant them greater rights than those accorded to religious communities categorised as 'non-traditional'. This 'privileging' of the dominant religions has been justified in terms of their national status, contribution to historical development, the need to protect them against unfair competition, and with reference to wider debates about how best to pursue the nation-building process.

Only in our two Catholic cases, Spain and Poland, did the constitutional issue acquire a considerable political salience, as in both cases the Roman Catholic Church fought against its exclusion from the public sphere. In Spain the church simply demanded recognition of its status as the church of the majority, whereas in Poland the hierarchy sought a more extensive national commitment to Christian values and argued that formal separation of church and state was inappropriate in the Polish context. Less clear is why the Catholic Church took a more outspoken position on constitutional recognition than did the Orthodox Church.

This has not, however, prevented the Orthodox from pushing their case in relation to other laws dealing with religion. On the issue of restrictive legislation affecting minority groups, it is the countries with an Orthodox and, to some extent, a Muslim tradition that have made the running, with national Catholic hierarchies generally supporting – or not actively opposing – the evolution of laws guaranteeing religious liberty. Though recent developments in Poland and Hungary, as well as in Latin America, suggest some Catholic ambiguities as to how far religious liberty should be extended, the impact of Vatican II's teaching on religious liberty and the role of Pope John Paul II in promoting human rights would make it hard for the hierarchy to play too active a role in promoting discriminatory legislation. In Greece, restrictions on minority rights date back to the pre-war period, with bans on proselytism affecting many groups and Orthodox bishops being given considerable say in decisions affecting the opening of non-traditional churches. More recently, Greece has liberalised some of its practice, largely under the impact of external pressures but, as we have seen, there remains a sense in which those belonging to minority faiths are seen as in some sense not properly Greek. Across the old iron curtain the 1997 Russian law on religion appears to have acted as a stimulus for some of the successor states, as well as their East-Central European neighbours, to begin discussing ways in which 'sect' activity might be curbed. In both Orthodox and Muslim countries such discussions have been tied into wider debates about the need for national unity in time of change and suggestions that excessive religious diversity along American lines might prove divisive in these fragile new states whose national churches have been weakened by years of harassment and persecution.

There is no single explanatory model that might explain the varieties of experience evident in the countries we have explored, but it might be worth returning to the four broad types of explanation set forth in the introduction. These related to prior regime type and the nature of the transition, to confessional differences, to socio-economic factors, and to the role of nationalism in states seeking to establish a new sense of identity and belonging.

Regime type and the nature of transition

The broad assumption here would be that the transition to a more pluralistic vision of religion's place in the political order would be more problematic in post-communist states than in post-authoritarian states of a more traditional nature. In addition, it might be expected that problems might also arise in states where the transition was less consensual, and in societal contexts where the general levels of tolerance were low. It is probably stating the obvious to suggest that the resolution of religious issues might be more problematic in states emerging from communist systems that to varying degrees were overtly hostile towards religion. On the one hand, in a number of these countries officials from the old regime were still in place and the disposition to control remained strong. On the other hand, there was occasionally a reactive tendency to over-compensation in which governments tried to make up for past persecutions by granting at least some religious communities state protection and 'recognition'. Equally, some religious leaderships traumatised and weakened by their past relationship with the state and now facing challenges from reformers within and religious competitors without, might have found the easiest solution to their problem to lie in appeals to a political leadership guilty about its predecessors' sins in this area. Yet in practice the impact of regime type is less significant than one might expect. Both the Spanish and Greek regimes were committed to a vision of Christian values shaping politics but, with the collapse of authoritarianism, responses to the questions of 'recognition' and 'restriction' have differed considerably. Hence the Spanish church, sometimes reluctantly, has found it easier to accept a more limited role in public life than its Greek counterpart. Equally, within the former communist countries we see similar differences emerging, for though nearly all the national churches have sought some form of 'recognition', there is no shared position when it comes to recognition of minority rights. So it appears that previous regime type alone offers little guide to the 'religious outcomes' emerging in newly democratising states.

It is also hard to see a clear relationship between the nature of the transition process and outcomes in terms of recognition and restriction, with the most consensual transitions – those in Spain and Poland – producing very different reactions from the two Catholic hierarchies. In Spain, the experience of past polarisation led to a consensual style of decision-making during the first years of the Spanish transition in which key actors made compromises in pursuit of the democratic goal. This was particularly evident in the debate over the place of the Catholic Church in the wording of the 1978 constitution where, as we have noted several times, a compromise solution was found. Poland, too, had a negotiated transition, though here the church's proclamation of moderation during the negotiations was lost somewhat once democracy was established and its key policy concerns were on the agenda. Here the legacy of late communism in Poland was the emergence of a confident, perhaps over-confident, church keen to assert its rights and expecting, perhaps wrongly, that the legitimacy built up in recent decades would engender popular support for a reassertion of Polish Catholicism's influence in the political arena. Transition in our other countries was either 'accidental', as in Greece, or a consequence of the Soviet collapse, and religious institutions played little role in bringing about change and thus acquired limited experience of the process of political negotiation. In addition, in countries such as Russia and Bulgaria religious leaders heading weakened churches initially lacked the confidence in the early 1990s to challenge the emerging religious pluralism. Overall, however, we have seen no common pattern in the way in which they have entered discussions revolving around religious issue. Where the transition may be more important, however, is in the subsequent pace and scale of liberalisation and/or democratisation. Here there are some patterns in the post-communist world for, by and large, arguments for the restriction of religious liberty are made most strongly in those countries where democratisation is most weakly established and consolidation is far from complete.

If the nature of the transition is less significant, it might well be that there is some form of relationship between the success or 'consolidation' of the democratic experiment and the growth of tolerance within the new political societies. Where one might expect societal values and attitudes to have a greater impact is in relation to minority issues, with the expectation that laws restricting religious liberty or minority rights might be likely in countries where general levels of tolerance were low. Evaluating the spread of 'pluralistic values' is problematic in many respects and a full set of comparative data is not available, but there is sufficient material to offer some preliminary conclusions regarding our five main case studies. Broadly speaking, the countries that have the most liberal regulatory regimes with regard to religious minorities, that is, Spain and Poland, also have the highest levels of social tolerance. Survey data on attitudes to religious minorities are not available for all of our countries, but studies of issues such as race and ethnicity would appear to support this conclusion. For example, a 1996 Eurobarometer poll asked people in various European countries about the extent to which they harboured racist feelings and just 4 per cent of Spaniards described themselves as 'very racist' and another 16 per cent as 'quite racist'. This was amongst the lowest recorded in the European Union states and contrasted favourably with the worst cases: Belgium (22 per cent and 33 per cent), France (16 per cent and 32 per cent), Austria (14 per cent and 28 per cent).[1] Another survey reported by Krassimir Kanev of the Bulgarian Helsinki Committee asked whether respondents would like to have people of another race living next to them. The results of this poll suggested that of the East European states Poland was amongst the more tolerant, with the Czech Republic, Slovakia, Hungary and Bulgaria all producing more negative responses. This survey showed an average of 9 per cent replying negatively in West European countries, 21 per cent in East European countries and 17 per cent in Poland.[2] Clearly this evidence should be used with caution, and impressionistic accounts from Poland certainly do not always confirm such high levels of tolerance, especially in relation to the few remaining Jews, and responses in Poland and Spain may be as much a product of the relatively small numbers of ethnic and religious minorities in these two countries as of greater tolerance of 'difference'.

Greece is a more complex case. On the one hand, many observers – including some Protestants – report high levels of social tolerance, especially in the cities, with regard to what people do in the privacy of their homes and churches.[3] This seems to be borne out by many opinion polls, including the Eurobarometer data on racism cited earlier, which records only 6 per cent of Greeks describing themselves as 'very racist'. And some studies comparing the attitudes of Greek and other Balkan populations suggest that the Greeks, though disliking Jews, Roma and Gypsies as much as their neighbours, are more accepting of the proposition that such groups should have the same rights as everyone else.[4] Against this, other observers point to the weakness of Greek civil society, the resistance of the state to accepting the activities of human rights groups, the tendency to see rights as something granted by the state rather than inhering in the individual, the resistance to the building of mosques and the vehement anti-Turkish sentiments expressed in some quarters, and the harsh treatment meted out to Jehovah's Witnesses in many local communities. Various commentators have suggested that the 'identification of Hellenicity with Orthodoxy has made it difficult for various minorities to become fully integrated into the dominant political culture' and that therefore 'the concept of multi-culturalism and ethnic pluralism remains underdeveloped'.[5] This trend is exacerbated at the constitutional level by Article 25, which suggests that 'the state shall have the right to claim that all citizens should fulfil the duty of social and national solidarity', a form of words which Pollis sees as assuming a transcendent, holistic notion of Greek identity.[6]

Turning to Russia and Bulgaria, the evidence for a correlation between public opinion and state policies towards religious minorities appears a little clearer. In both these countries survey data from the mid-1990s suggests relatively low levels of support for democracy as a political form.[7] There was also some support for the contention that order should take priority over democracy and that on occasions democratic rights might have to be restricted in order to ensure stability or national security. In Bulgaria, for example, 44 per cent of ethnic Bulgarians supported this notion in 1994, though the number had declined to 35 per cent three years later.[8] More importantly for our purposes, a number of studies suggest relatively low levels of tolerance, or acceptance of 'otherness' or 'difference', in both countries. In Bulgaria, despite claims of high levels of tolerance and mutual support in mixed communities during Todor Zhivkov's assimilation campaign in the 1980s, several reports confirmed that many Bulgarians viewed Turks and Roma as essentially lazy, criminally inclined, and as undesirable for neighbours or marriage partners. At the same time, studies repeated at various points during the 1990s show a very gradual decline in the levels of intolerance.[9] Another study asking specifically about attitudes towards 'religious sects' found that 58.1 per cent of Bulgarians believed they should not be allowed to propagate their views and 58.3 per cent described themselves as having 'personal antipathy' towards such organisations.[10] In the introduction we quoted data from Russia in the early 1990s which revealed high levels of suspicion of those considered 'deviant' (p. 2) and later surveys often, though not always, reinforced this image of intolerance. A 1997 survey reported 40 per cent supporting the contention that the rights of minority religious groups should be restricted, though less favoured any official privileging of the majority religions.[11] Another study in 1999 tested people's attitudes towards religious minorities and assessed whether denominations were viewed in a 'very positive', 'somewhat positive', 'somewhat negative' or 'very negative light. In this the Orthodox gained an overall 94 per cent positive rating, followed by the Muslims with 59 per cent and the Catholics with 58 per cent; the three groups with the most negative ratings were Jehovah's Witnesses with 47 per cent (and 14 per cent positive), Baptists with 45 per cent (25 per cent positive) and Pentecostals with 36 per cent (16 per cent positive). At least half of those polled responded with 'don't know' when asked about Lutherans, Methodists, Adventists and Moonies.[12] More recently a survey of 1,600 Moscow school children aged 15–17 revealed that 35.9 per cent believed religious sects should be banned, a figure that appears at odds with other reports of a more tolerant younger generation.[13]

All this suggests that there is some correlation between mass values relating to tolerance and the acceptance of diversity on the one hand, and the legal restriction of minority rights on the other. This might even be a relationship that extends beyond the countries studied here, for the parts of Western Europe where self-proclaimed racists were most open included countries such as France and Belgium that have begun in recent years to adopt a more restrictive legal approach to new religious movements.

Against this, one would have to note that overall these latter countries have a much stronger democratic tradition and a more supportive political culture than their Eastern counterparts, so it is not entirely clear how far one can draw this parallel. It is also the case that, whatever the value surveys show, in these cases democracy is strongly entrenched, something that reminds us of the need to be cautious of positing a simple relationship between the preferences of populations and the properties of the political system. Moreover, as with our other propositions, this broad assumption does not work for all of our cases, notably Greece where the general levels of tolerance are high but restrictions continue to affect minority religious communities.

Confessional difference

In all our cases attempts to restrict the rights of religious minorities have been more extensive in countries with an Orthodox and Islamic tradition. And, with the exception of Poland, the pursuit of 'recognition' or legal protection for the traditionally dominant religious communities has been more extensive in those same countries. This would appear to reinforce the argument that religious traditions and historical experience continue to play a role in shaping a country's political culture and the context within which policy-makers operate. How this might be so is less clear, and clearly it has little to do with current levels of religious adherence and practice. In most of our countries, the majority of the population consider themselves to be members of the dominant tradition but their knowledge of religious doctrine and regular involvement is far more limited. Most sources suggest that regular attendance in Orthodox churches is around 2–6 per cent in Russia, Bulgaria and Greece, though in the latter country the institution is more firmly embedded in daily social life. There is also no suggestion that policy-makers are primarily influenced by concerns over alienating the religious vote. Most studies suggest that the political behaviour of religious believers in many former Soviet bloc countries differs little from those of the population at large[14] – though it might be that in the earlier transition period politicians in some countries over-estimated the value of appealing to a perceived religious constituency. It would be equally mistaken to argue that certain religious traditions are simply incompatible with democracy and, as we noted in the introduction, most religious traditions are multi-vocal when it comes to political matters in general and the question of pluralism in particular.

Yet one can argue for a more indirect religious influence, focusing on the rather intangible ways in which the religious traditions and experience of the country – though not necessarily theological differences – might shape the context within which policy-makers create policy. For example, it has been suggested that the Russian Orthodox notion of *sobornost* and its vision of society as essentially holistic may have contributed to a legal culture in which individual or minority rights are subordinate to the needs of the wider community.[15] It could also be that the lack of a serious reform movement along the lines of the Reformation or Vatican II – absences seen as positive by most Orthodox – mean that few within the Orthodox Church have engaged seriously or extensively with social and political questions, let alone with the issue of democracy and religious rights. Whilst most Russian and Greek hierarchs support these in the abstract, the reality has proven more complex, even in Greece with its longer democratic traditions. In a context where society is viewed in a holistic sense and where the assumption is that to be Greek or even Russian is to be Orthodox, it is perhaps inevitable that some will urge the restriction of religious rights. So religious traditions are multi-vocal but at any one point in time it may be that the dominant voice or orientation in those traditions works for or against the development of a pluralistic vision of the polity and the place of religion within it. For example, even though Patriarch Bartholomew of Constantinople has argued that freedom of conscience is the greatest gift given to mankind, Metropolitan Kirill of Smolensk expressed doubt as to whether the principle had any roots in the Orthodox tradition. In a statement issued by Russian bishops in August 2001 it was argued that freedom of conscience was 'evidence of society's loss of religious aims and values, of mass apostasy, and de facto indifference to the activity of Church and to victory over sin'.[16] So, differing Orthodox voices, but in practical terms one trend tending to predominate in much of the Slavic, and even Greek, Orthodox world.

Though there are 'pluralistic' and 'egalitarian' elements in Orthodoxy, in Russia and Bulgaria the impact of the Soviet experience on both sets of hierarchs, and indeed the wider population, may have reinforced the predisposition to an authoritarian solution of the question of religious competition. In the Catholic cases the predominant tendency within the international church works in other ways, despite the more 'conservative' moral direction favoured by Pope John Paul II. As a result, though individual Spanish and Polish bishops may have reservations about religious liberty or hanker after a restoration of national Catholicism, the dominant ethos in the contemporary international church works against any active promotion of this vision. Thus national churches may seek some degree of constitutional recognition but they have not tended to link this to the restriction of the rights of 'others'. Whilst the Polish case might seem to contradict the religious tradition argument, the position adopted by the hierarchy stemmed in part from the perception of John Paul II's church that in countries where Catholics predominate their religious institutions and values cannot be confined to the private sphere. The international dimension may also explain why the Spanish church, arguing its case in the same year that the Pope was elected, did not seek more than a simple mention, whilst the Polish church argued for a more thorough-going acceptance of its values and priorities in the constitutional text. So, in contexts where a single religious community has historically dom-inated religious tradition does matter, but so do contingent factors such as timing – as in the Spanish case where the bishops sought constitutional recognition during a Vatican interregnum with no strong direction from Rome.

Modernisation, secularisation and religious economics

Under this heading several arguments were alluded to in our introduction. The first two arguments suggest that we are less likely to see the protection of dominant traditions and the restriction of religious liberty in the more thoroughly 'modernised' societies and in those where secularisation is more advanced. The third approach, associated with rational choice the-ory, suggests that the levels of religious liberty are likely to have more to do with levels of religious competition and the regulatory regime in place. The basic assumption of modernisation/secularisation arguments is that, in general, the public role of religion will shrink as societies be-come more modern and that individuals within any particular country will give decreasing respect to the political platforms of religious lead-ers. For their part, churchmen seeking to make an impact in the political marketplace or society as a whole will have to find non-theological ways of justifying their position, a lesson learned by an Orthodox Archbishop of Athens who encouraged his people to fast by focusing on the dietary benefits of the practice[17] – though it is unclear whether this suggestion was any more successful in encouraging fasting than a theological justi-fication would have been. For that reason it is perhaps not surprising to find Orthodox leaders in Russia justifying their demands for 'recognition' or 'restriction', not in terms of church interests, but with reference to na-tional identity and the threat posed to the new state by 'sects' who break up families and encourage anti-social behaviour.

More generally in the context of this study, the modernisation the-sis might lead us to expect that as one moved politically 'eastwards' the degree of religious liberty would decline and the traditionally dominant religious institutions would seek to regain, preserve or create a monopoly position. Here there does appear to be a crude correlation, for within Southern Europe it is the more 'easterly' Greek state that has struggled to come to terms with religious pluralism and permitted a considerable public protection of the dominant tradition. In the former communist world the same patterns emerge – with the most 'liberal' regulatory regimes to be found in Poland, Latvia and Lithuania, whilst the most restrictive are probably in Russia, Armenia and Turkmenistan. Once again one has to be wary of taking this correlation too far because there are clearly some exceptions, notably Kyrgzystan in the 'east', which during the 1990s maintained in practice a relatively free market in religion. If one combines the two regions together the picture become more complicated, because on most indices of modernisation Greece would clearly come in front of Poland yet, as we have seen, its national church enjoys a constitutional pre-eminence and supports a far more restrictive policy towards religious minorities. Russia is also an exceptional case insofar as its level of economic development is on paper similar to that of the Baltic states, though in other ways it is clearly far less 'modern'.[18] Clearly one would need a fuller explanation of the statistical data to take this argument further, though it might be worth noting Anthony Gill's analysis of Latin America that found a very limited correlation between levels of economic development and degrees of religious liberty in that continent.[19] Nonetheless there are some imperfect correlations between development and the political salience of religious issues. It does appear to be the case that as these countries settle into a 'normal' pattern of socio-economic development the importance of religious issues declines. Though the outbursts surrounding the Greek identity card debate in 2000 could be seen as raising questions about such assumptions, these can adequately be explained with reference to Steve Bruce's arguments about resurgence being primarily confined to times of cultural change and transition.

In terms of the rational choice approach the prediction that traditionally dominant churches will seek to protect and preserve their position is largely borne out by the Greek and post-communist cases, though in the Spanish case other considerations came into play in moderating the claims on the system made by the hierarchy. For example, in the post-communist societies the 'national churches', weakened by years of harassment, sought legal protection to reinforce their position. In the view of the churches this was essential to allow time for rebuilding prior to entering the religious free market prematurely created by 'liberals' in the early 1990s. In Poland the situation differed somewhat, with the church's position in the 1990s shaped in large part by its perception that its role in overcoming the old regime and hold on the spiritual affections of the majority of the population entitled it to special consideration.

Equally, political support for such protection arose less out of theological conviction than the perception that defending the national churches served wider political objectives. Thus in Russia some politicians appeared initially to believe that there might be a distinctive religious constituency capable of being mobilised for electoral gain. Alternatively, in Russia, Bulgaria, Greece and other 'eastern' countries not discussed here, politicians have sometimes located their defence of traditional churches in wider discourses about building or protecting national identity against the encroachments of globalisation and Westernisation. At the same time, politicians will consider the economic consequences of religious regulation, as in several Latin American countries where religious liberty often originated in special concessions made to Protestant investors or trading communities in order to attract them to the countries concerned. In the long term, however, Gill suggests that religious issues will generally lose their significance for countries when their political systems 'settle down' – perhaps a restatement of the modernisation thesis after all. Again, these arguments have some merit, and it is worth noting that in all of our countries with the partial exception of Greece the political salience of religious issues has gradually declined as the transition process recedes into the past and political preferences and cleavage lines begin to solidify.

Whilst this approach appears to shed some light on developments in transitional society, its claims to offer a comprehensive general theory are more problematic. In particular, as we have suggested in earlier sections, it downplays too much the role of culture and ideas. For example, it is arguable that in Spain the Catholic hierarchy did not simply offer rhetorical support for religious freedom despite its reservations, and that ideological shifts within the wider transnational church were important in shaping the context within which politicians and church leaders operated. Equally, in the Russian government's consideration of a new law on religion during 1997 economic considerations might have suggested a continued presidential veto of the draft law given the threat of some US interests to end their economic involvement in the country should it adopt a restrictive law. Against this a rational choice approach might note the more intangible political benefits of standing up for Russia's right to determine its own path of development. In the case of Bulgaria, the cessation of a sensationalist 'anti-sect' campaign followed the election of a more liberally inclined government in 1997. This shift might reflect a rational concern with Bulgaria's poor image in potential donor countries, but surely also was a product of an ideological perspective on 'otherness' that differed from that of its predecessors. But if policies in these areas are largely the product of contingency and political need what room is left for a general theory? At the same time, it is impossible to ignore the role of ideological shifts, as the Greek, Russian and Bulgarian governments gradually recognise that part of the process of integration into the most modernised sections of the world community entails acceptance of international norms and values in the religious sphere.

Nationalism and civil religion

The notion that religious issues are likely to acquire renewed political significance during times of cultural change would appear to be borne out by several of our case studies. As we saw in the previous chapter, much of the discourse over the public status of religion has been located in wider debates about national identity, especially in the Orthodox countries. Internally the debate has focused on the potential contribution of religious values to the stabilisation of the political order, as when the future Archbishop of Athens Christodoulos stressed the importance of Orthodoxy in preserving Greek homogeneity and spirituality.[20] More frequently, however, the internal debate has adopted the language of 'culture wars' in ways that can often be internally divisive, separating out the good from the bad members of the community. On occasions there are echoes of American debates of the 1970s and 1980s when there emerged a 'conservative' reaction to the perceived liberalism and permissiveness of the period, which united all 'right thinking' people regardless of religious belief or denomination in a struggle with the dominant liberal ethos.[21] Similar divisions can perhaps be found in some of our cases, as in Poland where we saw one senator denouncing those favouring a liberal abortion regime as not really Polish, or in Greece where some have argued that there exist two political cultures, one profoundly traditionalist and communally oriented and the other more outward-looking and open to new ways of doing things.[22]

More significant for our purposes, however, has been the emphasis on doing things 'our way' rather than imitating an outside world that may do things in a fashion inappropriate to 'our' political and cultural condition. This is not to accept uncritically arguments about the inevitability of civilisational conflict, but to recognise that for many of those involved in these debates in transitional societies there are fundamental cultural differences between 'East' and 'West' that cannot and should not be ignored. The arguments may focus on specific aspects of church–state relations, in particular the criticism noted in the previous chapter of Western models rooted in Enlightenment notions of 'separation'. They may also tie into suggestions that minority religions are not really 'ours' but represent transplants from another world and even threats to the security and wellbeing of the nation. Such arguments are utilised in relation to 'Muslims' in Greece and Bulgaria, though in Russia Islam is more readily accepted as a 'traditional' religion so long as its leaders adopt a largely quietist role. In Bulgaria, a number of writers have used language reminiscent of Huntington in pointing to their country as sitting on a civilisation fault line where they act as a 'bridge' or 'corridor' between Christianity and Islam.[23] There is consequently a tendency for nationalist politicians to promote the dominant religions and claim that the legal protection of national churches is an essential part of the rebuilding of national identity. Such arguments also surface in relation to proposals for integration into larger political units. Discussing the European Union, the Archbishop of Athens emphasised that genuine European integration could only be built 'with the pages of our histories, and not with forgetfulness'.[24] That these are not just elite arguments is suggested by survey data from Russia in the 1990s which showed 78 per cent of the population supporting the statement that Russia should develop 'according to its own traditions', and a very small minority wanting to move along the lines of the country's European neighbours.[25]

If the positive side of these debates is an attempt to preserve traditional cultures and ways of life against an encroaching, globalising world, the downside is a defensive mentality that sees threats all around.[26] In consequence, churchmen or politicians seek to privilege religious institutions seen as 'traditional' and restrict the rights of those 'threatening' the country's national and spiritual inheritance. Though monopoly may in the long term be harmful to religious institutions, the 'threat' is viewed as extensive enough to demand a response. This may not be a numerical threat – the number of people adhering to religious minorities is small in Greece – though in Russia and possibly Bulgaria it is arguable that as many people attend non-Orthodox as Orthodox places of worship on a typical Sunday (or Friday or Saturday). Nonetheless, the official and sometimes popular view is that religious minorities do undermine the homogeneity of the nation in times of change, a view reinforced by a media and popular perception which lumps all 'non-traditional' groups together and all too often sees them as external implantations or 'viruses'.

All these discussions reinforce Steve Bruce's argument about religious revitalisation being most likely in contexts of cultural defence and cultural transition, when religious issues become entwined with broader arguments about identity and belonging.[27] Such an interpretation is fairly explicitly supported by two Russian intellectuals who argued that the debates over the 1997 law on religious freedom had nothing to do with religion, but with the 'right of Russia to pursue an independent foreign and domestic policy, its right to build a new, non-communist life in accordance with its national interests and historical traditions'. The law would allow for 'an at least partial restoration of the Orthodox Church's influence on our way of life' and offer 'a chance to shape a new Russian consciousness and to revive a sense of Russian identity'.[28]

Politicians and religious leaders utilising such arguments might refer back to the ways in which the resolution of issues relating to 'recognition' and religious pluralism were handled prior to the authoritarian regime. They might then seek to recreate past relationships, though in most cases the world has moved on in ways that make a simple restoration impossible. In Bulgaria the church was for most of the twentieth century a largely subordinate institution and, though the modern state pays it constitutional respect as the national church, the present-day institution is weak and divided and thus in no position to build an influential relationship with the political order. The case of Russia is more complex, for here, as we have seen, critics charge that the Orthodox Church is seeking to resurrect its past ties to the state and some nationalist intellectuals argue explicitly for this in the context of the nation-building process. For its part, the church denies any intent to recreate what one hierarch described as a 'gilded cage' when close ties were achieved at the cost of a loss of independence. In other words, throughout the Orthodox and post-communist world the belief in a close partnership between church and state has survived the years of repression. In the modern era, however, the objective has been modified so as to seek recognition and support for its aims in limiting the impact of 'heresy' without paying the costs attendant on that relationship in the past.

In the Catholic countries it is arguable that the Spanish church learnt better from the past than its Polish counterpart in reading and responding to the new context within which they were operating. The latter, or at least part of its leadership, succumbed to a certain triumphalism following its major contribution to the collapse of communism and was perhaps 'over-ambitious' in pursuing its agenda during the early 1990s. In consequence, by pushing hard on issues such as abortion and constitutional 'recognition' it succeeded in alienating sections of the population hitherto sympathetic to the institution.[29] Here it seems that the sympathy of Cardinal Glemp and others for a revitalisation of the old national-Catholic model blinded them to the realities of the new order.[30] By way of contrast, history had a different impact on the Spanish Catholic Church, for here both religious and secular leaders remembered all too well the extreme polarisation around religious issue that characterised the civil war period and were thus anxious to avoid any revival of old hostilities. Thus both sides moderated their demands and sought compromises during debates over the constitution in 1977–8 and found a form of words that gave the church recognition without excessive privilege. The Spanish resolution of the religious liberty issue is also interesting insofar as it demonstrates the flexibility of religious institutions and the ways in which they can contribute to cultural and legal change. Here changes within the wider Catholic Church led an institution previously bitterly opposed to religious liberty to change its position from the 1960s onwards and to accept the establishment of full religious liberty after Franco's death. In other words, past relationships between church and state may have an impact upon how such issues are handled in the present, but the direction in which they will take religious institutions is less clear.

Political and religious elites in these circumstances may also look to the future, seeking to find ways of anchoring a new sense of national identity and belonging in some form of civil religion. In the American sense the modern concept of civil religion has a non-denominational meaning, though its origins lie in a predominantly Protestant vision of the world in which the values of congregational life are transferred to the wider community. The detachment of a civil religion from its specific denominational roots permits politicians not noted for their personal piety to make use of a country's religious heritage without necessarily adhering to the finer points of its teaching. As a result many people can ignore the divergence between the religious language and the practical behaviour of Bill Clinton or refrain from comment when Andreas Papandreou dedicated the Greek armed services to the Virgin Mary. In Russia and Bulgaria, the media has occasionally been less accepting of politicians who in the 1990s took to attending church, but at the cost of making elementary mistakes in the way they crossed themselves or mumbled their way through the prayers. Yet there is also a sense in which this 'conversion' process goes beyond the utilitarian, especially in the post-communist societies where many people in the early 1990s were searching for some form of ideological certainty. In the post-communist societies it may also reflect a commonly held belief that one of the roles of the state is to promote some form of ideological or normative value system.

Religious leaders take the view that there can be no such thing as a spiritual vacuum and any society has to choose some form of value system. Hardly surprisingly they suggest that a religious world-view is ultimately preferable to one rooted in secularism or individualistic relativism. Equally, for the politicians it is easier to utilise those religious traditions already having some sort of hold on the public mind. For that reason, whilst the promotion of a particular religion may seems at odds with the notion of civil religion in its American manifestation, it makes sense in many transitional societies. And in practice many national religion communities have in effect evolved along the lines of civil religion, in which the content of belief is less important than the social cohesion provided by the tradition. Kokosolakis referring to Greece notes that:

nationalism was underpinned by the Orthodox religion throughout the nineteenth and twentieth centuries, and as a result the secularisation of Greek society was never deep or widespread . . . the spirit of the Enlightenment and the Reformation had never penetrated into the structures of Greek society. Instead a civil religion developed which involved a fusion of popular and official religion along with Hellenic and national ideals which have informed the dominant ideology of Greek society to the present day.[31]

This view of Orthodoxy as a 'civil religion' is implicit in many of the speeches of the current Archbishop of Athens, with their emphasis on the dangers facing a society that neglects its traditions and spiritual heritage in a rapidly changing world. Here he seeks to avoid 'narrowly' religious arguments for the state to support the Orthodox Church, but to promote a vision of 'spirituality' able to draw in those Greeks who are at best lukewarm in their relationship with the institutional church. Up to a point this appears to work in that the vast majority of Greeks continue to accept the notion that there is a link between being Greek and being Orthodox.

In countries with a Western tradition this linkage is far weaker, and even in 'Catholic Poland' one survey showed that when asked 'what in your opinion makes someone a Pole?', the Catholic faith was ranked only tenth, with only 9.2 per cent saying it was very important and 41.1 per cent saying that it was not particularly important.[32] Yet many of the arguments we quoted from the Polish constitutional debate are in effect rooted in the notion of a 'civil religion' capable of providing values and meaning, as well as a bulwark against the infiltration of a an excessively individualistic, 'anything goes' mentality coming from the West. Given persistent political upheaval over several centuries none of the former communist countries has had the time to develop the rather amorphous American-style non-denominational version, and thus have to make use of existing traditions, with the 'national church' or religion proving the most obvious starting point. As in the USA politicians have little desire to see churchmen offering comment on their political programmes or private lives, but they do see their utility as providers of the means of civilising society and offering some form of value cement. In most cases this is the often unconscious assumption underlying their defence of the national religious communities.

At this stage one has to ask whether it is possible to find any general patterns or explanatory models, or whether the most important factors are contingent, dependent upon the day-to-day needs of politicians and a product of circumstances that are peculiar to each country. As we suggested in the previous section, an analysis of policy-making in this area cannot exclude references to the positions of *political elites*, to their need to build constituencies of support in a context where political identities are still in transition. In some cases *individuals* may be extremely important in shaping the evolution of policy, as was the case in Spain where Cardinal Tarancón encouraged a firm but cautious approach to the intricacies of constitutional definition, or more recently in Greece where the selection of an ambitious church leader with a flair for publicity has put religious issues back on the political agenda. *Timing* is also important, with Tarancón opting for constitutional moderation in 1978, a transitional year for the Vatican, whilst the Polish bishops entered the constitution-writing process with a Polish Pope firmly in place and keen to emphasise the role of religion in public life. *International factors* have been influential in relation to the production of 'anti-sect' legislation, as several laws emerging in the former Soviet bloc appear to be modelled in part on the Russian model, whilst anti-sect campaigners refer to legal cases in Germany or the decisions of several European parliaments relating to this question.

If the search for theory is maintained, are some of the approaches we have outlined more useful than others in shedding light on our cases? There are rough correlations between indices of 'modernisation' and the resolution of recognition/restriction issues, though these are not exact. For example, a 1997 per capita income hierarchy would be Spain, Greece, Poland, Russia, Bulgaria, whilst a ranking in terms of religious pluralism would probably be Spain, Poland, Greece, Bulgaria, Russia. There is also some suggestion that as the patterns of political behaviour and socio-economic development 'settle down' religious issues become less contentious, except, as suggested by Bruce, where cultural transition and direction are at issue.

In general, and without wishing to resort to cultural determinism or notions of inherent civilisational conflict, it does appear that cultural factors are better predictors of policy outcomes than other factors, particularly with regard to the restriction of minority rights. There does appear to be, not surprisingly, a correlation between the broader level of societal tolerance and the degree of restriction or freedom available to minority religious groups. Equally, the problems facing minorities are generally greater in the countries of an Orthodox or Islamic tradition than those where Catholicism or Protestantism has traditionally predominated – though why this should be so needs further exploration. With regard to 'recognition' the picture is more ambiguous, though one could make a distinction between the simple Catholic claim for a public status and the more explicit Orthodox tendency to link this to the restriction of minority rights. If one were to broaden the picture to analyse demands for the privileging of religious perspectives on the policy agenda the situation gets yet more complex, for by and large here it is the Catholic Church that has made the running on issues such as abortion whereas the Orthodox, though in principle opposed, have rarely elevated this to a first-order issue. At the risk of stating the obvious, it does appear that without a considera-tion of the historical or cultural legacy and the political self-confidence of nations undergoing transition one cannot fully comprehend the context within which political, social and religious actors make their choices – rational or otherwise.

The purpose of this study was primarily to describe and analyse the ways in which 'third wave' countries making the transition from author-itarianism to democracy, or at least a more liberal regime, handle the is-sues of religious 'recognition' and/or restriction. In most of our countries religious issues have rarely taken centre-stage, though in some religious institutions or programmes have enjoyed occasional periods in the politi-cal limelight. With regard to wider questions of democratisation, we have followed the 'transitologists' in focusing on the role of key institutions and elites, stressing the role of religious leaders in determining the key de-mands made by spiritual institutions. And to the extent that such people enjoy respect in their societies the positions they adopt may well have an influence, however marginal, in the shaping of public attitudes towards democracy and thus affect the chances of consolidating a democratic order and mind-set amongst the population. For example, if the Polish church argues against abortion on the grounds that it possesses special knowledge in this area, it is effectively, whatever the rights and wrongs of its position, asking that some issues be removed from the purview of democratic institutions – a tension that is inevitable for all traditional religious faiths which reserve the right to judge the morality of the sur-rounding society. Equally, when the Russian Orthodox Church actively promotes the restriction of minority rights it could be suggested that it is publicly reinforcing those elements in post-Soviet political culture that are suspicious of 'otherness' or 'difference', rather than encouraging ele-ments within that tradition more conducive to democratic development. For these reasons, if no others, the politics of religious liberty in transi-tional societies has a significance that transcends the narrowly religious. It suggests that religion will periodically erupt into the public domain, that the 'privatisation' of religion is far from complete, and that historical legacies and contexts will continue to shape the ways in which politicians and political systems handle the public role of religion.

Notes

1. Eurobarometer Opinion Poll, No. 47.1, 1996.
2. K. Kanev, Report submitted to the Bulgarian Council of Ministers in September 1999 in relation to Bulgaria's commitments under the Framework

Convention for the Protection of National Minorities. I am grateful to Dr Kanev for giving me a copy of this report.

3. This was also stated by Fotis Romeo, General Secretary of the Greek Evangelical Alliance. Interview, May 2000.
4. Eurobarometer Opinion Poll, No. 47.1, 1996; Kanev Report, Tables 19, 22 and 23.
5. N. Demertziz, 'Greece', in R. Eatwell (ed.), *European Political Cultures: Conflict or Convergence* (London: Routledge, 1997), p. 113.
6. A. Pollis, 'Greek national identity: religious minority rights and European norms', *Journal of Modern Greek Studies*, 10: 2, 1992, p. 176.
7. *Central and Eastern Eurobarometer*, No. 6, March 1996, reports 80 per cent of Bulgarians and 86 per cent of Russians as dissatisfied with democracy; against this one might note one finding which shows regular churchgoers in Bulgaria (and Ukraine) to have more pro-market, pro-Western orientations than the population as a whole. S. White et al., *Religion and Political Action in Postcommunist Europe* (Strathclyde: Studies in Public Policy, No. 307, 1998), p. 22.
8. Kanev Report, Table 12; a 1998 survey reported by George Fotev noted that 43.7 per cent of Bulgarians favoured full religious freedom whilst 26.8 per cent opposed it. G. Fotev, *Ethnicity, Religion and Politics* (Sofia: Pensoft Publishers, 1999), p. 112.
9. Kanev Report, Tables 1–6; on more positive assessment in the context of Zhivkov's assimilation campaign see some of the essays in A. Zhelyazkova (ed.), *Relations of Compatibility and Incompatibility between Christians and Muslims in Bulgaria* (Sofia: International Centre for Minority Studies, 1997).
10. N. Todorova, 'Religion in post-communist Bulgaria', in I. Borovik and G. Babinski (eds.), *New Religious Phenomena in Central and Eastern Europe* (Krakow: Nomos, 1997), pp. 176–80.
11. *Nezavisimaya gazeta*, 25 December 1997.
12. K. Kaariainen and D. Furman, 'Religiosity in Russia in the 1990s', in M. Kotiranta (ed.), *Religious Transitions in Russia* (Helsinki: Aleksanteri Institute, 2000), p. 56.
13. Taken from Paul Steeve's website quoting RIIA Novosti. Posted 15 May 2000.
14. S. White and I. Mcallister, 'The politics of religion in post-communist Russia', *Religion, State and Society*, 25: 3, 1997, pp. 235–52.
15. S. White, 'Russia', in Eatwell, *European Political Cultures*, p. 196; see also Oleg Khakhordin's distinction between Catholic, Protestant and Orthodox conceptions of civil society. 'Civil society and Orthodox Christianity', *Europe-Asia Studies*, 50: 5, 1998, pp. 949–68.
16. Quoted in *KNS*, 12 April 2001.
17. G. Mavrogordatas, 'Church–state relations in the Greek Orthodox Case', paper presented to the ECPR Joint Sessions on 'Church and State in Europe', Copenhagen, 14–19 April 2000.
18. In 1997 GNP per capita terms the ranking of the eleven countries would be Spain, Greece, Poland, Russia, Latvia, Lithuania, Bulgaria, Georgia, Turkmenistan, Armenia and Kyrgyzstan. Figures taken from *The Europa World Year Book, 2000* (London: Europa Publications, 2000).

19. A. Gill, 'The political origins of religious liberty: initial sketch of a general theory', Paper presented at ECPR Joint Sessions, Workshop on 'Church and State in Europe', Copenhagen, 14–19 April 2000.
20. *Athens News*, 30 April 1998.
21. J. D. Hunter, *Culture Wars: The Struggle to Define America* (New York: Basic Books, 1991).
22. See the discussion in Demertziz, 'Greece', p. 118.
23. N. Bogomilova, 'Tsivilizationni i natsionalni izmereniya na religiyata', in G. Bakalov (ed.), *Religiya i tsyrkva v Bylgariya* (Sofia: Gutenburg Publishing House, 1999), pp. 28–38.
24. Speech quoted on Greek Orthodox Church website, Ecclesia: http://www.ecclesia.gr/English/Archbishop.html.
25. White, 'Russia', pp. 203–4.
26. Some Russian Orthodox churchmen have commented to me on the way in which it is the new converts, often from communist backgrounds, who are the most defensive and ideologically zealous on behalf of their new faith which they promote in the style of Dostoyevsky's Grand Inquisitor.
27. S. Bruce, *Religion in the Modern World* (Oxford: OUP, 1996), chapter 5.
28. *Nezavisimaya gazeta*, 20 August 1997.
29. This argument was made to me in a private conversation by a Vatican official who felt that whilst the Polish Church's objectives were often just they pursued them in ways that failed to recognise the need to build up constituencies of support in a democratic order.
30. J. Casanova, *Public Religions in the Modern World* (Chicago: Chicago University Press, 1994), p. 110.
31. N. Kokoslakis, 'Greek Orthodoxy and modern socio-economic change', in R. Roberts (ed.), *Religion and the Transformations of Capitalism* (London: Routledge, 1996), p. 254.
32. E. Nowicka, 'Roman Catholicism and the contents of Polishness', in Borovik and Babinski, *New Religious Phenomena in Central and Eastern Europe*, pp. 81–92.

Select bibliography

BOOKS, ARTICLES, PAPERS

Alivizatos, N., 'A new role for the Greek Church?', *Journal of Modern Greek Studies*, 17: 1, 1999, pp. 23–40

Almond, G. and Verba, S., *The Civic Culture* (Princeton: Princeton University Press, 1963)

Anderson, J., *Religion, State and Politics in the Soviet Union and the Successor States* (Cambridge: Cambridge University Press, 1994)

'Authoritarian political development in Central Asia: the case of Turkmenistan', *Central Asian Survey*, 14: 4, 1995, pp. 509–27

Kyrgyzstan: Central Asia's Island of Democracy? (Reading: Harwood, 1999)

'Religion, state and society in the new Kyrgyzstan', *Journal of Church and State*, 41: 1, 1999, pp. 99–116

Ash, T. Garton, *The Polish Revolution* (London: Granta and Penguin, 1983/1991)

Ashford, S. and Timms, N., *What Europe Thinks: A Study of West European Values* (Aldershot: Dartmouth, 1992)

Bacon, E., 'Church and state in contemporary Russia: conflicting discourses', *Journal of Communist Studies and Transition Politics*, 18: 1, 2002, pp. 97–116

Bakalov, G. (ed.), *Religiya i tsyrkva v Bylgariya* (Sofia: Gutenburg Publishing House, 1999)

Balodis, R., 'Religious organisations in the Latvian state: their rights and obligations', *Religion, State and Society*, 27: 2, 1999, pp. 233–8

Beeson, T., *Discretion and Valour: Religious Conditions in Russia and Eastern Europe* (London: Fount, 1982)

Bell, J. (ed.), *Bulgaria in Transition: Politics, Society and Culture after Communism* (Boulder: Westview, 1998)

Bellah, R. and Hammond, P. (eds.), *Varieties of Civil Religion* (New York: Harper & Row, 1980)

Berger, P., *The Sacred Canopy: Elements of a Sociological Theory of Religion* (New York: Archer Books, 1990)

Bonimo-Blanc, A., *Spain's Transition to Democracy: The Politics of Constitution Making* (Boulder: Westview, 1987)

Borovik, I. and Babinski, G. (eds.), *New Religious Phenomena in Central and Eastern Europe* (Kraków: Nomos, 1997)

Bourdeaux, M., *Land of Crosses: The Struggle for Religious Freedom in Lithuania, 1939–78* (Chulmleigh: Augustine Publishing Company, 1979)

Boyle, K. and Sheen, J. (eds.), *Freedom of Religion and Belief: A World Report* (London: Routledge, 1997)

Bowker, M. and Ross, C. (eds.), *Russia after the Cold War* (Harlow: Longman, 2000)

Brasslof, A., *Religion and Politics in Spain: The Spanish Church in Transition, 1962–96* (London: Macmillan, 1998)

Bremmer, I. and Taras, R. (eds.), *New States, New Politics: Building the Post-Soviet Nations* (Cambridge: Cambridge University Press, 1997)

Bria, I., *Romania: Orthodox Identity at a Crossroads of Europe* (Geneva: WCC Publications, 1995)

Bruce, S., *Religion in the Modern World* (Oxford: Oxford University Press, 1996)
Choice and Religion (Oxford: Oxford University Press, 1999)

Bruce, S. (ed.), *Religion and Modernisation* (Oxford: Oxford University Press, 1992)

Brzezinski, M., *The Struggle for Constitutionalism in Poland* (London: Macmillan, 1998)

Callahan, W., *The Catholic Church in Spain, 1875–1998* (Washington DC: Catholic University of America Press, 2000)

Carillo, S., *Eurocommunism and the State* (London: Lawrence & Wishart, 1977)

Carr, R., *Modern Spain* (Oxford: Oxford University Press, 1986)

Carter, S., *Russian Nationalism: Yesterday, Today, Tomorrow* (London: Pinter, 1990)

Casanova, J., *Public Religions in the Modern World* (Chicago: Chicago University Press, 1994)

Clogg, R., *A Concise History of Greece* (Cambridge: Cambridge University Press, 1992)

Clogg, R. (ed.), *Greece in the 1980s* (London: Macmillan, 1983)

Close, D. (ed.), *The Greek Civil War, 1943–50: Studies of Polarisation* (London: Routledge, 1993)

Corley, F., *Armenia and Karabakh: Ancient Faith, Modern War* (London: Catholic Truth Society, 1992)

Costa, D. and Stavrou, T. (eds.), *Greece Prepares for the Twenty First Century* (Baltimore: Johns Hopkins University Press, 1995)

Cracraft, J., *The Church Reform of Peter the Great* (London: Macmillan, 1971)

Crampton, R., *A Concise History of Bulgaria* (Cambridge: Cambridge University Press, 1997)

Crouch, M., *Revolution and Evolution: Gorbachev and Soviet Politics* (London: Philip Allan, 1989)

Davies, N., *God's Playground: A History of Poland* (Oxford: Clarendon Press, 1981)

Dawisha, K., *Eastern Europe, Gorbachev and Reform* (Cambridge: Cambridge University Press, 1988)

Diamond, L. (ed.), *Political Culture and Democracy in Developing Countries* (London: Lynne Reinner, 1994)

Di Palma, G., *To Craft Democracies* (Berkeley: California University Press, 1990)

Dreifelds, J., *Latvia in Transition* (Cambridge: Cambridge University Press, 1996)

Dunlop, J., *The New Russian Nationalism* (New York: Praeger, 1985)

Eatwell, R. (ed.), *European Political Cultures: Conflict or Convergence* (London: Routledge, 1997)

Edles, L., *Symbol and Ritual in the New Spain* (Cambridge: Cambridge University Press, 1998)

Ellis, J., *The Russian Orthodox Church: Triumphalism and Defensiveness* (London: Macmillan, 1996)

Evans, M., *Religious Liberty and International Law in Europe* (Cambridge: Cambridge University Press, 1997)

Featherstone, K. and Ifantis, K. (eds.), *Greece in a Changing Europe* (Manchester: Manchester University Press, 1996)

Featherstone, K. and Katsoudas, D. (eds.), *Political Change in Greece: Before and After the Colonels* (London: Croom Helm, 1987)

Filatov, S. et al., *Religiya i politika v postkommunisticheskoi rossii* (Moscow, 1994) *Religiya i prava cheloveka: na puti svobode sovesti III* (Moscow: Nauka, 1996)

Fleet, M. and Smith, B., *The Catholic Church and Democracy in Chile and Peru* (Notre Dame: University of Notre Dame Press, 1997)

Fotev, G., *Ethnicity, Religion and Politics* (Sofia: Pensoft Publishers, 1999)

Friedrich, C. and Brzezinski, Z., *Totalitarian Dictatorship and Autocracy* (New York: Praeger, 1956)

Gachelidze, R., *The New Georgia* (London: University College of London Press, 1995)

Gill, A., 'The political origins of religious liberty: initial sketch of a general theory', paper presented at ECPR Joint Sessions, Workshop on 'Church and State in Europe', Copenhagen, 14–19 April 2000

Gomulka, S. and Polonsky, A. (eds.), *Polish Paradoxes* (London: Routledge, 1990)

Graham, R., *Spain: Change of a Nation* (London: Michael Joseph, 1984)

Gunther, R. and Blough, R., 'Religious conflict and consensus in Spain: a tale of two constitutions', *World Affairs*, 143: 4, 1981, pp. 366–412

Gunther, R., Sani, G. and Shabad, G. (eds.), *Spain after Franco: The Making of a Competititve Party System* (Berkeley: University of California Press, 1988)

Gunther, R. (ed.), *Politics, Society and Democracy: The Case of Spain* (Boulder: Westview, 1993)

Halkias, A., 'Give birth for Greece: abortion and nation in letters to the editors of the mainstream Greek press', *Journal of Modern Greek Studies*, 16: 1, 1998, pp. 111–38

Hammer, D., *Russian Nationalism and Soviet Politics* (Boulder: Westview, 1989)

Havel, V., *Living in Truth* (London: Faber, 1986)

Heywood, P., *The Government and Politics of Spain* (London: Macmillan, 1995)

Higley, J. and Gunther, R. (eds.), *Elites and Democratic Consolidation in Latin America and Southern Europe* (Cambridge: Cambridge University Press, 1992)

Hooper, J., *The Spaniards* (London: Penguin, 1986)

Hughey, J., *Protestants in Modern Spain* (South Pasadena: William Carey Library, 1973)

'Church, state and religious liberty in Spain', *Journal of Church and State*, 23: 3, 1981, pp. 485–95

Hunter, J. D., *Culture Wars: The Struggle to Define America* (New York: Basic Books, 1991)

Huntington, S., *The Third Wave: Democratization in the Late Twentieth Century* (Norman: University of Oklohoma Press, 1993)

Inglis, T., Mach, Z. and Mazanek, R. (eds.), *Religion and Politics: East–West Contrasts from Contemporary Europe* (Dublin: University College of Dublin Press, 2000)

Khakhordin, O., 'Civil society and Orthodox Christianity', *Europe-Asia Studies*, 50: 5, 1998, pp. 949–68

Kotiranta, M. (ed.), *Religious Transitions in Russia* (Helsinki: Alaksanteri Institute, 2000)

Koumoulidis, J. (ed.), *Greece in Transition: Essays in Modern Greek History, 1821–1974* (London: Zeno Publishers, 1977)

Lannon, F., *Privilege, Persecution and Prophecy: The Catholic Church in Spain, 1875–1975* (Oxford: Clarendon Press, 1987)

Lawlor, T. and Rigby, M., *Contemporary Spain* (London: Longman, 1998)

Leftwich, A., 'From democratization to democratic consolidation', in D. Potter (ed.), *Democratization* (Cambridge: Polity, 1997), pp. 517–36

Linz, J. and Stepan, A., *Problems of Democratic Transition and Consolidation* (Baltimore: Johns Hopkins University Press, 1996)

Mavrogordatas, G., 'Church–state relations in the Greek Orthodox case', paper presented at ECPR Joint Sessions, Workshop on 'Church and State in Europe', Copenhagen, 14–19 April 2000

McDonough, P. et al., *The Cultural Dynamics of Democratisation in Spain* (Itahaca: Cornell University Press, 1998)

McIntyre, R., *Bulgaria: Politics Economics and Society* (London: Pinter, 1988)

McNair, J., *Education for a Changing Spain* (Manchester: Manchester University Press, 1984)

Michel, P., 'Religious renewal or religious deficiency: religion and democracy in Central Europe', *Religion, State and Society*, 20: 3–4, 1992, pp. 339–44

Michnik, A., *Letters from Prison and Other Essays* (London: University of California Press, 1985

The Church and the Left (Chicago: Chicago University Press, 1993)

Millard, F., *Polish Politics and Society* (London: Routledge, 1999)

Minkenburg, M., 'Religion and policy effects: church, state and party configurations in the policy-making process', paper presented at ECPR Joint Sessions, Workshop on 'Church and State in Europe', Copenhagen, 14–19 April 2000

Monsma, S. and Soper, J., *The Challenge of Pluralism: Church and State in Five Democracies* (Oxford and New York: Rowman and Littlefield, 1997)

Mouellán, A., *La iglesie católice y otras religious en la España da hoy* (Madrid, 1999)

Mujal-Leon, E., 'The left and the Catholic question in Spain', *West European Politics*, 5: 2, 1982, pp. 32–54

O'Donnell, G., Schmitter, P. and Whitehead, L. (eds.), *Transitions from Authoritarian Rule: Southern Europe* (Baltimore and London: Johns Hopkins University Press, 1986)

Papandreou, A., *Democracy at Gunpoint* (London: Penguin, 1970)

Papastathis, C., 'Church and state in Greece in 1998', *European Journal of Church and State*, 6: 1, 1999

Payne, S., *Spanish Catholicism* (London: University of Wisconsin Press, 1984)

Perez-Diaz, V., *The Rebirth of Civil Society* (London: Harvard University Press, 1993)

Pettifer, J., *The Greeks: Land and People since the War* (London: Viking, 1993)

Pollis, A., 'Greek national identity: religious minorities, rights and European norms', *Journal of Modern Greek Studies*, 10: 2, 1992, pp. 65–84

Poulton, H. and Taji-Farouki, S. (eds.), *Muslim Identity and the Balkan State* (London: Hurst & Co, 1997)

Preston, P., *The Triumph of Democracy in Spain* (London: Methuen, 1986)

Franco: A Biography (London: HarperCollins, 1993)

Preston, P. (ed.), *Spain in Crisis* (London: 1976)

Przeworski, A., 'Democracy as a contingent outcome of conflicts', in J. Elster and R. Slagstad (eds.), *Constitutionalism and Democracy* (Cambridge: Cambridge University Press, 1988), pp. 61–3

Ramet, P. (ed.), *Eastern Christianity and Politics in the Twentieth Century* (Durham: Duke University Press, 1988)

Religion and Nationalism in Soviet and East European Politics (Durham: Duke University Press, 1989)

Ramet, S., *Whose Democracy? Nationalism, Religion and the Doctrine of Collective Rights in Post-1989 Eastern Europe* (Oxford: Rowman & Littlefield, 1997)

Nihil Obstat: Religion, Politics and Social Change in East-Central Europe and Russia (Durham: Duke University Press, 1998)

Roberts, R. (ed.), *Religion and the Transformations of Capitalism* (London: Routledge, 1996)

Sajo, A. and Avineri, S. (eds.), *The Law of Religious Identity: Models for Post-Communism* (The Hague: Kluwer Law International, 1999)

Sapiets, M., 'The Baltic churches and the national revival', *Religion in Communist Lands*, 18: 2, 1990, pp. 155–68

Scwab, P. and Frangos, G. (eds.), *Greece under the Junta* (New York: Facts on File, 1970)

Shterin, M. and Richardson, J., 'Effects of the Western anti-cult movement on development of laws concerning religion in post-communist Russia', *Journal of Church and State*, 42: 2, 2000, pp. 247–71

Sigmund, P. (ed.), *Religious Freedom and Evangelization in Latin America: The Challenge of Pluralism* (New York: Orbis, 1999)

Stavros, S., 'The legal status of religious minorities in Greece today: the adequacy of their protection in the light of current human rights perceptions', *Journal of Modern Greek Studies*, 13: 1, 1995, pp. 1–32

'Human rights in Greece: twelve years of supervision from Strasbourg', *Journal of Modern Greek Studies*, 17: 1, 1999, pp. 3–21

Stepan, A., 'Religion, democracy and the "twin tolerations"', *Journal of Democracy*, 11: 4, 2000, pp. 37–57

Szacki, J., *Liberalism after Communism* (Budapest: Central European Press, 1995)

Tabyshalieva, A., *Vera v Turkestane* (Bishkek, 1993)

Taras, R., *Consolidating Democracy in Poland* (Boulder: Westview, 1995)

Tokes, R. (ed.), *Opposition in Eastern Europe* (London: Macmillan, 1979)

Tsvetkov, P., 'The politics of transition in Bulgaria: back to the future', *Problems of Communism*, May–June 1992, pp. 34–42

Urban, J. and Solovei, V., *Russia's Communists at the Crossroads* (Boulder: Westview, 1997)

Vardys, S., *The Catholic Church, Dissent and Nationality in Lithuania* (Boulder: Westview, 1978)

Vardys, S. and Sedaitis, J., *Lithuania: The Rebel Nation* (Boulder: Westview, 1997)

Veremis, T., *The Military in Greek Politics: From Independence to Democracy* (London: Hurst, 1997)

Wald, K., *Religion and Politics in the United States* (Washington DC: CQ Press, 1997)

Ware, T., *The Orthodox Church* (London: Penguin, 1993)

Weigel, G., *The Final Revolution: The Resistance Church and the Collapse of Communism* (New York: Oxford University Press, 1992)

White, W., *Russia's New Politics: The Management of a Postcommunist Society* (Cambridge: Cambridge University Press, 2000)

Witte, J. and Bourdeaux, M. (eds.), *Proselytism and Orthodoxy in Russia: The New War for Souls* (New York: Orbis, 1999)

Wyman, M., *Public Opinion in Post-Communist Russia* (London: Macmillan, 1997)

Woodhouse, C. M., *Modern Greece: A Short History* (London: Faber, 1998)

Young, L. (ed.), *Rational Choice Theory and Religion* (London: Routledge, 1996)

Zhelyazkova, A. (ed.), *Relations of Compatibility and Incompatibility between Christians and Muslims in Bulgaria* (Sofia: International Centre for Minority Studies, 1997)

JOURNALS AND NEWSPAPERS

Argumenty i fakty
Athens News
BBC Summary of World Broadcasts
Brigham Young University Law Review
Church History
Democratization
The Economist
East–West Church Ministry Report
Europe-Asia Studies
European Journal of Church and State
The Georgian Times
Iberian Studies
Independent
Izvestiya
Journal of Church and State
Journal of Communist Studies and Transition Politics
Journal of Democracy
Journal of Ecumenical Studies
Journal of Modern Greek Studies

Journal of Politics
Keston News Service
Kommersant Daily
Moskovskie novosti
Nasha gazeta
Nezavisimaya gazeta
Obektiv
Ogonyok
Problems of Communism
Rationality and Society
Religion in Eastern Europe
Religion, State and Society (formerly *Religion in Communist Lands*)
RFE/RL Research Report
Rossiiskaya gazeta
Rossiiskie vesti
Russkaya mysl'
Rus pravoslavnaya
Slovo Kyrgyzstana
The Tablet
Transition
Turkmenskaya iskra
Vechernii Bishkek
The Warsaw Voice
West European Politics
World Affairs

Index